The
South
Atlantic
Quarterly
Spring 1996
Volume 95
Number 2

The *South Atlantic Quarterly* (ISSN 0038-2876) is published quarterly, at $66.00 for libraries and institutions and $26.00 for individuals, by Duke University Press, 905 W. Main St., 18-B, Durham, NC 27701. Second-class postage paid at Durham, NC. POSTMASTER: Send address changes to *South Atlantic Quarterly*, Box 90660, Duke University, Durham, NC 27708-0660.

Photocopying. Photocopies for course or research use that are supplied to the end-user at no cost may be made without need for explicit permission or fee. Photocopies that are to be provided to their end-users for some photocopying fee may not be made without payment of permissions fees to Duke University Press, at $1.50 per copy for each article copied. Registered users may pay for photocopying via the Copyright Clearance Center, using the code and price at the bottom of each article-opening page.

Permissions. Requests for permission to republish copyrighted material from this journal should be addressed to Permissions Editor, Duke University Press, Box 90660, Durham, NC 27708-0660.

Library exchanges and orders for them should be sent to Duke University Library, Gift and Exchange Department, Durham, NC 27708.

The *South Atlantic Quarterly* is indexed in *Abstracts of English Studies, Academic Abstracts, Academic Index, America: History and Life, American Bibliography of Slavic & East European Studies, American Humanities Index, Arts & Humanities Citation Index, Book Review Index, CERDIC, Children's Book Review Index (1965–), Current Contents, Historical Abstracts, Humanities Index, Index to Book Reviews in the Humanities, LCR, Middle East: Abstract & Index, MLA Bibliography, PAIS,* and *Social Science Source.* This journal is a member of the Council of Editors of Learned Journals.

ISSN 0038-2876

ISBN for this issue: 0-8223-6435-2

Real Sports

The
South
Atlantic
Quarterly
Spring 1996
Volume 95
Number 2

James T. Fisher

Editor's Note

Late in the month of June during each year of my childhood, the Pittsburgh Pirates came to New York for a series with the Mets. I looked forward to the series all through the winter and spring because I knew that on one of those nights my father would come home early from work and we'd make the long, mostly silent trip to Shea Stadium. By the time we hit the traffic around LaGuardia Airport my heart would be starting to pound and it would not relent until I saw the number 21 posted in the lineup on Shea's outfield scoreboard, indicating that my idol, Roberto Clemente, would occupy his customary third spot in the batting order that evening. But I was equally intent upon locating "the Gunner," Bob Prince, the Pirates' extremely garrulous broadcaster whose voice was my constant companion through the long nights of the baseball season, when the 50,000-watt signal of KDKA Pittsburgh blanketed thirty-eight states and parts of Canada. I saw Clemente perform perhaps a dozen times in person and slightly more often on television in the pre-ESPN era, but I heard Bob Prince call hundreds of games: not

The *South Atlantic Quarterly* 95:2, Spring 1996.
Copyright © 1996 by Duke University Press.
CCC 0038-2876/96/$1.50.

just the *voice* of the Pirates, he embodied the Buccos' character and personality.

In reading the essays for this special issue of *SAQ* on "Real Sports," I was fascinated by the diverse ways in which the authors explore the *media* of sports, both in the contemporary sense—as in print and broadcast journalism—and in the environmental and aesthetic contexts traditionally implied by the term. Students of the humanities have become familiar enough in recent years with the cultural politics of mediation—and of representation—but the worlds of sports have remained generally immune from such concerns. Before reading these essays, I might have been tempted to say that it was a good thing too, as the prospect of a "sports studies" movement is not pleasant to behold. Yet in sharing their enjoyment of games, the contributors to this issue offer themselves—good sports, all—as mediators of the imaginative passions that inspire all real sports.

On behalf of all the contributors, I wish to thank *SAQ* Managing Editor Candice Ward for her outstanding editorial supervision of this issue. While carefully scrutinizing all of our work, she has remained a "real sport" and has sustained throughout the original spirit of our enterprise.

Carlo Rotella

Three Views of the Fistic Summits from College Hill

Lafayette College is on College Hill, overlooking the rest of Easton, Pennsylvania, a large town wedged into the junction of the Delaware and Lehigh Rivers. It is a standard arrangement of college and town, although the hill is steep and Third Street bends significantly where it becomes College Avenue at the hill's base, the effect being to separate college from town with particular emphasis. Lafayette looks like a college, which means that its buildings and grounds speak in appropriately reserved ways of accrued time and money; most of Easton, which tends toward the low-rise brick styles of the industrial era, has the quiet, stark feel of Edward Hopper's paintings.

There is no boxing on College Hill. If you have cable, you can watch a fight on television, which since the 1950s has been most people's principal avenue to the ring, but there is a school of thought that argues you ought always to feel a little bad for doing it: television is a villainous agent in the narrative of boxing's decline as craft and institution (of which more to come). On a typical day, there is probably no boxing on TV anyway.[1] If you desire daily access, whether to

The *South Atlantic Quarterly* 95:2, Spring 1996.
Copyright © 1996 by Duke University Press.
CCC 0038-2876/96/$1.50.

fight or to watch, your principal avenue to the ring runs through town to the Larry Holmes Training Center.

Anybody who has seen the introductions before a Larry Holmes fight can tell you there is boxing in Easton. Holmes, introduced by ring announcers as "The Easton Assassin," was heavyweight champion of the world from 1978 to 1985. To get to his gym from College Hill, you drive down the hill, negotiate the traffic circle in the town's central square, cross Larry Holmes Drive and the Lehigh River, then take a right onto Canal Street, a stretch of road separated from the river to your right by railroad tracks behind a screen of overgrown weeds. The gym, a long, low building among several facing tracks and river, is on your left after the auto-body place. Inside, there is a red, white, and blue ring with a couple of rows of folding chairs arranged on two sides of it; there are pairs of heavy bags and speed bags and a wall of mirrors for shadowboxing; two other walls are hung with rows of fight posters and framed photographs. In some photographs, a stone-faced boxer presents a fist; in others, a smash-nosed man in street clothes offers what seems to be a genuinely happy smile. The pictures have the feel of history: in the whiff of horse-and-wagon antiquity surrounding the stylized "fistic" poses, and in the dated dandyism that informs the fighters' taste in clothing. Until recently, life-size cutouts of Holmes and Muhammad Ali in action squared off across the room from one another, standing among the smaller photographs like two heroes leading armies to battle. (The cutouts were taken down and moved to Holmes's new nightclub, leaving a pair of blasted-looking silhouettes in dried, yellowish glue on the gym's wall, after Holmes lost to Oliver McCall in April 1995.) In the afternoons there are a few young men and kids learning the craft with various degrees of diligence and skill, perhaps a couple of older ones just working up a sweat, and sometimes an older gentleman in street clothes, with his shirttail hanging out, who knows everything. Holmes trains there weekdays at 5:00 P.M.; when he has a fight coming up, increased numbers of wanderers-in give the place the air of a crossroads. For $35 per month you can train there too.

Or you can read a good book. From College Hill, the other route providing reliable daily access to fights and fight people goes through representations of the ring in various texts—essays, journalism, novels, poetry, cultural criticism, paintings, movies. My path to the textual ring runs through the boxing essays of A. J. Liebling (1904–1963), collected in *The Sweet Science* and a posthumous companion volume entitled *A Neutral Corner*.[2] *The*

Sweet Science was not the first writing on boxing I read—it was probably one of Robert E. Howard's blood-soaked pulp allegories of Anglo-Saxon regeneration through beefcake—but I read Liebling at an impressionable age and his essays have served ever since to organize and clarify for me a central problem that gives shape to boxing literature: What meanings can be found in a fight? Liebling crafted an oeuvre around showing his own path to the ring—the people he met, the books he read, the cities he traversed, the bars in which he idled, what he knew and how he knew it—and the problems and the pleasures of his style have to do with explaining what that education prepared him to see in the ring once he got there. His prose shows him running all over the cultural map—from Stendhal to Archie Moore, from the *New York Journal–American* to the scholarly quarterlies, from Gertrude Stein to Philadelphia Jack O'Brien, from the nineteenth-century British journalist Pierce Egan to the fourteenth-century Tunisian historian Ibn Khaldūn—as he assembles the mix of idioms needed to articulate the range of meanings at play in a fight. Students at Lafayette typically want to know what the hell Liebling is doing when, in his account of the Moore–Marciano fight, he compares light-heavyweight Archie Moore not only to the great lightweight Benny Leonard, but also to Margot Fonteyn, Arthur Rubinstein, Orson Welles, Faust, Ahab, and Sisyphus, as well as to a Japanese print entitled "Shogun Engaged in Strategic Contemplation in the Midst of War" and to intellect itself confronted by naked force (in the person of Marciano).

In those comparisons, Liebling shows how ripples of meaning spread out from particular forms and usages of the ring. The fight world has useful ways of analyzing the pattern of ripples: a good big man beat a good little man; a fighter stepped back when he should have stepped in to avoid the hook; a recent fight repeated or varied the lessons of another fight that happened long ago; quality of training will find a way to display itself in the ring. Any reader of the fights must know what fight people know, but there are, of course, other ways of reading a fight. The ripples extend in all directions, into other ways of knowing: pursuing an extended tail-and-dog analogy between the ring and the world outside it, Budd Schulberg asserts that boxing, "the most basic and complex of all our sports," forms a richly signifying "appendage to the various dog-shapes civilization has assumed over the past five thousand years."[3] All manner of interpreters have found in pugilism a simple binary structure capable of carrying a variety of meanings that extend far beyond the fight world's boundaries: rituals of gender, maps of morality or psychology, allegories of all stripes; social, economic, and cultural orders violently parsed; epic, tragedy, comedy, history; aesthetics, science, craft. I will not review them here; others have made necessarily partial lists.[4]

Because the pattern of ripples spreading out from fighters' ring styles embraces both the fight world and the world beyond it, the problem of reading the fights entails resolving the tensions among different orders of meaning. You can choose to see just a fragment of the pattern—you can reduce a fight to a technical boxing problem, and you can reduce a fight to a poetic or political or moral artifact—but you will have given up on seeing the relationships among fragments that suggest a larger whole. In *Beyond a Boundary*, Liebling's contemporary C. L. R. James makes the same point about reading cricket. He sees all manner of "social passions . . . using cricket as a medium of expression," and his readings of the game's "significant forms" invest cricket with a social, cultural, and aesthetic history embracing the rise and fall of British Victorianism and colonialism; but James insists that all bridges of logic extending beyond the boundaries of the game must be anchored in the technical details of the game itself. Declaring that "any extended cricket analysis which is not based on historical facts or the technique of the game tells more about the writer than what he is writing about," James then details W. G. Grace's batting and bowling styles in order to prove that Grace both embodied everything worth knowing about pre–Victorian England and invented modern cricket.[5] The book's opening image—James as a child climbing up a chair to get to both the bookshelf and the window from which he could see the cricket ground—sets a pattern for James's pursuit of the meanings of cricket into Thackeray and Trotsky and colonial history, but all of his arguments are also rooted in the game itself and in the cricket world's own analytical traditions.

What follows here, then, goes to and through the ring: it begins in the techniques and history of boxing, but goes well beyond the ring into literature, the social landscape of Easton, and post–World War II cultural and social history, in asking what meanings can be found in a fight. The answers are based in readings of style: how Liebling assembles an essay on boxing; how Holmes fights his fight. Liebling tells us about the relation of boxing to "culture" in both the anthropological and the Arnoldian (Matthew, not Schwarzenegger) sense, and his signature style—prodigiously digressive and allusive, extravagantly juxtaposing various registers of speech, structured around mapping his own path to the ring—dramatizes the problem of reconciling fight talk with the kinds of talk available to literary critics, historians, social scientists, and the conventionally "cultured." Holmes tells us about the relation of boxing to the social landscape beyond the ring, and *his* signature style—built around the left jab, good defense, subtle footwork, a solid chin, and the conservation of resources—dramatizes the negotiation of asset and liability that characterizes boxing, business, and the texture of life in an industrial town at a postindustrial crossroads. Read together, the two stylists, Liebling and Holmes, suggest the dimensions of a larger relation between the ring and the social and textual worlds that contain it.

There was no doubt that the fight had caught the public imagination, ever sensitive to a meeting between Hubris and Nemesis, as the boys on the quarterlies would say, and the bookies were laying 18–5 on Nemesis, according to the boys on the dailies, who always seem to hear.[6]

Liebling wrote almost all of his boxing essays for the *New Yorker*, a weekly magazine nicely suspended between the daily papers and the scholarly quarterlies. He was proud of having learned his craft by writing for the dailies, which were strong on reporting but strictly limited in prose style and in the range of interpretive response to the news they pursued. Those limitations were—and still are—especially evident on the sports page. (He liked to tell a story about being fired from a menial job at the *New York Times* because he tried to relieve the drudgery of the sports pages by putting some private jokes in the box scores of high school basketball games.) Liebling sampled the quarterlies, on the other hand, as a reader with esoteric enthusiasms rather than as a professional scholar. (He was also proud of having been thrown out of Dartmouth for missing mandatory chapel services.)[7] The quarterlies were weak on reporting and on making sense of the urban world in which Liebling's authorial persona usually moved, and their language and interpretive repertoire could be limited or obscure, but they did engage with a range of literary and historical matters that were off-limits to the dailies. The *New Yorker* of the 1940s and 1950s valued good reporting and an insider's perspective on things beyond the direct experience of its readership, while also offering poetry, conventionally "serious" literary prose that eschewed "popular" formulas, and critical connection to the world of high culture (literature, drama, music, opera, dance, painting). One of Liebling's favorite tactics in writing for the *New Yorker* about subject matter fit for the dailies—and, more generally, about the social strata that Harold Ross, his editor at the magazine, described as "lowlife"—was to make authorial theater out of behaving as if he were writing about it for the quarterlies.

If Liebling wanted to establish that he was a good reporter who could work on the dailies, an insider with the know-how to make sense of transactions in the ring (always knowing the odds because, like the boys on the dailies, he knew all the right fight people), he also wanted to establish that he was not just another hack filing copy for the *Journal–American*. He could speak the stylized cant of the dailies, but he always did so in the ironic mode: for example, "Rocky Marciano, the reigning heavyweight champion, scaled the fistic summits, as they say in *Journal–Americanese*, by beating Jersey Joe Walcott."[8] He had an equally distanced sense of how the boys on the quarterlies might cover the fights: Liebling used mock-heroic and mock-scholarly diction to show himself reading into a boxing match a set of cartoonishly "cultured" meanings appropriate to the quarterlies. In "Ahab and Nemesis," he describes the moment when Rocky Marciano (Nemesis) got back on his feet after being knocked down by Archie Moore (Hubris): "I do not know what took place in Mr. Moore's breast when he saw him get up. He may have felt, for the moment, like Don Giovanni when the Commendatore's statue grabbed at him—startled because he thought he had killed the guy already—or like Ahab when he saw the White Whale take down Fedallah, harpoons and all."[9] Sandwiched between Don Giovanni and Ahab, the pointedly unscholarly "killed the guy already" reminds us that Liebling is mixing registers for effect.

The effect, here and elsewhere, is to foreground his efforts to find and communicate the meanings to be found in a boxing match. Each essay makes a secondary narrative out of Liebling's self-appointed task of assembling the language needed to represent the ring, language that he shows himself gathering not only from fight people and the dailies, but also from a bookshelf stuffed with texts both standard (Homer, Melville, Stendhal, Camus) and not so standard (Pierce Egan, Ibn Khaldūn). The drama of writing the ring sometimes parallels and sometimes plays against the drama in the ring, but the relation between the two—between strategies for making meaning in books and the meaning to be found in the strategies and trans-actions of the ring—creates a productive tension that dominates the inner life of Liebling's boxing essays. In addition to telling the stories of fights and fighters, his essays meditate upon how to write those stories and how the writer of the ring places himself among other literary figures.

Liebling therefore makes a literary spectacle out of dragging in language from all over the cultural map in an effort to represent and interpret the details of a fight. In some of his paragraphs, the various registers pile up so rapidly that the potential unwieldiness of the combination and the smoothness with which he masters it threaten to become the point of the exercise. Here, for instance, is the aftermath of Moore's knockdown of Marciano in "Ahab and Nemesis":

> After being knocked down, Marciano had stopped throwing that pat-terned right-and-left combination; he has a good nob. "He never trun it again in the fight," Whitey [Bimstein, a trainer] said next day, but I differ. He threw it again in the fifth, and again Moore hit him a peach of a right inside it, but the steam was gone; this time Ahab [i.e. Moore] couldn't even stagger him. Anyway, there was Moore at the end of the second, dragging his shattered faith in the unities and humanities back to his corner. He had hit a guy right, and the guy hadn't gone. But there is no geezer in Moore, any more than there was in the master of the *Pequod*.[10]

The "good nob" comes direct from Pierce Egan, the great journalist–impresario of the nineteenth-century London prize ring; almost all of Liebling's boxing essays make reference to Egan's mannered prose. Whitey Bimstein, whom Liebling calls his "private eye," contributes technical analysis of Marciano's tactical adjustment in the dialect of fight people ("trun" for "thrown"), allowing Liebling's own expertise to be displayed through a corrective gloss in a gentler register ("but I differ," as opposed to, say, "the hell he didn't"). Ahab appears twice, extending Liebling's reading of the fight as a parallel to *Moby-Dick* in which the "cerebral and hyper-experienced" Moore's educated faith in self and intellect leads him to glorious ruin at the hands of large, impersonal forces, embodied in his "White Whale"—the stronger, younger, far less polished Marciano. Liebling also liked to imagine boxing as a kind of academy—Stillman's Gym in New York was for him "the University of Eighth Avenue"—dedicated to promulgating eternal truths both historical and artistic. Thus Moore's "shattered faith in the unities and humanities" describes the foundations of ring tradition being shaken by the "gauche" Marciano rising from the canvas: the classically trained Moore cannot believe that there can be an exception to one of boxing's structuring truisms—that every guy will go if you hit him right. "If a boxer did not believe that," Liebling explains, "he would be in the position of a Euclidian without faith in the hundred-and-eighty-degree triangle."[11] (Later, he speculates on the explanation that Moore's "Faustian mind" might have come up with to explain Marciano's seemingly miraculous recovery: "He may have thought that perhaps he had not hit Marciano *just* right; the true artist is always prone to self-reproach."[12]) Finally, the "geezer" of ring talk and the epithetical reference to "the master of the *Pequod*" (unless you know *Moby-Dick*, you won't know that Liebling is still talking about Ahab) together balance the registers of the daily and the quarterly. Liebling maintains that balance throughout the essay: describing Moore's fading chances of victory later in the fight, for instance, he writes, "It was in the fourth, though, that I think Sisyphus began to get the idea he couldn't roll back the Rock."[13] The "Rock" gets the capital-R treatment not only as an inflated Symbol appropriate to the quarterlies (Moore becomes Camus's existential hero struggling against history), but also because the dailies and the kind of people who read them often called Marciano (born Rocco Marchegiano) "the Rock."

All this ironic distance, serving to position Liebling as familiar with but not native to the various strata of language and culture through which he pursues the meanings of a fight, makes it seem as if there are invisible quotation marks around most of what he says. That jokey, needling quality can make Liebling hard to take: there is something about his prose, to borrow a phrase from Jim Thompson, that's like biting down on tinfoil. But it is precisely where a literary cutey-pie (to borrow a boxing term for a deceptive, trap-setting fighter) like Liebling seems jokiest that one should look for his most serious claims: that boxing is great art (an argument made by James for cricket); that boxing is a fit subject for great artists and critics (an argument akin to the one made by Ishmael for whaling, and done via a similarly audacious survey across the cultural spectrum); and that Liebling's uniquely comprehensive expertise as a writer of boxing, displayed in his eclectic command of idioms, subsumes and exceeds the reach of both writers who don't know any better than to use "fistic" and those who know all too well how to use "hubris."

The same set of impulses drove Liebling's tendency to write about boxing as if he were reviewing poetry. The processes of literary culture are put into burlesque motion around the subject of boxing when he reviews fighters as artists, offering evaluations of major and minor figures in the canon: Cassius Clay's early work indicates a major new talent on the make, for example, while the classicist Archie Moore has been underappreciated in an age of declining technical virtuosity. Liebling's essays continually trace and reinforce a network of intertextuality binding texts (e.g., his own to those of Egan, Malory, and Homer), themes (e.g., the perpetual struggle of classically trained boxers to keep the "sweet science" from being dragged in the mud by rough brawlers), and characters (e.g., underappreciated poets, overvalued goons, colorful supporting players). Liebling also lampoons the world of secondary texts: he cannot devote his full attention to the artists and the primary texts (the fighters themselves and their fights) because, like a critic obliged to tangle with other critics, he is constantly interrupted by know-it-all secondary figures—trainers, managers, hangers-on—who compete to purvey their own interpretations of primary texts. Most of the fighters, like poets, are too immersed in their craft to bend his ear.

One sign that Liebling's treatment of fighters as artists adds up to more than an exercise in cleverness, however, lies in his reversing rather than repeating the usual writer–fighter analogy. Typically, writers use fighters to think about what it means to write. Joyce Carol Oates, for example, suggests that the writer's sense of "kinship, however oblique and one-sided, with the professional boxer" proceeds from parallels between training for a fight and writing for publication: "That which is 'public' is but the final stage in a protracted, arduous, grueling, and frequently despairing period of preparation."[14] Her list of "serious" writers on boxing includes Swift, Pope, Byron, Hemingway, and Mailer, but does not include Liebling, whom Oates finds "relentlessly jokey" (i.e., insufficiently serious).[15] Liebling, on the other hand, uses the language of literary criticism to think about what it means to fight. His habit of treating fighters like artists provides a way to get at what matters to him about boxing as well as a way to get at the problem of chasing ripples out from the ring into the textual world.

What matters most to Liebling is mastery of style in the ring and the well thought out content it expresses: "The boxer who interests me is the *reasoner* in the ring," as opposed to the slugger, more "popular with the unthinking crowd," who rushes in "to occupy the other fellow's gloves with his face while he slugs away at the face in front of him."[16] In his essays, Liebling always goes to a fight "hoping to see art vindicated" over slugging (punching without science) and showy "prancing" (energy wasted in superfluous motion); in a fight crowd, he is a person of discernment besieged by coarse uninitiates howling for the wrong kind of action. Liebling's favorite fighters, then, are craftsmen and stylists: Archie Moore, whose subtlety earns him the relatively obscure status of "a boxer's boxer, as Stendhal was for a long time a writer's writer"; Floyd Patterson, whose "driving earnestness . . . transcended pugnacity" to become a devotion to reasoned pugilism that evoked "the rage of a literary stylist trying to get something down on paper";[17] and Cassius Clay (not yet Ali and not yet a champion when Liebling died in 1963), who showed in his early genre work the promise of maturing into a major artist of pathbreaking originality.

A boxing match, then, means an opportunity to see the logic and traditions that undergird the sweet science as an artistic discipline dramatically enacted: the violent contrast of styles, new practitioners compared to old masters, genius and training and will challenging the limitations of the form (limitations of body, mind, and circumstance). Liebling looks forward with a sense of incipient plenitude to visiting a dedicated fighter's training camp or to seeing a good fight: "Not only rivers and the life cycle have a continuous quality that gives a fellow something to hold on to. The processes of art, too, are self-renewing."[18] He is not overly disturbed, therefore, when the self-taught Swedish puncher Ingemar Johansson knocks out the artist Floyd Patterson in their first fight because the self-renewing processes of art can be seen at work in Johansson's victory. After all, the puncher has exercised reason and craft to exploit in textbook fashion a flaw in the boxer's style: Johansson knocks Patterson down the first time with a classically short, straight right thrown inside the arc of Patterson's left hook. But in a subsequent essay, Liebling becomes the traditionalist aghast when Johansson prepares for the rematch with Patterson by guzzling milkshakes, bringing his fiancée to camp, and otherwise contravening boxing tradition in ways that speak of chaos rather than innovation. Johansson then represents "the seed of the dissipation of authority and the germ of the disintegration of discipline,"[19] a crisis resolved when Patterson diligently adjusts his style and demolishes the profoundly limited Johansson in the rematch.

Liebling entitled his essay on the rematch, a paean to the capacity of boxing to dramatize its artistic self-renewal, "A Blow for Austerity." However, it is not austerity in and of itself, but rather Patterson's austere genius that Liebling wishes to see vindicated for the good of boxing. He also roots vigorously in more than one essay for the anything-but-austere Cassius Clay, whose "amplitude" in and outside the ring Liebling sees as the mark of a potential genius capable of leading the sweet science into another heroic age. Liebling was charmed by Clay's reasoning in the ring and by the tongue-in-cheek self-importance with which he both advertised and mitigated his overweening ambition. Other fight people were not so taken with Clay's semi-ironized hubris, and some were especially put off by his habit of concocting rhymed assessments of his adversaries. "Anti-Poetry Night," an account of Clay's victory over Harlem heavyweight Doug Jones before a Madison Square Garden crowd that booed the decision, makes an extended defense of Liebling's "fellow-littérateur" Clay, "the heavyweight poet from Louisville, Kentucky," whose latest work has met with a loutish response from a public that fails to appreciate his gift.[20] In fight commentary that doubles as literary criticism, Liebling describes Clay's advantage in reach over the much shorter Jones as a critic would evaluate a rising master's early genre work: "The poet towered above his chosen subject."[21] The genre in this case is the marquee fight against a tough young heavyweight with only average speed and ring sense, and the rising master's successful rendition of Jones portends future greatness for Clay even as it exposes his present lack of polish.

One can see why a witty, articulate boxer like Clay would have appealed to Liebling. Not only was Clay a young heavyweight with preternaturally fast hands who showed promise of ruling the fight world; he could recite original poetry while doing sit-ups (a trick that Liebling wanted "to see T. S. Eliot try").[22] Much as Liebling reversed and resisted the writer's habit of using boxing to think about writing (never saying that writing is like boxing, but frequently saying that boxing is like writing), one is tempted to read his paralleling of boxers and literary artists the other way around: his mock evaluations of boxers as artists also consider his own status as a writer of literate boxing essays, among other generic miscellanea. His hero, after all, was Archie Moore, a great artist who, like Liebling but unlike Clay, did his best work in a minor genre, the light-heavyweight division.

Liebling, whose oeuvre spans a range of light-heavyweight genres, wants to make literature out of marking the path that leads down from his middle-class origins through "lowlife" and then up into "high culture." He aspires to go conventionally low in order to get to the conventionally high—an aspiration common among literary students of urban culture and sports, and, more generally, among children of the middle class who find themselves drawn to both the street and the library.[23] Liebling developed a literary anthropology of lowlife that documented the world of fight people, saloon people, Broadway types, racetrack touts, and seedy reporters. These hustlers led lives that resembled those of artists—usually austere, sometimes inspired—and that emphatically did not follow his family's upward-curving social trajectory from the Lower East Side to middle-class security in the Rockaways. He also wanted to write his way into the highbrow canons of literary culture and criticism, albeit as a disruptive and parodic force wielding a cultural authority acquired in parts of the social landscape that his *New Yorker* readers avoided in person.

Liebling's model in this project was Pierce Egan, "a hack journalist, a song writer, a conductor of puff-sheets, and, I am inclined to suspect, a shakedown man," as well as "the greatest writer about the ring who ever lived."[24] He introduces Egan with a new heroic epithet in each essay (the Sir Thomas Malory of the London Prize Ring, the Edward Gibbon, the Homer, and so on); slipping into Egan's voice becomes another running gag. The introduction to *The Sweet Science* concludes with a pitch-perfect Eganism that links Liebling's book to Egan's journal *Boxiana*: "I can think of nothing more to say in favor of the Present Extension of the GREAT HISTORIAN'S Magnum Opus."[25] Egan, who seems to have been at every boxing match, dog fight, and bar brawl in early nineteenth-century London, has been described elsewhere as "a first-class journalist and . . . an important figure on the lower slopes of literature" who provided Dickens with authoritative material on the bottom third of England's social strata, and romantic slummers like Byron with an insider's guide to the world of pugilism.[26] Egan offered, as Liebling describes it, "a panorama of low, dirty, happy, brutal, sentimental Regency England that you'll never get from Jane Austen." Austen and even Hazlitt ("a dilettante" whose essay

Figure 1. A. J. Liebling (January 1963). UPI/Bettmann News-
photos. Reproduced by permission of the Bettmann Archive.

"The Fight" visits Egan's bailiwick) were marooned too far up the slopes
of literary culture to get a good view of the action down below. Liebling
sees Egan as positioned to link high and low, largely cutting out the un-
interesting social and cultural middle, a role emphasized in his accounts
of "that curious pattern of good fellowship and snobbery, not mutually exclusive, that has always existed between Gentleman and Player."[27] Egan,
slangy and distinctive, gave Liebling a model of literary writing that could
smoothly shuttle between high and low.

Fittingly, Liebling made a place for himself on the lower slopes of
American letters that was roughly analogous to Egan's. Picture Liebling
(Figure 1), a gouty fat man, typing away between meals in a modest bunga-
low which overlooks the trailer parks of popular literary culture (home to
pulp writers like Robert E. Howard, best known as the creator of Conan the
Barbarian), but stands significantly downhill from the neat rows of ranch
houses and tudors that house critically respected novelists and poets, repu-
table critics, and the relatively few essayists and academics who achieve a

general readership. As Fred Warner, one of the editors of *A Neutral Corner*, points out in trying to explain Liebling's marginal place in American letters, "It is still strangely difficult in this country to evaluate properly a writer who didn't chiefly write fiction, poetry, or plays, and in the academy there are still not many people who know and esteem Liebling's work." [28] Liebling was a reporter, and a kind of cultural critic (although of a genus that does not encourage a rush to his work among readers of C. L. R. James or Roland Barthes, to name two of Liebling's contemporaries with things to say about sports and culture), and he wanted to be known as a literary man. However awkward a problem of evaluation he might present, Liebling was clearly a literary figure in several senses: he had a terrifically eclectic command of language and letters, and what he wrote drew life from its connections to literary artifacts major and minor; he published in the *New Yorker*, cheek by jowl with some of the most widely esteemed poets, fiction writers, and critics of his day; and he made it his business to evaluate critically the work of poets who gave significant form to the everyday materials available to them. One must include under this definition of "poets," as he did, though, not only litterateurs but also welterweights, chefs, and reporters.

Liebling's literary resumé ranges across genres, always with one foot in reporting and the other in something else—history, aesthetics, literature. He was one of the great press critics, unrivaled in slicing up bad journalistic writing and reasoning, but ready to defend competent reporters and writers hamstrung by the corporate imperatives and impoverished political culture of the news business. Among the best war correspondents of the World War II era, he was the most sophisticated reader and writer, the most committed to framing that war on the human scale of individual people and daily life, and one of the least sentimental (except regarding the French, for whom he had a terrible weakness). *The Earl of Louisiana*, his 1961 portrait of Earl Long, is still one of the most engaging American political biographies. With fellow *New Yorker* essayist Joseph Mitchell, he mapped midcentury New York in ways that established a pattern for American nonfiction: his influence can be traced in the writing of the New Journalists, in practically any contemporary issue of the *New Yorker* and other high-end cosmopolitan magazines, or, for that matter, in *Sports Illustrated* or the daily paper. He contributed mightily to the haphazard effort in American letters to represent what happens in those interstices of urbanism that do not fall neatly into the generic realms of upper, middle, and lower class. He wrote about food more than a decent person should; and he wrote great essays on boxing.[29]

Being the best multiple-threat press critic, the most literate war correspondent, and the best lowlife essayist, food writer, and fight writer around is kind of like being the light-heavyweight champion of the world: an enormous achievement of craftsmanship but a relatively minor distinction. The light-heavyweights are overshadowed on one side by the middleweight division, with its own deep tradition of boxing excellence—Sugar Ray Robinson, still considered by many to be the best pound-for-pound fighter of all time, was a middleweight—and, on the other side, by the heavyweights, who always capture the lion's share of the public imagination. Many great middleweights and heavyweights have fought as light-heavyweights, but few have enjoyed great renown on the strength of their light-heavyweight bouts. Liebling was like a classic light-heavy who finds himself too heavy to box comfortably as a middleweight and too light to join the heavies; he was a fine essayist and reporter in whose rotund breast beat the heart of an expansive, digressive novelist.

After Liebling wrote what he called "a favorable review" of one of Archie Moore's victories, the light-heavyweight champion sent him a note of thanks signed "the most unappreciated fighter in the world, Archie Moore."[30] Moore yielded to the light-heavy's classic temptation: he challenged heavyweight champions, who beat him. Fight people always want to know if the light-heavy champ is going to "move up" to the big time and seek the heavyweight title. Only one has done it successfully: Michael Spinks won a close decision against Larry Holmes (although many think Holmes was robbed). Moore, probably the greatest light-heavy of all time, lost to heavyweight champions Marciano, Patterson, Ezzard Charles (three times), and even to the future champion Cassius Clay. A true light-heavy, who does not grow naturally into a heavyweight as he ages and who reaches the optimum balance of speed and precision with power at a fighting weight of 160 to 175 pounds, usually ends up distorting his body (by beefing up), his style, or both when he takes on a significantly bigger man—but the temptation to go after the heavyweight crown is powerful.

Liebling certainly had good material with which to move up in the conventional hierarchy of literary genres: during his years as a reporter he had done the "research" for a series of novels in the manner of his urban-realist heroes—Dickens, the French masters, Crane—and he entertained thoughts of embarking on such projects, but he only dabbled in prose fiction. He also started and abandoned a play based on his war reportage. Once he had found his mature essayistic style, Liebling did not make any sustained attempts at publishing fiction, poetry, or drama. Perhaps he no longer had any interest in them; perhaps he realized that the change in genres would distort his style and undermine the balance of good humor and elegant diction that made it work. When "a literary friend" criticized as "too obvious" an image of blood mixed with milk that appeared in Liebling's war reportage, he pardoned the friend for "mistaking me for a creative writer."[31] Liebling did not necessarily feel uncreative as an essayist, nor did he feel unappreciated (except possibly by the part of himself that aspired to write fiction and drama), but nobody seemed eager to recognize him as a literary heavyweight.

Instead of forcing the issue by trying to "move up," Liebling made a virtue of his light-heaviness. Both in style and in substance, his boxing essays present him as uniquely positioned across the lines that divide culture into high and low, literary and popular, and thus as well placed to draw a uniquely broad range of meanings—technical, historical, literary, dramatic, aesthetic, sociological, political—from a boxing match. His cultivation of a necessary distance from any one way of knowing or articulating the fights, as well as the exclusiveness of his claim to expertise, irritates some other writers on boxing—like Oates and Gerald Early, both of whom pass over Liebling as a patronizing joker in their reviews of boxing literature.[32] Oates can say, with an utterly straight face, things like "in the brightly lit ring, man is *in extremis*, performing an atavistic rite or *agon* for the mysterious solace of those who can participate only vicariously in such drama: the drama of life in the flesh. Boxing has become America's tragic theater."[33] Early tends to reduce boxing to racial theater. Both may, then, feel themselves unfairly subsumed and dismissed by Liebling's pervasive contention that he can read the spreading pattern of meanings proceeding from a fight more expertly than those whose path to the ring is more circumscribed or less coolly mapped than his own—the boys (and girls: Liebling was narrow-minded on that score, among others) on the quarterlies, the characters who frequent the fight clubs, illiterate (for all their expertise in the history and technique of boxing) fight people, and literate dilettantes slumming in lowlife.

A. J. Liebling lives on College Hill—the library has eleven of his books, and at least one professor on campus teaches "Ahab and Nemesis"—but boxing has a textual rather than a physical presence at Lafayette. As at most pricey, exclusive colleges, there is an occasional drunken fight (not to be confused with boxing), usually between chesty young men who allow the knowledge of how much they stand to lose curb an already inexpert animosity toward one another: they do not want to get expelled; they do not want to get into trouble with their parents; they do not want to get sued; they do not necessarily know how to hit each other correctly; and deep down they do not really want to risk ruining their own or their adversary's placid and class-appropriate physiognomy. They mostly shove one another with theatrical vehemence and yell hard, wounding things. Art Statum, who won an NCAA heavyweight boxing championship at North Carolina A&T, used to instruct Lafayette students in the manly art of self-defense (no sparring, just drills and conditioning). The college stopped offering those lessons some years ago, and Statum, having retired from coaching and teaching at Lafayette, now volunteers as a roving peacekeeper ("verbal intimidation," he assures me, "nothing physical") at a nearby middle school. Statum looks back with fondness on the college boys he instructed in the craft of boxing—they worked hard, he says, even if they lacked "the killer instinct"—but he thinks that some of Lafayette's administrators were glad to see him leave College Hill. I asked Statum if they were uncomfortable with the idea of a large Black man teaching a violent craft to young White men. He said, "What do you think?" [34] (Other faculty members have suggested that Statum was "not perky enough" or was "too old-fashioned" to teach recreational sports at a college.)

While Statum was telling me this over lunch in a restaurant fronting Easton's central square, Larry Holmes walked in with a lawyer, who waited, not too patiently, as the two warhorses did some preprandial cutting up. Statum offered, with broad irony, to buy lunch for Holmes, who is a millionaire several times over. Holmes responded, with mock concern, that he did not have change for a dollar—an insult of unclear import, but apparently a reference to the fact that amateur champions do not make any money. Statum, twenty-one years older than Holmes, said, "I can still take you," to which Holmes answered, "I'll check back with you when I'm sixty-five." "Six," said Statum, "I'm sixty-six." He seemed to feel that that settled the discussion; Holmes and his lawyer went away.

Holmes, who is still active as a fighter at this writing, won the heavy-weight title in 1978 (taking the WBC title from Ken Norton) and held it over a remarkable seven-year span of nineteen defenses until he lost the controversial decision to Michael Spinks in 1985. When Holmes beat a depressingly diminished Muhammad Ali (who had once employed him as a sparring partner) in 1980, he put an end to the era of Ali and ushered in the five-year period of his own undisputed ascendancy. After losing a second close decision to Spinks, Holmes retired in 1986, then came out of retirement to fight Mike Tyson (who knocked him out) in 1988. After re-retiring, Holmes came out of retirement again in 1991 and lost a title bout by decision to Evander Holyfield in 1992. Having beaten less distinguished opponents in 1993 and 1994, Holmes, then forty-five years old, positioned himself for yet another title shot, against Oliver McCall on 8 April 1995. He fought well against McCall, but lost again, bringing his lifetime record to 61–5.

When he came into the restaurant that day in April 1995, Holmes still had under his left eye the mark of a deep gash opened ten days before by McCall during an unlovely but decisive series of punches in the ninth round of their fight. Holmes had been ahead on most cards until the ninth, fighting in his signature conservative style: wasting no energy, scoring with his still-potent left jab, slipping punches with subtle head movements, foiling his much younger opponent's attack with punch-entangling arms and a knack for crossing up McCall's predictable footwork. Holmes often looks awkward, as when he retreats to erase an attacking opponent's advantage in position, blinking furiously (he has had eye troubles) and pawing with his long arms to smother punches; then there are moments when he looks improbably smooth, as when he stands in the middle of the ring with his hands low and evades a series of punches with unexcited three-inch re-positionings of his chin.

The pawing and slipping, as well as the jab-heavy offense and impeccable, unhurried footwork, are aspects of a style shaped to conserve his resources. That measured style, exaggerated in the last ten years as he has gone from a mature to an old fighter, reconciles two sometimes conflicting imperatives: Holmes protects his physical assets, the fighter's brain and its bodily frame, with superb defensive technique, but he must also protect his record and especially, when he held it, the heavyweight title by winning the fight, which means risking damage in order to damage his opponent. Every fighter has to work through that calculus, but Holmes's solution—defensive boxing and low-risk offensive maneuvers leading toward victory by decision (unless his opponent makes a big mistake and gets himself knocked out)—has become increasingly rare among heavyweights. Since the advent of television, promising young heavies have been rushed along, with minimal seasoning, toward the chance of big-money fights and thus place their confidence in offense—which paying customers have always valued more anyway—rather than in their underdeveloped defensive skills, which take longer to learn and require more experience and expert instruction. Holmes throws twenty left jabs for every right hand, the ratio of a defensive specialist looking patiently for an opening. Between rounds of sparring in the gym, a trainer massages and pummels the muscles of Holmes's left shoulder and arm so that they will not stiffen up; he does not attend similarly to the right side.

Still, for all his anachronistically sound craftsmanship, Holmes lost the McCall fight. McCall is not a particularly skilled boxer, but he is a bruiser, and he won a close but clear decision over a much older man whose resources have dwindled. Holmes, whose increasingly friable and avoidable right hand has lost most of its utility as a punching instrument, could not hurt McCall. He spent too much time on the ropes trying to sucker the skeptical McCall in close, where Holmes hoped to score with that suspect right hand, and he faded in the late rounds as McCall came on with vigor. Holmes was in excellent shape for a man of forty-five, but it was apparent to all that he had lost a great part of his speed and force: even at thirty-five he could still have cut to ribbons a literal-minded musclehead like McCall without getting hit much in return. The loss to McCall drastically reduced Holmes's chances of regaining the championship and securing big-money battles against George Foreman (a year older than Holmes, and the last of Ali's notable opponents still in action) and Mike Tyson. (When he came out of retirement to fight the latter in 1988, Holmes accurately predicted that Tyson would go to jail; in 1995, as Tyson's jail term drew to a close, Holmes angled unsuccessfully for a bout with him early in his post-incarceration comeback, "so I'll get him when he's rusty like he got me."[35]) Before the McCall fight Holmes had promised to retire for good if he lost, but everyone knew he would fight again (and he has): he believes that he can protect himself from injury, and there are too many beatable champions out there. By the time this essay is published in 1996, Holmes ought to have retired once more, but he will probably still be active. If he can line up the right flawed champion and the right ringside judges, he may have even won himself a piece of the fragmented heavyweight title by then. That I can even suggest such a possibility is a measure of the heavy-weight division's disarray, of the lasting virtues of Holmes's style, and of the marketing value of fight fans' nostalgia: an ex-champion from the era of Ali still draws television viewers and can make decent money in the ring.

The money is not just an excuse. Holmes has always been a business-man—rather than a wild man—in the ring where he made his fortune, and in the last decade he has become a businessman who fights rather than a fighter with some businesses on the side. Back before he hit the big money, Holmes once went up the hill to fight at Lafayette, stopping one Joe Gholston by TKO in the Kirby Field House in 1976. "I made $1,500 when I fought at Lafayette. That's it," he told me, characteristically going straight to the bottom line. Since then, Holmes has made a great deal of money in the ring, kept much of it, and learned how to manage his financial assets in the same belt-and-suspenders way he has managed his resources in fights. In April 1995, a few days after I saw him in the restaurant, he talked to me about money, life in Easton, and the ring. We were sitting in his office on the fifth floor of L&D Holmes Riverside Plaza, an office building he put up in the 1980s. He paid cash for it, he said, not to flaunt his millions but to avoid paying interest on a bank loan. (He will slip punches with his hands down not to flaunt his skills, but because he does not need to block those punches and can therefore save his energy for something else.) From a suite of offices here, with panoramic views of Larry Holmes Drive and the river junction around which Easton grew as a mill town and nexus of waterways, he manages a portfolio of holdings that includes the building we sat in, another one (known in good developerese as "Phase Two") just completed next door, a new nightclub in Phase Two, another nightclub (for sale), a parking lot, his gym just across the river on South Side, a big house on the edge of Easton (with a fancy security system, a boxing glove–shaped pool, and a garage full of handsome cars), various promotional enterprises, and whatever else he has in the works. He also donates money and time to local charities, especially those dedicated to helping children.

Holmes sat behind his desk, facing his view. He wore a black shirt, leather vest, and off-white pants. The cut under his eye had healed, but the mark remained. When he is not fighting or training, he wears glasses, which perch slightly askew on his broad face. Small, hard eyes and a patient, evaluating manner give him a stony presence, only slightly disarmed by the glasses and a gap between his front teeth. Holmes is a big heavyweight, at 6'3" and a current prime fighting weight of about 240 pounds. He has long arms and legs, making for a long reach. Stripped for action, he never looked like a bodybuilder and looks even less like one these days: although he has always been big and strong enough to move his adversaries around in the ring, his muscles are massy and smooth rather than blown up and well defined, his torso rounded rather than chiseled, and he is solid through the middle rather than extra-wide at the shoulders. He is, in short, a man of substance built to defend himself with a minimum of fuss (Figure 2). Some big athletes look grotesque when they do normal things, like sit at a desk, with their abnormal bodies, but Holmes looked comfortable in his office.

He also seemed to enjoy his work. While we talked he occasionally excused himself to take business calls, murmuring decisive-sounding phrases like "ask her how much can we get it for," and "I'm on another long-distance call . . . give him to Dick," in a mellow phone voice. As we stood at the window to look at his view, he was full of plans scaled to a big developer's imagination. He would like to see pleasure boats come up the Delaware to Easton from Philadelphia, with the river and riverfront developed to bear the traffic and profit from it. He would like to see Easton's rivers spruced up, in any case: "See that log in the river? They should get rid of it, clean it up. See that island there? No, over *there*. Get rid of it! It's a *eyesore*! This could be a nice place." He would also like to see people park their cars more decorously on Larry Holmes Drive so that drivers pulling out of the driveway of his building can see both ways down his street. He enjoys his work, but he seems disappointed at the world's failure to arrange itself as he wants it: he does things the right way, thrifty and reasoned both in the ring and outside it, but neither fight people nor his neighbors always appreciate that kind of virtue.

Life in Easton has been rewarding for Holmes, who has gradually shaped his relationship to the town to suit his wealth, if not his expectations. He moved to Easton from Georgia with his mother when he was five and grew

Figure 2. Larry Holmes, undisputed heavyweight champion of the world, in 1984. Reproduced courtesy of Larry Holmes.

up in a housing project, a position of maximum exposure to the harshest forces at play in the social landscape. He has arrived, in middle age, at a position of relative insulation from those forces: rich and secure, owner of a fine house, with an office built to command one of the Lehigh Valley's most picturesque and historically resonant vistas. And yet he began our talk by saying, "Why do you want to talk about Easton? *Fuck* Easton"; then he offered a wide chilly smile and said he was just kidding. It suggested a complicated relationship of fighter to town.

On the one hand, Holmes has often said that his decision to remain in Easton, even after he had won the title and made his fortune, was good for both himself and his family. Easton is a "quiet, beautiful" town where he can raise "regular kids" who "don't think they are better than other people," and he credits the town's traditional calm with keeping his attention on training hard and saving his pennies. "You can go out for a beer or whatever, but most nights after ten o'clock it's time to go home. . . . Plus there are no Joneses to keep up with." At a press conference held in Easton before the McCall fight, a reporter asked Holmes why he did not consider himself washed up at the age of 45, given that the 38-year-old Ali had been sadly over the hill when Holmes destroyed him in 1980. "Ali burned the candle at both ends," Holmes answered. "I never did. Thanks to Easton, my lifestyle has been at a minimum."

On the other hand, Holmes feels that many of his neighbors and local government officials have never given him the credit he deserves for staying when he could have moved away; for spending his money in town, supporting local charities, and putting Easton on the map. (It is hard to imagine the national press sending reporters here en masse except to interview Holmes.) The town did rename an avenue in his honor, boosters do tout him as a civic asset, and there are people here who speak proudly of Easton as the "home of Holmes," but he feels underappreciated, especially in comparison to the region's other world champion, race-car driver Mario Andretti. Holmes senses a coldness in Eastonians, even those who show him off to visitors: "They just like to say 'Hello, Larry'—because I'm famous—and I say 'hello' back, but there's nothing in it." Solicit opinions of Holmes around town and many people, especially those who do not know him and who speak under cover of anonymity, say that he is "rich and arrogant," that his buildings are "ugly" and "hog the best spot" in town, that the criminal behavior of his brothers, Jacob and Mark, reflects badly on him. One woman told me, with strong emotion in her voice, that "a lot of people around here" take offense at the red and white color scheme of Holmes's ring equipment because he is "using the colors" of the local high school, from which he did not graduate. Eastonians in local bars said they would not watch the Holmes–McCall fight because the pay-per-view fee was too high. (It is hard to imagine them attending an out-of-town fight in large numbers and rushing the ring after the hometown fighter's victory, as Liebling describes Rocky Marciano's rooters from Brockton doing in New York.) Holmes also thinks the town's government and business community should be more inclined to reward him for investing in—and attracting money to—Easton. In particular, it galls him that his plans to develop the riverfront encountered local opposition.

Holmes thinks the problem is rooted in race: like Statum at Lafayette, he is a Black man in a largely White community. "If I was White, nobody would oppose me putting up a five-million-dollar building. . . . I bring fame, but I get no credit." Especially since he became champion, Holmes has been willing to air his ideas about race. His blunt rhetorical style is less suited to building a following among White people and the press than, say, Ali's witty theatrics, and he probably did not further endear himself to even his local boosters by bringing Al Sharpton to Easton several years ago to support him in accusing the police department of having beaten and harassed his brother. It is hard to judge, though, how much the opposition to Holmes's riverside buildings was motivated by racial animosity and how much by anti-redevelopment traditionalism. In design the L&D Holmes Plaza gestures cordially toward the town's brick architecture and homey scale, but it also stands as a sign of postindustrial redevelopment at the river junction from which sprang a town still resolutely industrial in its self-conception.

It is, as I said, a complicated relationship between fighter and town. Holmes sums it up by saying, "As fair as they haven't been to me, let me say this: without them knowing it, Easton has been great to me."

Easton has not been the source of Holmes's wealth; rather, it has been the space in which he stored it (in real property, above all) and the forum in which he expressed it: "The ring generated all my money," he says. "I haven't made a penny out of Easton." The fame and especially the money Holmes won in the ring have allowed him to significantly reconfigure the form of Easton and his position in it. The blank square of the ring, to which he has made his way almost daily for twenty-seven years, has been a kind of money-making machine—training, will, and accrued ring acumen go in, money comes out—and the practiced moves he still makes in the ring's circumscribed space have enabled the much more expansive set of moves he has made in the social landscape: to the secure house outside town, to the well-appointed office downtown. Pretty good, as he says, for a seventh-grade dropout. As he tells it now, he has gone into each fight with a clear sense of how his path would carry him through the ring and back into the world beyond it:

> I fought for one thing: money. For instance, I knew I couldn't beat Tyson: I wasn't ready, I was two years rusty. I was confident, though, that I could protect myself, not get hurt. I fought him for three million dollars. I'm always thinking, "I'm fighting to get money for something"—my wife and kids, a house, a pool, a car. I wrote it on the wall. Every fight had a goal. The Tyson fight—the goal was money to pay for this building we're sitting in.

Sports sentimentalists, a group that includes almost every sportswriter and most fans, will never gush over Holmes as they did over Marciano or Ali, and students of culture will probably not flock to him as they have to Ali and Joe Louis. Holmes fights in a style that does not galvanize the popular or critical imagination; rather, it seems designed to galvanize the imaginations of bankers who make small business loans. It is a style suited to the principles of upward social mobility as pursued by the striving poor rather than the fortuitously gifted. Holmes accepts risk when he has to in order to realize gain—he risks getting hurt when he goes in to hurt an opponent—but he is careful to do so only when a plausible opportunity presents itself. He conserves his resources and protects himself, always looking to get ahead, to build up points, to build on what he has.

Sustained upward mobility from the lower classes through sports is supposed to be a cruel lie—and almost all of the time it is, especially for boxers—but Holmes has followed the cliché's improbable curve all the way up. He seems at once bemused and inspired by the difficulty of being a Black millionaire. Americans tend to think of a million dollars as the amount it takes to definitively insulate one from our sharkish social processes, but Americans also tend to think of being Black as inevitably exposing one to social processes at their most annihilating. For Holmes, the ring has been a public arena in which he risks physical and professional annihilation for a carefully calculated return—enough money to redefine and secure his place in the social landscape.

"The worst thing in the world," said Al Sharpton, speaking at Lafayette in February 1995 during Black History Month, "is to endure pain and to adjust to it." He meant that American Blacks must not stop demanding justice even in the present climate of backlash against their proper sense of a historical grievance requiring redress. Holmes, then in training for the McCall fight, sat on the podium behind Sharpton, who said he was happy to have his old friend watching his back on College Hill. Holmes, who tried not to look as if he were thinking about McCall's footwork during Sharpton's talk, nodded slightly in affirmation during the best parts. If asked, though, Holmes might well have qualified Sharpton's point about pain. When he rode down from College Hill in the dark after lending his good name and considerable presence to the occasion of Sharpton's talk, his route took him through a landscape bearing the imprints of the fortune he acquired by enduring and adjusting to pain, as well as by inflicting it.

Now, as for why you should feel bad about watching the fights on television, it has to do with a story of decline that embraces both Liebling and Holmes, both boxing and Easton.

There is nothing like a story of decline to flatten, interpret, and explain complexity, and an argument for present decline also establishes the credentials of its purveyor because it implies an understanding of and association with a past golden age. Since decline gives narrative coherence to the overlap of persisting older orders and succeeding newer ones, we tend to use it to understand all kinds of things—cities, politics, movies, kids, sports, and anything else of which anyone can say that it used to be better but has since gone to hell. (Oddly enough, academic scholarship, which purveys declines of all stripes, has managed to sustain the idea of its own processes of supersession as intellectual progress, even while calling into serious question the very idea of progress.) The continuing story of the sweet science's postindustrial decline, like the story of Easton's postindustrial decline (to which I will soon turn), identifies the 1950s as the moment when the old order began visibly to collapse.

The story of boxing's decline took lasting form in the 1950s, molded by

Liebling and other members of the ring intelligentsia. Liebling made that story a thematic building block of his oeuvre: he never missed a chance to say how much he hated television. In his most extended disquisition on why you should go to the fights in person rather than watch them on TV, Liebling argues that the pleasures of being there include telling the fighters what to do and analyzing the fight for the benefit of everyone else within earshot. He then gives a hypothetical example of how you can demonstrate expertise by offering extravagantly tenuous comparisons between the fight going on in front of you and a fight between Panama Al Brown and Edouard Mascart that you attended in Paris in 1927. First you draw the attention of those around you to a fanciful similarity between one of the present fighters and Brown: "'Reminds me of Panama Al Brown,' you may say as a new fighter enters the ring. 'He was five feet eleven and weighed a hundred and eighteen pounds. This fellow may be about forty pounds heavier and a couple of inches shorter, but he's got the same kind of neck.'" You have thus laid the groundwork for an expert conclusion to be drawn at the end of the fight:

> If he wins, you say, "I told you he reminded me of Al Brown," and if he loses, "Well, well, I guess he's no Al Brown. They don't make fighters like Al any more." This identifies you as a man who (a) has been in Paris, (b) has been going to fights for a long time, and (c) therefore enjoys what the fellows who write for quarterlies call a frame of reference.[36]

Some of this makes a familiar self-portrait of Liebling. Obviously, American fight fans would not care if you had been to Paris, but people who read the *New Yorker*, not to mention the quarterlies, might—especially in the 1950s, when American expatriates and French existentialists were important literary figures. Liebling had, of course, been to Paris and written about its food, fights, horse racing, and other assorted attractions; during World War II he had chronicled his own return to Paris from Normandy with the Allied forces. Liebling had also been going to fights, and writing about them, for a long time; and his richly allusive prose offered at least a semblance of familiarity with the quarterlies and the world of culture they represented for him. His list, then, constitutes a resumé detailing his own frame of reference, which significantly overlaps but also significantly exceeds his readers': those who have read Camus are unlikely to know fight people or other lowlife characters, and vice versa. Liebling's portrait of a ringside aficionado is thus also a self-portrait of an intellectual who makes a public spectacle of his frame of reference. The self-portrait positions Liebling in relation to the ring: in Paris and at the fights, between the critics on the quarterlies and the colorful fight people who serve as critics for the ring, among the well-read but also among those who know the fight world's history, against television but privy to the public imagination as it is displayed by a fight crowd. Liebling also positions himself in time with a thumbnail narrative of boxing's decline: "They don't make fighters like Al anymore." The essays in *The Sweet Science*, especially, argue that boxing has entered "a lean aesthetic period" in the age of television (hence the importance of going to the fights to counteract its effect). Liebling feared that the 1950s had ushered in an age of fewer good, experienced fighters and trainers, and therefore fewer good fights.

It bears noting that Liebling did not employ the decline formula unless he felt he had to, and never without ironic qualification; in his self-portrait, the nostalgic blowhard eulogizing Panama Al Brown at the fights does not inspire blind confidence in his analysis. As a press critic, Liebling could spot a decline narrative (on which urban journalism and sportswriting rely heavily) a mile away, and he was by nature and training suspicious of received wisdom and the formulas that convey it. Liebling further distanced himself from the notion of decline by showing himself to be compensating for the warping effect of nostalgia on his judgment. At the end of "Ahab and Nemesis," for instance, Marciano's defeat of Moore at Yankee Stadium gets Liebling thinking back to the first boxing card ever held there, in 1923, "in a time that is now represented to us as the golden age of American pugilism." He concludes that "old Ahab Moore could have whipped all four principals on that card [Jess Willard, Floyd Johnson, Luis Angel Firpo, and Jack McAuliffe II] within fifteen rounds, and that while Dempsey may have been a great champion, he had less to beat than Marciano."[37] In other words, golden age–and–decline is a dubious formula suffused with autobiographical sentiment.

It also bears noting that Liebling's account differs from the more facile and widely circulated narratives of decline driven by racial and ethnic anxiety that arose in the 1950s to explain changes not only in the ring but in the American social landscape. As the great South–North migration changed American urbanism, Black fighters finally began to eclipse

Irish, Italian, and Jewish fighters. (Hispanic fighters would come to predominate in many of the lower weight classes.) Whatever Liebling's conventional assumptions about race (and they are harder to pin down than
readers like Oates and Early allow[38]), his pantheon of first-rank ring poets
was all-Black, and he treated racial and ethnic successions as mildly interesting sociological phenomena which mattered only to the extent that they
shaped what happened in the ring. The dividing lines he cared most about
separated good trainers from bad ones, the tribe of boxers from the tribe of
sluggers. Building his account of decline on observation of the ring and an
awareness of the historical moment, he did precisely what C. L. R. James
advised by starting from inside the boundaries of the sport and then working outward to the world beyond it. Liebling concluded that television, in
combination with long-wave social trends of the twentieth century, was
eroding both the craft and the institutions of boxing.

In the introduction to *The Sweet Science*, Liebling asserts that boxing is in
decline because "there exist certain generalized conditions today, like full
employment and a late school-leaving age, that militate against the development of first-rate professional boxers. (They militate as well against the
development of first-rate acrobats, fiddlers, and *chefs de cuisine*.)"[39] To "full
employment" (an exaggeration even in the 1950s) and nearly universal secondary education (though of significantly lower quality in those parts of the
American social landscape that tend to produce boxers), we might add two
other "generalized conditions" of leisure and work. First, baseball, football, basketball, and other team sports grew fantastically during the first
half of the century, and the amateur and professional institutionalization
of these sports helped to shrink the pool of prospective fighters. (Liebling
made a point of being horrified by Marciano's new-order fans, uncolorful
rah-rah types who seemed to belong at a high school football game.) Second, some observers believed that by midcentury the proliferation of labor-
saving devices and the reduction of the heavy manual work required by
extractive and manufacturing industries during their more labor-intensive
eras had cut into the "production" of boxers in the rough. For example,
according to Nat Fleischer, who was Madison Square Garden's house intellectual, "The trades that developed our greatest fighters were those which
had to do with swinging a hammer, mining, or hauling heavy loads." Fleischer, certainly not the first American male to long for a more vigorous
and accomplished golden age in the receding high-industrial moment, saw

"an amazing decline" in the craft of pugilism since the late-nineteenth-and early-twentieth-century era of Bob Fitzsimmons (a blacksmith), Jack Dempsey the Nonpareil and Jack McAuliffe (both coopers), Jim Jeffries (a boilermaker), Jack Johnson and Harry Wills (both stevedores), and the heavyweight Jack Dempsey (a miner).[40]

These structural changes in leisure and work reduced the number of prospective boxers willing to apprentice themselves in the ring, but the midcentury advent of television accelerated the process of contraction. "The immediate crisis in the United States, forestalling the one high living standards might bring on, has been caused by the popularization of a ridiculous gadget called television," which, Liebling perceptively explains, "is utilized in the sale of beer and razor blades."[41] Regular boxing shows—weekly and sometimes more often—were a mainstay of early television, and TV exposure and TV money were rapidly destroying the network of local clubs and gyms where young men mastered their craft. Why pay to see a club fight when you can watch a stadium fight between nationally ranked contenders on TV for free? That collapse of the club network, and the related thinning in the ranks of experienced old hands who could make a living by teaching young apprentices, attenuated the capacity of pugilism to renew itself. There could not be, then, as many fighters with the training and experience essential to technical virtuosity as there used to be. This complex process played out with particular force in the United States, world capital of boxing since early in the century, where television had its greatest influence over leisure and sports.[42]

The midcentury narrative of scientific pugilism's decline in America offers a parody of postindustrial transformation in which a few promoters and fighters enjoy increased profits (with the aid of technological advances, in the form of television), while many more suffer through the "downsizing" of the boxing business and its reformulation as television spectacle. Like all narratives of decline, this one begs some big questions about its fundamental principles. It is true that after World War II the raw numbers of top-flight boxers decreased sharply: Fleischer claims that early in the century "the difficulty in ranking fighters lay in selecting ten from an outstanding field of possibly fifteen or more. . . . Today's headache comes from trying to find a sufficient number of worthies in any division after the first three or four have been listed."[43] It is difficult to accept, though, that the best fighters of the postwar period have been inferior to those of previous eras. The lower weight classes have gone through "golden ages" since the 1950s (think of Marvin Hagler, Sugar Ray Leonard, Roberto Duran, and Thomas Hearns, to name one circle of ring poets who produced master-works in the 1980s), and even in the case of heavyweights, the division most sharply affected by television, one might argue that current train-ing practices and nutrition can make contemporary fighters both stronger and faster than their predecessors. If both boxers in the ring are at least competent, the stronger and faster one usually wins, which means that it is possible to imagine even a pretty good postindustrial heavyweight like Riddick Bowe—let alone Ali or a young Holmes or Tyson—presenting a combination of speed and power that would have overwhelmed sainted high-industrial figures from Jeffries to Dempsey.

Whatever its manifest weaknesses, though, the story of boxing's decline demands at least a hearing, especially if extended to the present and espe-cially if applied to the heavies. Looking beyond the television-enhanced drama and cultural import of Muhammad Ali's career during the 1960s and 1970s, a narrator of decline could plausibly argue that the rise of television has bequeathed us a period in which relatively few competent boxers, who are relatively unseasoned because they do not have to fight up through local and regional strata to hit the big time, compete for as-tounding purses without necessarily knowing much about boxing. Neither Oliver McCall nor Bruce Seldon, both of whom had fewer than thirty pro-fessional victories and both of whom, at least temporarily, held pieces of the world heavyweight title after 8 April 1995, is particularly impressive as a boxer, or even as a puncher. They are undoubtedly in superb physical condition—both built like V-shaped Michelin men, true to the pumped-up Arnoldian (Schwarzenegger, not Matthew) ideal of the 1980s and 1990s, yet retaining a boxer's speed and suppleness—but neither defends him-self with more than paint-by-numbers expertise, and neither throws crisp combinations of punches. McCall hits harder than Seldon does, but he is not a great puncher; Seldon has the better jab, but it is not in the same class as Holmes's. George Foreman, also recognized in the spring of 1995 as a champion of sorts by some of the many governing bodies and un-official authorities in boxing, can still punch very hard, but he is too old and slow to defend himself from a precise hitter. Any heavyweight with a jab and a command of basic footwork should be able to cut him to pieces while staying out of his way. Were he alive today, Liebling would probably be decrying this present "lean aesthetic period" among the heavies and welcoming the return of Mike Tyson, who originally learned the fighter's trade from Cus D'Amato, a trainer with pretelevision credentials for whom Liebling had a great deal of respect.

Liebling esteemed Archie Moore above all other fighters in part because his later career represented the old order's last stand. Moore began fighting in 1936, and he was still going in the 1960s. He fought 228 professional bouts, a depth of experience that made for complete mastery of the sweet science's principles. (Tyson, the premier heavy since Holmes's reign ended, is still well short of fifty professional bouts.) Moore's loss to Marciano in 1955 forms the closing frame of *The Sweet Science*: "Ahab and Nemesis," however self-aware it is about the tendency of decline narratives to achieve explanatory force at the expense of complexity, closes Liebling's account of an old order in decline in the 1950s (although in the early 1960s he began to hope that Cassius Clay might usher in a new golden age).

When Liebling died in 1963, before the Age of Ali, thirteen-year-old Larry Holmes was still years away from the ring, although he was already in the habit of beating up his peers (including Sal Panto, future mayor of Easton). Had Liebling lived to see Holmes fight, he probably would have appreciated the pretelevision resonances in the Easton Assassin's style. It is also likely, though, that Liebling would not have esteemed the workmanlike Holmes as he did Moore or Clay; he would probably have decided that Holmes lacked what Liebling's semimythical friend Colonel Stingo called "the divine inflatus," that artistic amplitude found only in true heavyweight poets. Holmes and Liebling would have seen eye-to-eye, though, on the matter of boxing's decline.

"I'm the last of the good heavyweights," Holmes likes to say. By "good" he means at least three things. First, he means that he is the last classical stylist among the heavyweights, skilled in the manly art of self-defense. He means the same thing that Liebling meant when he called Moore "the old classicist" and "the last of the good pre-television heavyweights." George Foreman, a great puncher of Holmes's respectable vintage, is not "good" in this technical sense: "They say Foreman got hit 200 times in his last fight," Holmes points out; "I didn't get hit 200 times in my whole career." Even in his pugilistic dotage, Holmes still has a rigorous left jab: a hard, straight punch thrown with defensive and offensive purpose, not the pro forma tap or inert stiff-arm that many heavies use for a jab. Second, Holmes means that he is a good draw. With the exception of Riddick Bowe, who "has a sense of humor" and is not a bad boxer, the heavyweight division lacks "personality," he says. Holmes and Foreman are still active in their mid-forties because they command respect, but the rest are either nobodies (Bruce Seldon), "assholes" (Oliver McCall), or unlikely to stay active for long (Mike Tyson, who "hasn't changed" and will end up back in the joint or worse). Third, Holmes means "good" in a moral sense. He wants to distinguish himself—a family man, a businessman, an old-style "race man" working quietly in the wings of Ali's and Sharpton's television-savvy political theater—from loutish younger heavies who "beat up women," train badly, use drugs, buy decisions, and suck up to Don King.

Holmes is dissatisfied, though, with being the last of the good heavyweights in a time when few are equipped to appreciate that distinction. He complains that even the ringside judges lack the subtlety of perception needed to recognize the quality of his work, forcing him to dumb down his style accordingly. Liebling was satisfied with his relation to the history of boxing, presenting himself as an older man, intimately connected to the prewar ring world, whose cultural work it was to witness and narrate, from ringside, boxing's present decline. Holmes, who is still fit enough in his mid-forties to do his work in the ring, wants to improve his place in its history.

He keeps fighting because the money is still good, but also because he wants to add luster to his reputation by regaining the heavyweight championship. He is, of course, already a distinguished figure among champions, having held the title for seven years, and he will be remembered as a tough and canny heavyweight with anachronistically sound boxing skills, a great chin, and terrific self-possession in the ring. But Holmes will not be remembered as one of the greatest heavyweight champions, mostly because his style in the public arena—his conservative fighting style and modest Eastonian persona—did not command a wider following. The transition from Jimmy Carter's America to Donald Trump's may yet come to be widely understood as an appropriately resonant historical backdrop against which Holmes's tenure as champion will gain a larger meaning, but for now his reputation does not enjoy the extra-pugilistic resonance with which Hitler and World War II endowed Joe Louis or Vietnam and the U.S. urban crisis endowed Ali. Moreover, some people feel that Holmes did not fight enough great adversaries, a charge leveled at all heavyweight champions except Ali, who had the three-man wrecking crew of Liston, Frazier, and Foreman (not to mention his draft board and Howard Cosell) to help make him great. Ali was too spent by 1980 to do Holmes the favor of giving him an epochal struggle.

It may seem unfair, then, but if the fight world's historical memory were a landscape, Holmes's reputation would be a cast-iron footbridge of under-stated classical elegance over which strollers made their way from a colossal statue of Ali to Tyson's truncated obelisk. Even Marciano, who retired un-beaten in 1956 after knocking out Moore, would rate at least a big chunk of granite set in a nice grove. The reputation of Marciano, who fought out of Brockton, an industrial town of Eastonian scale and type, famously irri-tates Holmes: Marciano, after having beaten the old classicist Moore, re-tired, and died relatively young, figuratively got up off the canvas one more time to become Holmes's nemesis. Holmes won his first forty-eight pro-fessional fights, leaving him one short of Marciano's perfect lifetime record of 49–0, but then lost to Spinks. After the fight, Holmes testily responded to inquiring reporters, "Marciano couldn't carry my jockstrap." They made more of Holmes's heretical bad sportsmanship than they ever had of his victories. It is easy to see, though, why Marciano's presence in the first rank of champions would irritate Holmes. Even though purists regard Marciano as a loutish and indifferent boxer, he was a world-historical puncher who took a punch to give one, the type that crowds love best. It also rankles that people seem not to hold it against Marciano that he did not have to fight great champions in their prime, or that he only defended his title six times. Furthermore, and crucially, Marciano was the last of the great White heavy-weights, insanely popular not only with the boxing press, but also with the so-called White ethnics of Italian, Irish, and Eastern European descent who dominated the industrial social order of places like Brockton and Easton. If Marciano were from Easton and still alive, his shoes would never touch the street: every time he left the house, White-ethnic mobs of young men (with connect-the-dots mustaches, baseball caps, and baggy clothes) and old men (with full mustaches, logos of veterans' organizations on the caps, no baggies) would scoop him up and carry him around on their shoulders.

None of this is lost on Holmes. In the lobby of L&D Holmes Plaza, there is a "Wall of Fame" hung with handsomely mounted photographs of boxers. Some of the pictures are inscribed with a congratulatory note and signature. These inscriptions have in common a guileless tone of summer-camp friendliness ("To my friend," "Take good care of yourself") and a tendency to assure Larry Holmes of his place in boxing history: "To a great champion" (Tony Zale and Jack "Kid" Berg); "Your the greatest" (Willie Pep); "To Larry with sincere wishes to a great champion" (Billy Soose, who adds his own credentials: "Retired middle weight champion of the world"). Petey Hayes says it most baldly: "You can be classified with the great champions of all times." There are, of course, several photographs of Black and Hispanic fighters on the wall, but none of them bears an inscription assuring Holmes of his greatness. (Alexis Arguello reminds him to "be a good son," though.) The wall, then, exudes a soft chorus of White-ethnic voices, all telling Holmes that he deserves a monument of his own. In a town full of sports-obsessed White ethnics who do not like Holmes as much as he thinks they ought to, these voices offer authoritative counterpoint from the experts.

At least in his relationship to Easton, though, Holmes may be trying to buck historical forces that run deep in the community's fabric. The local resentment he perceives from Eastonians can be seen as an aspect of a more general historical grievance related to Easton's narrative of decline. As in the story of boxing's decline, the 1950s is the beginning of the end in the town's historical memory. Easton's narrative of decline enjoys a semiofficial status, informing as it does the city's comprehensive plan for downtown redevelopment. "Downtown [Easton] has stayed much the same over the past 40 years," says the consultants' report on which the city's plan is based, "but the world around it has changed. The dominance of the automobile, hence suburban shopping centers and malls, is not expected to abate."[44] The same postindustrial transformation—condensed by Liebling in the figure of the television, and by the consultants in that of the automobile—which caught up with the sweet science in the 1950s has been tough on Easton as well. Suburbanization of capital and population, deindustrialization of the older central cities, contraction of the manufacturing sector and expansion of the service sector, a thoroughgoing reconfiguration of the social and political landscape, the succession of ethnic and racial neighborhood orders during an age of interlocking South-to-North and city-to-suburb migrations—all these processes have diminished the town and its way of life as they were during the industrial golden age. However, no clearly defined new order has emerged to replace the old. Easton still conforms in significant ways to the high-industrial template that evolved in the Midwest and Northeast before World War II: White ethnics dominate the population, 70 percent of the city's housing units were built before 1940, and jobs that involve making and fixing things still command special respect. City planners hope to profit from tourism—to make downtown Easton "a destination again" in a decentralized age—by enhancing and exploiting the "historical" value of the industrial order's surviving elements. The story of Easton's decline, as retold by its planners, points toward a future in which the old neighborhood and the plant will attract tourists to the coal-and-steel belt the way chin beards and horse-drawn buggies attract them to the nearby Amish country.

Seen in the light of this transformation, Holmes personifies aspects of postwar history with which many people in Easton have not made their peace. He is a wealthy man in a town that used to be more prosperous, an agent and proponent of postindustrial redevelopment in an industrial town, and a Black Southerner come North into a White-ethnic preserve during the great postwar migrations of people and capital. That Holmes has come to prominence via a morally and pugilistically virtuous ring style that bespeaks prewar and pretelevision antecedents—a throwback to the boxing culture of the industrial era—only suggests an irony at his expense. Most of the people who follow the fights, or at least the heavyweights, in the Age of Tyson are not ready to appreciate Holmes either. He cannot win either of his two historical battles until the town's culture refits itself to the historical moment or until the transitional era he represents in boxing history acquires new significance.

In August 1995, a rumor circulated in the press that Easton was planning to erect a statue of Holmes in the town's central square, at a cost of $150,000. Officials in City Hall quickly scotched the rumor, and Holmes himself told an interviewer that, while the statue was "a great idea," he understands "what is going on in the city of Easton. . . . They don't have time to worry about a statue for Larry Holmes." When asked if he might put up the money himself, as ex-mayor Sal Panto had suggested, Holmes said, "If I spent $150,000 on a statue of myself, that means to me, 'Larry Holmes, you've got a fucking big head.' . . . I don't want people to think that I think I'm better than them." He wanted to sound like a man who was satisfied with what he had: "I'm just getting finished with one project. . . . And I have a street named after me. I'm the happiest man in the world."[45]

Then, since he was in training for his next fight (which he won), he went to the gym and got back to work on his own monument.

＝＝＝＝＝

"The ring is a continuum with fixed values and built-in cultural patterns, like Philadelphia or the world of Henry James," observes Liebling the aphorist.[46] In a sense, he is right: Holmes the aging scientist lost to McCall the younger free-swinger—a reduced but recognizable restatement of the principles enacted by Moore and Marciano forty years earlier. Before the fight, Holmes even intoned Moore's classicist mantra: "McCall has a good chin, but if you hit him right. . . ." The processes of art are indeed self-renewing. On the other hand, putting Liebling in conversation with Holmes shows the ring's values and patterns of meaning to be anything but fixed; they alter and shift under pressure from the historical moment and the observer's perspective. What Liebling sees in the ring overlaps with what Holmes takes from it, but most of what each knows lies outside the zone of overlap.

Liebling and Holmes have led me on a long, meandering path, into matters of literary form and postindustrial transformation, in finding my way to the ring from College Hill and tracing the pattern of the meanings that spread out from the ring. Both of them, though, offer good models of purposeful meandering. Liebling made the "labyrinthian digression" an element of his style—wedded to a mixture of registers, breadth of allusion, and juxtaposition of boxing and "culture." The point was always to delineate his path to the ring in order to show what meanings he was prepared to find there. Holmes, for his part, now bangs directly at his opponent for only a few seconds in each round, whiling away the rest of the time in apparent digressions from scoring—clinches, sessions of resting on the ropes, stretches of purely defensive blocking and slipping—in which he wears the other fighter down and lays the groundwork for exploiting another opening. The point is always to win the fight and thereby to acquire in the ring the money and acclaim it takes to place himself advantageously in the world beyond it.

If we pay attention to the significant forms of their work, stylists like Liebling and Holmes lead us by branching paths into those traditions—of fighting, of writing, of urbanism—that join the ring to the social and textual worlds that contain it, present to past, quarterlies to dailies, College Hill to Easton. "There is still a kick in style," concluded Heywood Broun on the occasion of classicist Benny Leonard's defeat of slugger Rocky Kansas in 1922, "and tradition carries a nasty wallop."[47]

Notes

Thanks to Larry Holmes, Dick Lovell, and Art Statum, who were generous with their time and opinions in interviews; John O'Keefe, for material on redevelopment in downtown Easton; and John Mosedale, who once loaned my brother *The Sweet Science*.

1 In late 1995, the Fox Network began to experiment with occasional prime-time matches on free television, a series built around Mike Tyson's return to the ring and his effort to unify the heavyweight championship.

2 A. J. Liebling, *The Sweet Science* (New York, 1982 [1956]); and *A Neutral Corner: Boxing Essays by A. J. Liebling*, ed. Fred Warner and James Barbour (San Francisco, 1990).

3 Budd Schulberg, *Sparring with Hemingway and Other Legends of the Fight Game* (Chicago, 1995), 35.

4 For reviews of boxing literature, each of which says as much about its author's path to the ring as it does about the literature, see Schulberg, *Sparring with Hemingway*, esp. 187–90; Gerald Early, *The Culture of Bruising: Essays on Prizefighting, Literature, and Modern American Culture* (Hopewell, NJ, 1994), esp. 5–45; Joyce Carol Oates, *On Boxing* (Garden City, NY, 1987), esp. 26–28, 50–62; Tom Sawyer, *Noble Art: An Artistic and Literary Celebration of the Old English Prize Ring* (London, 1989); and Arthur Krystal, "Ifs, Ands, and Butts: The Literary Sensibility at Ringside," *Harper's* (June 1987): 63–67. An excellent book on boxing that confines itself to what the fight world knows is Thomas Hauser, *The Black Lights* (New York, 1986), an account of the long and tortuous path to the ring taken by Billy Costello as he prepared to defend his super-lightweight title against Saoul Mamby, who has in latter years joined Larry Holmes's crew of seconds.

5 C. L. R. James, *Beyond a Boundary* (Durham, NC, 1993 [1963]), 54, 171.

6 A. J. Liebling, "Ahab and Nemesis," in *Sweet Science*, 295.

7 For details of Liebling's life and his various autobiographical glosses on it, see Raymond Sokolov's excellent biography *Wayward Reporter: The Life of A. J. Liebling* (New York, 1980).

8 Liebling, "Ahab and Nemesis," 288.

9 Ibid., 300.

10 Ibid., 300–301.

11 Ibid., 293.

12 Ibid., 301. Moore concluded in retrospect that he had indeed hit Marciano right and that Marciano was dazed and ready to be knocked out, but that an overexcited or perhaps more darkly motivated referee saved Marciano; see Archie Moore and Leonard B. Pearl, *Any Boy Can: The Archie Moore Story* (Englewood Cliffs, NJ, 1971), 85–88.

13 Liebling, "Ahab and Nemesis," 301.

14 Oates, *On Boxing*, 26.

15 Ibid., 53. Oates admires and quotes from George Garrett's essay "My One-Eyed Coach," probably the sharpest and most concise use of boxing to meditate on writing and reading; see *Reading the Fights*, ed. Joyce Carol Oates and Daniel Halpern (New York, 1990), 253–58.
16 A. J. Liebling, "The Men in the Agbadas," in Warner and Barbour, eds., *Neutral Corner*, 192; and "Ad Lib," in Warner and Barbour, eds., *Neutral Corner*, 148.
17 Liebling, "Ad Lib," 148; and "An Artist Seeks Himself," in Warner and Barbour, eds., *Neutral Corner*, 85–86.
18 Liebling, "Artist Seeks Himself," 84.
19 A. J. Liebling, "A Blow for Austerity," in Warner and Barbour, eds., *Neutral Corner*, 118.
20 A. J. Liebling, "Anti-Poetry Night," in Warner and Barbour, eds., *Neutral Corner*, 213.
21 Ibid., 222.
22 A. J. Liebling, "Poet and Pedagogue," in Warner and Barbour, eds., *Neutral Corner*, 164.
23 Budd Schulberg's novel *The Harder They Fall* (New York, 1947) is narrated by just such a child of the middle class, who wants to write a great boxing novel but earns his keep writing press releases for fight-fixing mobsters.
24 A. J. Liebling, "Introduction," in *Sweet Science*, 8.
25 Ibid., 12.
26 John Ford passed that judgment on him in his introduction to a collection of pieces from Egan's journal; see *Boxiana*, ed. John Ford (London, 1976), 5.
27 Liebling, "Introduction," 10–11.
28 Fred Warner, "Afterword," in Warner and Barbour, eds., *Neutral Corner*, 244–45.
29 Liebling's books include *They All Sang: From Tony Pastor to Rudy Vallée* (by Edward J. Marks, as told to A. J. Liebling [1934]); *Back Where I Came From* (1938); *The Road Back to Paris* (1944); *The Telephone Booth Indian* (1944); *La République du Silence/The Republic of Silence* (edited with Eugene Jay Sheffer [1946, 1947]); *The Wayward Pressman* (1947); *Mink and Red Herring: The Wayward Pressman's Casebook* (1949); *Chicago: The Second City* (1952); *The Honest Rainmaker: The Life and Times of Colonel John R. Stingo* (1953); *Normandy Revisited* (1958); *The Press* (1961); *Between Meals: An Appetite for Paris* (1962); *The Jollity Building* (1962); *The Most of A. J. Liebling* (1963); and *Liebling at The New Yorker: Uncollected Essays* (edited by James Barbour and Fred Warner [1994]).
30 Liebling, "Ahab and Nemesis," 289.
31 A.J. Liebling, *Mollie and Other War Pieces* (New York, 1964), 286.
32 See Oates, *On Boxing*, 53; and Early, *Culture of Bruising*, 12, 20–21.
33 Oates, *On Boxing*, 116.
34 Art Statum, interview by author, Easton, PA, 18 April 1995.
35 Holmes is quoted from his remarks at a press conference in Easton on 21 March 1995 and from an interview by the author on 26 April 1995.
36 A. J. Liebling, "Boxing with the Naked Eye," in *Sweet Science*, 17.
37 Liebling, "Ahab and Nemesis," 306.
38 See Oates, *On Boxing*, 53; and Early, *Culture of Bruising*, 12, 20–21. Early can think of no more cutting thing to say of Ishmael Reed's essay "The Fourth Ali" than that Reed, "a black intellectual," writes like Liebling, a "white boxing writer."
39 Liebling, "Introduction," 2.

40 Nat Fleischer, *50 Years at Ringside* (New York, 1958), 274–75.

41 Liebling, "Introduction," 3.

42 For another version of this argument, see Randy Roberts, "The Wide World of Muhammad Ali: The Politics and Economics of Televised Boxing," in *Muhammad Ali: The People's Champ*, ed. Elliot J. Gorn (Urbana, 1995), esp. 28–31, 38–39. Roberts draws upon the wisdom of fight manager Jack "Doc" Kearns, who, like Liebling and Fleischer, argued that television was bad for boxing.

43 Fleischer, *50 Years*, 274.

44 Abeles Phillips Preiss & Shapiro, Inc., and Norman Mintz Associates, "A Strategy to Make Downtown Easton a Destination" (report submitted to the Easton Economic Development Corporation and the City of Easton, October 1993), 12.

45 Dave Boyer, "No False Idol for the Champ," *Easton Express–Times*, 1 September 1995, B: 1.

46 A. J. Liebling, "The University of Eighth Avenue," in Warner and Barbour, eds., *Neutral Corner*, 19.

47 Quoted in Liebling, "Ahab and Nemesis," 288.

Philip Deloria

"I Am of the Body": Thoughts on My Grandfather, Culture, and Sports

Like his father before him, my grandfather, Vine Deloria, Sr., was an Episcopalian minister. A powerful orator, his sermons moved people in extraordinary ways, and he was, by all accounts, beloved by the congregations of the South Dakota reservation parishes he tended. In 1954, he traded the Great Plains for New York City, where for several years he directed the national church's Indian mission programs. Some claim that the conversion of a majority of Sioux Episcopalians was due to the proselytizing of my grandfather and his father. In a different time, he would almost certainly have been appointed Bishop of South Dakota.[1]

But my grandfather was also an Indian. In the 1950s, he spoke out strongly against the federal government's plan to force Indian assimilation by "terminating" tribal governments, and this won him no friends in the church hierarchy.[2] Lakota culture tolerates a far greater degree of contradiction than the Episcopal Church, however, and Sioux people saw him as both a Christian minister and a respected elder. My brother and I used to play anthropologist with him, recording

The *South Atlantic Quarterly* 95:2, Spring 1996.
Copyright © 1996 by Duke University Press.
CCC 0038-2876/96/$1.50.

his inexhaustible store of songs and tales on our father's reel-to-reel. And actual anthropologists, as well as linguists and historians, would visit my grandfather, seeking to plumb his knowledge of old words and oral history.

At the time, I missed the fact that my grandfather was a man of extraordinary physical vitality. At seventy-one, he had no trouble playing George Mitterwald to my Bert Blyleven, bent into a crouch and holding out his old-fashioned catcher's mitt—a flat, weathered pancake, slightly dented in the middle. He liked to pass the football around too, and threw a nice, tight spiral with good distance. While I ran triangle patterns around the yard, he would stand in place, cocking, firing, and invariably parking the ball right in my hands. At eighty-three, when he helped perform my wedding ceremony, his voice boomed throughout the church, distorting the sound system until it was quickly turned off. I recall watching him a few years later grasp a half-rotten post and vault a barbed-wire fence after I had parted the strands for him to slide through. Marveling, I wondered what he must have been like in his thirties.

My grandfather died of Alzheimer's disease in 1990. As his mind discarded parts of his life and personality, older memories acquired new vitality, and he often gave visitors a peek into his life as a young man sixty years ago. I last saw him on a day when a lifetime of significance had become distilled in a snatch of music and a story. A descant verse that accompanied the song "School Days" counterpointed "reading and writing and 'rithmetic" with the attractions of the nonacademic curriculum: "domestic-nestics and basketballs." He had learned it as a boy while attending Kearney Military Academy in Nebraska, where he sharpened his love of both music and basketball. The story, on the other hand, grew out of the usual, painful preliminaries:

Who are you?
Your eldest grandson, Philip.
Oh. Do you live here?
No. I'm visiting you from Connecticut, where I'm going to school.
Ah. Connecticut . . . Connecticut Aggies, Connecticut Aggies.
Suddenly, time is running out and St. Stephen's College needs a touchdown to beat the Connecticut (Agricultural and Mechanical College) Aggies. Playing fullback, Vine Deloria takes an option lateral, fakes a run, and then heaves the ball fifty-five yards downfield into the waiting arms of a receiver.

The pass not only sealed the victory for St. Stephen's, but set a record as the longest forward pass in college football history (Figure 1).[3]

═════

The more I thought about this exchange, the more compelling it became. At some primal level, my grandfather seemed to define himself neither as a Christian minister nor as a Lakota elder, but as an athlete. Could it be that sports were more important to his personal makeup than race or religion? Perhaps, but he probably never parsed his life so neatly. He came to maturity during a brief moment when sports functioned as a complicated nexus between Indian and Euro-American cultures; for those fifty-odd years, all the confusions of centuries of cultural collision were put on display at ballparks and on gridirons. Yet even as Indian men shared a playing field and a set of sporting rules and cultural understandings with non-Indians, they drew very different meanings from athletic competition. For my grandfather, race, religion, culture, and family were inextricably tangled with his feats on the playing field.

Born at Wakpala, South Dakota, in 1901, my grandfather belonged to a generation of native people who were supposed to be "disappearing," assimilated into the American "melting pot" or simply dying off. The massacre at Wounded Knee, that all-purpose marker of vanishing Indianness, was barely a decade past. The General Allotment Act (or "Dawes Act"), meant to assimilate native people by dividing up communal land into individual plots in order to inculcate Jeffersonian agrarianism, was swiftly becoming a corrupt vehicle for the mass dispossession of Indian landholders. The federal government would soon bolster existing restrictions on religious dancing and other cultural practices. The Supreme Court was about to rule, in *Lone Wolf v. Hitchcock*, that Congress exercised plenary power over Indian people and could thus abrogate any treaty at any time. Agents and "boss farmers" controlled many aspects of reservation life, and Indian children were torn from their families and sent to boarding schools to be forcibly made "White."[4]

It is customary to sum up these policies in terms of domination, resistance, and conflict: Did White Americans erase native culture? Did Indianness survive? Any change, of course, tends to be coded as declension—in this case, as the incremental death of "traditional" native culture. Alternatively, one can celebrate the vitality of "culture" itself as a meta-

Figure 1. Vine Deloria, Sr., at St. Stephen's (Bard) College, c. 1923.
Courtesy of Bard College and Vine Deloria, Jr.

concept, pointing to the inevitability and legitimacy of its continual re-figurings.[5]

My grandfather's world existed someplace between these understandings. Lakota people retained an essential control over their culture, even at its most transformative moments. In the eighteenth and nineteenth centuries, they had made over their world as they claimed European horses, rifles, and steel trade goods as their own. In fin-de-siècle America, the descendants of these people hunted cattle as they had the nearly extinct bison, celebrated their Sun Dance within strategically altered Fourth of July ceremonies, remade their warrior societies and women's groups as church sodalities, started a fashion craze for cowboy clothes, and amassed enormous herds of horses. Again and again, they created new Indian worlds, fusing diverse cultures or fitting themselves into the interstices between a core native "tradition" and new practices introduced from the American periphery.[6]

To celebrate these remakings too uncritically, however, would be to ignore the disparate power relations that existed both on the reservations and in the cities. If Sioux people refigured their world, they did so within the constraints of American rules and regulations. But, ironically, the same society that imposed such limits on Indians also offered a certain power to native people who could find and push the right cultural buttons. The intercultural world that took shape in the early twentieth century formed in response to both Indian and non-Indian imperatives and constraints.[7]

My grandfather grew up remembering, on the one hand, harsh government agents and missionary proselytizing and, on the other, enormous church convocations where powerful native men sang the Lakota hymns of the Brotherhood of Christian Unity. His parents raised him to be fluent in the language and the ways of his ancestors yet equally able to move competently through American society. When his mother died in 1915, my grandfather boarded the train to Kearney, Nebraska, to attend an Episcopalian military school. He wore a uniform, studied hard, and rose to the top rank of Cadet Colonel. While he learned English and went by the name of "Pete," however, the boys with whom he lived learned to speak Lakota as well. Rather than simply "assimilating," my grandfather helped to create a new, cross-cultural world for himself and his companions. Athletic competition was a key part of that world, and, while at Kearney, he lettered in football, baseball, and basketball.[8]

The idea of "sport" was nothing new to native people. Lacrosse, a popular but relatively latter-day American pastime, dominated the eastern region of Indian America for centuries. Colonial commentators noted the presence of "Indian football," which involved kicking and pitching a stuffed deerskin through enormous goals. For Sioux people, horse racing, speed and endurance running, and many other "games" in which men and women competed were also ways of training themselves for the exigencies of a demanding physical life. Like American sports, Indian contests had rules, traditions, and multiple layers of cultural meaning, with performances at once signifying status or rank, individual ability, religious observance, and group identity. While many of these older sporting practices continued on the reservations, native people also welcomed the introduction (often by missionaries) of American-style football, baseball, and basketball, easily enfolding these newcomers into extant cultural traditions.[9] By the late nineteenth century, reservation teams had begun to compete with one another and Indian boarding schools had become hotbeds of athletic talent, with players sometimes "raided" by non-Indian schools. This new kind of athletic competition was often part of a refigured warrior tradition, but it also provided an entrée into American society—a chance to beat Whites at their own games, an opportunity to get an education, and, even at its most serious, an occasion for fun and sociality.

In 1922, my grandfather won a scholarship to St. Stephen's College in Annandale–on–Hudson, New York, a small school with close ties to the Episcopal Church. (During the 1930s, St. Stephen's became more secular and was renamed Bard College.) For a long time—perhaps even his whole life—my grandfather assumed that the scholarship had materialized from the same church and Indian-targeted philanthropy that had enabled his older sister, Ella, to attend Oberlin College. When local parishioners just happened to drop by with a new suit of clothes, for example, my grandfather saw their generosity in terms of the church's long-standing desire to Christianize native people and to support its Indian clergy in particular. I suspect, however, that his having lettered in several varsity sports— football, baseball, track, and lacrosse—during every one of his four college years was not incidental. In Bard College's official history, he is listed as "St. Stephen's greatest athletic hero."[10]

If sports were an important part of a new Indian world, they were instru-
mental to transforming and reshaping modern American culture at the
turn of the century. As football players collided in bone-crunching maneuvers and baseball players stared each other down, they reaffirmed an
American masculinity then in the midst of a crisis of self-doubt. The uni-
fying power that accompanied the spectatorial experience offered comfort
and a sense of identity to those who were worried about the rise of an
anonymous mass society. As compelling and meaningful performances,
sporting events were perfect commodities for a society in which an ethos
of production was giving way to one of consumption.[11]

Nowhere were these cultural needs felt so keenly and sated so thoroughly as in colleges and universities. Beginning with the Ivy League
athletic programs of the 1870s, intercollegiate sports had evolved into a
crucial signifier of (male) identity.[12] The Yale–Harvard football game, for
example, defined and reinforced an elite New England sense of self.[13] While
the two sides maintained a pretense of being locked in mortal combat, a
discourse of good sportsmanship and the institution of identically posh,
crimson and blue–themed tailgate parties sustained their commonalities
as (re)producers of the same elite class. And upper-crust American manhood, it was obvious, could survive the taming of the frontier, the threat of
effeminating urban modernity, and the challenges of reorganized family
relations and politically active women. As Yale's mascot-keepers patrolled
the sidelines with Handsome Dan the bulldog (several generations of
which were stuffed and are now on display in the university gymnasium),
players and spectators together experienced a test or performance of crucial values—toughness, tenacity, and (quite literally) good breeding.

Small colleges and state universities emulated the Ivy example, cre-
ating athletic programs in order to boost institutional self-esteem, rally
alumni, and establish distinctive identities. In 1919, the new president of
St. Stephen's, B. I. Bell, who was determined to enhance the reputation
of his tiny, somewhat stodgy school, instituted an intercollegiate athletic
program. Given that the college had barely 100 students, this move was
unquestionably bold.[14] In Bell's first year, St. Stephen's played local high
schools, but by 1922—my grandfather's freshman year—the schedule included games with St. Lawrence, CCNY, and Providence College. In 1925,

the college's increasingly impressive list of opponents included Trinity, Williams, Middlebury, and Colby, as well as St. John's and Norwich. My grandfather captained the football team, whose high point was a decisive win over the University of Rochester in 1925. The basketball team also won major victories that year against Colgate, Hamilton College, and—in a move toward big-time legitimation—Yale.[15]

The success enjoyed by St. Stephen's in the early 1920s was readily available to colleges that were willing to play ringers. In fact, when St. Stephen's hired a new football coach in 1924, he brought with him ten players whose tuition bills were covered by phony promissory notes. The ensuing scandal forced the college to drop football after the 1925 season.[16] The team's previous coach appears to have engaged in a more subtle form of unconventional recruiting, seeking atypical but potentially successful students like my grandfather. Native men were indeed perfect recruits for such college teams. The success of the Carlisle Indian School football team, which began playing the Ivies and other big-time schools in the late nineteenth century, made it clear to coaches and sports fans alike that Indian communities were producing great athletes who could enrich a football or baseball program. And, unlike Black athletes, Indians had long been enmeshed in the discourse of American assimilation. "Giving the Indian a chance" was a culturally appropriate move, a shouldering of the White Man's Burden. The often underprepared Indian athlete, of course, invariably walked the fine line between ringer and scholar–athlete.

Racial discrimination abounded. My grandfather had especially keen memories of being given clothing because he also remembered not being allowed to try on clothes in Annandale stores. But Indian athletes, especially those who advanced the team, could also receive a surprisingly genuine welcome in many quarters. John "Chief" Meyers, a Cahuilla catcher with a powerful bat and a fourth-grade education, found himself the toast of Dartmouth College for a semester in 1905. Meyers, who later achieved fame with the New York Giants and the Brooklyn Dodgers, joined a fraternity and won a large following in Hanover before the school discovered his falsified credentials.[17]

Indians fit neatly into the nostalgic, antimodern image of professional and college sports. If athletes in general were emblems of post-frontier masculinity who embodied a reassuring sense of *Gemeinschaft*, my grandfather and other Indian athletes proved to be even more complex, evocative symbols for White spectators. In the early twentieth century's tête-à-tête with cultural primitivism, "Indians" could be objects not simply of racial repulsion but also—as they reflected nostalgia for community, spirituality, and nature—of racial desire.[18] My grandfather's performances on the field offered White spectators not only enactments of manhood and identity but spectacles of a lost time of "natural" physicality and strength, affirming social evolution and successful Christianization, the assimilation of difference and the ways in which assimilation could strengthen a multicultural, "transnational" America.

Bard College's official history, for example, pointedly notes my grandfather's origins as a "full-blooded Sioux Indian."[19] Sportswriter Grantland Rice, in commenting on Anishinabe Hall of Famer Albert "Chief" Bender, explicitly identified a set of racial essences that he thought made Indians great "natural" athletes. The Indian's "heritage is all outdoors," observed Rice. "His reflexes are sharp. He takes the game as it comes to him. He rarely gets excited or off balance. . . . Given the same chance, he has the white man lashed to the Post."[20] Physical power and mental equilibrium ("the stoical spirit of the Chippewa tradition") were the racial gifts that Indians brought to the stadium—when non-Indians let them in.

Balance and stoicism were especially important. Indians were survivals of a "premodern" American time and place, yet they rode the currents of modernity with calmness and equanimity. Anxious Whites could learn from them. Such notions as these deemphasized and devalued the traditional rhetoric of "assimilation" by encoding the *difference* of the pre- or antimodern, "primitive" physicality of native men as more compelling. Viewing Indian bodies displayed on the diamond, gridiron, or court, spectators and commentators naturalized the meanings they had constructed for "Indian" difference, enabling their own rhetoric to spice the stew of melting-pot America as it was blended in athletic performance.

Although my grandfather was the only Indian at St. Stephen's, he was one of many native men who took advantage of the window of opportunity opened by the converging forces of primitivist nostalgia and competitive college and pro sports. When considering Indian athletes, it is easy to slide into the "heroic" mode, focusing on Jim Thorpe and perhaps a few other outstanding individuals—"Chief" Bender, Hopi Olympic medalist Louis Tewanima, or William "Lone Star" Dietz, who head-coached football teams at Purdue and Louisiana Tech as well as the NFL Boston Redskins. But more obscure gridirons and dugouts all across America were also peppered with Indian athletes and coaches.

Many of these careers were launched at the Carlisle Indian School, a boarding school founded in 1879 to teach Indian youth the basics required for assimilation into White American culture. The school emphasized manual skills, such as tinsmithing and harness-making for boys and "domestic arts" for girls. In 1893, however, Carlisle began fielding a football team which, like that of St. Stephen's, rapidly became competitive. Ironically, this "extracurricular" activity contributed as much to the integrating of modern Indian and American culture as the rudimentary book-learning and obsolete manual-labor training on which the school prided itself.[21]

A number of Carlisle students who returned to the reservation "went back to the blanket," while others became leaders of "progressive" factions within tribes. Carlisle athletes, however, rarely returned to the reservation (at least, not immediately). They tended to continue playing sports, bouncing among colleges, professional leagues, and the minor league and semipro teams. Joseph Guyon, for example, an Anishinabe from White Earth, Minnesota, played football at Carlisle in 1911 and 1912. Five years later, as something of a ringer at Georgia Tech, he was named an all-American tackle in 1917 and running back in 1918. Going on to play professional football with the Canton Bulldogs, the Kansas City Cowboys, and the New York Giants, Guyon was inducted into the National Professional Football Hall of Fame in 1966. Stockbridge–Munsee Jimmy Johnson, a 1903 all-American at Carlisle, played for the next two years at Northwestern. Bemus Pierce, a New York Seneca who in 1896 was the first Indian all-American, went on from Carlisle to play for assorted professional football teams. Pete Calac and Gustavus Welsh, among others, followed similar trajectories, while Frank Mt. Pleasant joined Thorpe and Tewanima on U.S. Olympic squads. There were many other Carlisle players who never made it into the professional leagues, but still enjoyed careers in sports at the semipro and minor league levels or as coaches and scouts.[22]

Although Carlisle students also went on to become anthropologists, ministers, or journalists, professions that implied a more thorough degree of assimilation, athletes were different. American society valued them all the more for *not* becoming "White." Many Indian men refused that distinction, however, using "primitive" sports to acquire an "assimilatory" education more advanced than that offered by the Indian boarding school. Harold S. Jones—a Santee Sioux who, unlike my grandfather, did eventually become the Episcopal Bishop of South Dakota—played semipro baseball to finance his undergraduate education. Louis Bruce, Sr., a Mohawk, played with the Philadelphia Athletics and the New York Yankees prior to careers in dentistry and the ministry. His son, Louis Bruce, Jr., who would later become Commissioner of Indian Affairs, attended Syracuse University on scholarship as a pole-vaulter. Oklahoma Choctaw Ted Key attended Murray State Junior College for two years on a football scholarship, then played a year of professional football to fund his final year at Central State University. Jimmy Johnson had no trouble gaining admission to Northwestern's dental school after he announced his intention to continue playing football.[23]

When Carlisle closed in 1918, its preeminent place in Indian sports fell to the Haskell Institute, an Indian boarding school in Lawrence, Kansas. Basically a high school, Haskell was stocked with a full complement of Indian athletes, some of whom had already played for four years at Carlisle. Haskell was successful enough in the mid-1920s to build a 10,500-seat football stadium, which was usually packed for games with Tulsa, Bucknell, Michigan State, and Wichita, among others. Like Carlisle, Haskell continued to funnel Indians onto college, professional, and Olympic teams in track, basketball, football, baseball, wrestling, and boxing. Other Indian schools—especially Sherman in Riverside, California—ran similarly successful programs.[24]

━━━━━━

Sports—and Indian athletes—had special meanings for White American spectators, while Indians often found athletic competition equally significant but for very different reasons. In its early days, government recruiters had to coerce and sometimes even kidnap students for the Carlisle Indian School. Some students, however, like Luther Standing Bear, who enrolled in 1879, did so voluntarily, with a "traditional" sense of mission: "I was thinking of my father and how he had many times said to me, 'Son, be brave! Die on the battlefield if necessary away from home.' This chance to go East would prove that I was brave."[25] By the early twentieth century, however, such psyching up was no longer necessary, as native boys at Carlisle, Haskell, Sherman, and a variety of other schools seized the opportunities offered by sports and established a new intertribal athletic tradition on most reservations.

Carlisle, where Indian talent from around the country was first concentrated, acquired something of an Indian national team by default. Between 1907 and 1914, during Glenn "Pop" Warner's second coaching stint at the school, the football team went 73–22–5, playing such powerhouses as Yale, Harvard, Army, Navy, Alabama, and Notre Dame. When Carlisle beat Harvard in 1907, Indian newspapers around the country celebrated it as a second Little Bighorn. *The Arrow*, Carlisle's own newspaper, boastfully proclaimed: "Indians Scalp Harvard—The 'Big Four' now the 'Big Five.' " [26]

This inter-Indian athletic culture that grew up around schools like Carlisle and Haskell, and around individuals like my grandfather, flowed back to numerous reservations where American sports became an increasingly integral part of community life. Native people who did not make the journey to Carlisle, Haskell, or the other schools often enjoyed equivalent athletic experiences closer to home. In Pine Ridge, South Dakota, for example, Cleveland "Moot" Nelson discovered sports at Holy Rosary Mission School during the same years when my grandfather was playing for St. Stephen's. Nelson, whose uncle had played a short stint with the Chicago White Sox, went to St. Francis Catholic Indian School on the neighboring Rosebud Reservation because he wanted to play on its well-known basketball team. Although a small, reservation high school, St. Francis sent its Scarlet Warriors to the National Catholic Tournament eight years in a row during the 1930s. On the reservation, everyone turned out for their games. [27]

Many St. Francis basketball players went on to play with the Sioux Travellers, an exhibition club that toured the country, occasionally matching up with the Harlem Globetrotters. [28] Indian promoters such as William Conquering Bear sponsored other, less well-known but equally well-traveled exhibition teams. Conquering Bear also put together local organizations like the Wakpamni Lakers, which included men's baseball and basketball, women's softball, and boys' Little League teams. [29] While Harvard and Yale supporters were drawing a sense of community and identity from watching "The Game," the entire Rosebud community, indeed the Sioux people as a whole, were doing the same when they gathered in local gyms to watch the Travellers, the Lakers, or the local high school team.

The complexities of intercultural performance played a significant role in the new Indian world of the early twentieth century. Like the Globe-trotters, who fused athletic exhibition with a familiar minstrelsy tradition, Indian athletes were expected to display White cultural understandings of "Indianness" to their predominantly White audiences. Perhaps no team better illustrates this kind of self-conscious "Indian play" than the Oorang Indians, who played a full NFL schedule in 1922 and 1923, the same years when my grandfather was throwing passes against the Connecticut Aggies. The team, owned by an eccentric dog breeder and used primarily to adver-tise his canine products, consisted almost entirely of Carlisle and Haskell graduates.[30] Jim Thorpe, Joe Guyon, and other alums joined a smattering of Indian men recruited from other schools or straight off the reservations. With no hometown, the Indians—like the Globetrotters—played all their games "away" and proved to be an enormous draw. When they arrived in a town, the players would don blankets and headdresses and wander around the train or bus station, performing a hackneyed "naive Indian in the big city" act for spectators far less worldly than themselves. At halftime, the team would lead the stylish "Oorang Airedales" around the field and perform Indian dances, as well as staging knife- and tomahawk-throwing contests, bear-wrestling exhibitions, and World War I "Indian combat" re-enactments. Football was showcased in only one brief act of a theatrical production in which primitive Indian difference was dramatized on the field for the consumption of non-Indian audiences.

The players, of course, interpreted the game and the halftime show com-pletely differently: both were part of the long tradition of Indians playing "Indians," a tradition with a certain bicultural sophistication and an ar-ray of meanings clustered around labor, adventure, and conviviality. Many of the players saw exhibition football in the same light as a touring Wild West show—a chance to make some money and to have some fun. "White people thought we were all wild men," recalled quarterback Leon Bout-well, "even though almost all of us had been to college and were generally more civilized than they were. It was a dandy excuse to raise hell and get away with it."[31] If athletics meant different things to Indians and non-Indians, then, there were also significant points of overlap, such as Indians miming "Indianness" or taking the assimilatory step toward college. Sports served as a meeting place for transformation and persistence; for distinct, even mutually exclusive Indian and White interpretations, and for shared understandings. The fluidity of this meeting ground allowed Whites to bracket racial discrimination, Indians to move more confidently in non-Indian society, and an entire bicultural athletic world to come into being.

That world, however, could not sustain itself through the rapid changes occurring for both Indians and non-Indians in American society. The anti-modern valorization of racial difference was central to the entire pursuit, and it lost much of its compelling power during the Great Depression and the Second World War. After the war, a new push to "terminate" tribes and force Indians to become White and modern closed the windows of opportunity that had opened during the first half of the century. My grandfather's protests against the federal policy which would have dissolved reservations and destroyed tribal political identity represent his attempt to defend the validity of the intercultural world in which he grew up. But "termination" meant complete and total cultural homogeneity, and that policy, refusing to tolerate any difference, destroyed the world of my grandfather's youth. By the late 1940s, native people, who had little desire to eradicate their distinctiveness, found themselves viewed as recalcitrant and backward rather than "pure" and "primitive."

No longer recruited or welcomed elsewhere, Indian athletes excelled in smaller venues closer to home. Eventually, however, modern and post-modern disorientation and the culture of celebrity began to catch up with native people as well. In the "pure" days of 1912, for example, everyone back at Hopi knew runners with better wind and faster legs than Olympic medalist Louis Tewanima. Sports represented a complex mix of mimetic performance, metaphoric revenge, cultural acceptance, pan-tribal unity, financial windfall, and educational opportunity, but it was not the stuff of life and death. After winning silver medals in the 5,000- and 10,000-meter races, Tewanima returned to Hopi, gave his medals away, and settled down as a farmer, with no sense of epochal breaks between those experiences.[32]

For postwar Indian athletes, that sense of "everydayness" began to fall by the wayside, and many communities responded by drawing webs of kinship and unity ever tighter, keeping sports stars humble even as they were making them local celebrities. It grew increasingly difficult for Indian players to leave the tiny, nurturing pond of the reservation. Those players who made the jump found that university programs and minor league farm systems had become much more bureaucratized and impersonal, that sports organizations and native people now moved along very different trajectories. They rarely intersected.[33]

My grandfather's grandfather, Saswe, had had a vision in which he committed several generations of his family to serve as mediators between Lakota and non-Lakota people. Saswe had been a "medal chief," an interpreter, a go-between. His son, Tipi Sapa, had bridged the gap between Christian mission and native spirituality. When my grandfather graduated from St. Stephen's, however, he clashed with my great-grandfather over the nature and meaning of that familial obligation in the new, intertwined Indian–White world in which they found themselves. My grandfather, reenvisioning the commitment with twentieth-century eyes, desperately wanted to become a professional football player and coach; looking back toward the late nineteenth century, his father wanted, with equal desperation, for him to enter the ministry. It was, as they say, no contest. A few days after my grandfather was ordained a deacon, his father died. On receiving his degree from General Theological Seminary, the Episcopal Church's flagship institution, my grandfather traded New York for a series of backcountry South Dakota chapels on the Pine Ridge and Rosebud Reservations.

What must it have been like for him, watching each year pass and seeing his dreams of playing and coaching become more distant? Torn between his own desires and his deep loyalty to church and family, he turned his lack of playing time into something of a penance. If he could not compete at the same level, he would compete nonetheless. He played first base on the Martin town team, fielding complaints from parishioners who did not think it right for a man of the cloth to slide into second base with his spikes up. He coached the Bennett County High School football team and put together a baseball program for Indian kids, bringing his athletic experience back to the reservation.

Sports became a critical part not only of White American culture during the early twentieth century but also of a modern inter-Indian cultural system. The same 55-yard pass could carry multiple meanings for both Indians and non-Indians; some were shared, some were not. Likewise, my grandfather's turning at the end of his life to his athletic past meant more than the simple loss or rejection of his other identities. Like the complex mix of motivations, attitudes, and traditions that Indian players brought to the field, my grandfather's sports experience became intertwined with his personal sense of spirituality and his place as an Indian in America. He made those connections in explicitly familial terms, looking back to his father and grandfather and finding in his physicality not simply performance or pleasure but a way of serving, a special gift that informed his intellect, spirituality, and moral sensibility.

"I am not like either of my ancestors; one of the spirit, the other of the mind," he wrote in a get-well letter to former Indian Commissioner John Collier:

> I am of the body. I have a good, strong body. Nevertheless, may the *spirit* of my grandfather, Sasway, guided into me by the *wisdom* of my father, Tipi Sapa, impart to you on this paper, by my *physical strength*, the unseen healing resources of the earth, which rise up from the ground when we need them, by the power of the Great Spirit, and restore you to good health.[34]

My grandfather took up Saswe's obligation, devoting his physical gifts to the power of the Great Spirit and the restoration of good health to Lakota and non-Lakota people alike. When life and mind began to depart, however, he came full circle, returning to a memory of pure physicality. All else—intellect, memory, spirituality, culture—had been made manifest through his body.

Notes

1   See Vine V. Deloria, Sr., "The Establishment of Christianity among the Sioux," in *Sioux Indian Religion: Tradition and Innovation*, ed. Raymond J. DeMallie and Douglas R. Parks (Norman, OK, 1987), 91–111; and Sarah Emilia Olden, *The People of Tipi Sapa* (Milwaukee, 1918).

2   See Donald Fixico, *Termination and Relocation: Federal Indian Policy, 1945–1960* (Albuquerque, 1986).

3   According to Reamer Kline, the Connecticut Aggies were not beaten but tied by this touchdown; see his *Education for the Common Good: A History of Bard College—the First 100 Years (1860–1960)* (Annandale–on–Hudson, 1982), photo caption.

4   On Wounded Knee as a marker, see, for example, Ralph Andrist, *The Long Death: The Last Days of the Plains Indian* (New York, 1966); or almost any recent television documentary, especially Kevin Costner's *500 Nations*. On the General Allotment Act, see Frederick Hoxie, *A Final Promise: The Campaign to Assimilate the Indians, 1880–1920* (Lincoln, 1984); and Janet McDonnell, *The Dispossession of the American Indian, 1887–1934* (Bloomington, 1991). On government restrictions and legal decisions, see John Wunder, *Retained by the People: A History of American Indians and the Bill of Rights* (New

York, 1994). On boarding schools for Indian children, see Tsianina Lomawaima, *They Called It Prairie Light: The Story of Chilocco Indian School* (Lincoln, 1994); and Michael Coleman, *American Indian Children at School 1850–1930* (Jackson, MS, 1993).

5   One of the most thoughtful treatments remains James Clifford's *Predicament of Culture: Twentieth-Century Ethnography, Literature, and Art* (Cambridge, MA, 1988).

6   See Peter Iverson, *When Indians Became Cowboys: Native People and Cattle Ranching in the American* West (Norman, OK, 1994); Emily Greenwald, "Allotment in Severalty: Decision-Making during the Dawes Act Era on the Nez Percé, Cheyenne River Sioux, and Jicarilla Apache Reservations" (Ph.D. diss., Yale University, 1994); Frederick Hoxie, "From Prison to Homeland: The Cheyenne River Reservation before World War I," in *The Plains Indians of the Twentieth Century*, ed. Peter Iverson (Norman, OK, 1985), 55–75; and "Exploring a Cultural Borderland: Native American Journeys of Discovery in the Early Twentieth Century," *Journal of American History* 79 (1992): 969–95; Helen Blish, with drawings by Amos Bad Heart Bull, *A Pictographic History of the Oglala Sioux* (Lincoln, 1967). See also J. B. Carroll, "The Fourth of July Dishonored," in *The Indian Sentinel* (Washington, DC, 1910), 28.

7   See Philip Deloria, *Playing Indian: Native People and the Creation of American Identities* (New Haven: Yale University Press, forthcoming); and Michael Taussig, *Mimesis and Alterity: A Particular History of the Senses* (New York, 1993).

8   See Vine Deloria, Sr., "The Standing Rock Reservation: A Personal Reminiscence," *South Dakota Review* 9 (1971): 167–95. See also Luther Standing Bear, *My People, The Sioux* (Boston, 1928), in which White boys at these schools are described as more apt to learn Lakota than Indian boys were to learn English (189). My copy of Standing Bear's book, which originally belonged to my Great-Aunt Ella, has her gloss in the margin of this page: "Just like Vine at Kearney!"

9   See Thomas Vennum, *American Indian Lacrosse: Little Brother of War* (Washington, DC, 1994); Stewart Culin, *Games of the North American Indians: Twenty-Fourth Annual Report of the Bureau of American Ethnology to the Smithsonian Institution, 1902–1903* (Washington, DC, 1907); Edward H. Dewey, "Memoranda and Documents: Football and American Indians," *New England Quarterly* 3 (1930): 736–40; Peter Nabokov, *Indian Running* (Santa Barbara, 1981); and Kendall Blanchard, *The Anthropology of Sport: An Introduction* (South Hadley, MA, 1985), esp. 91–120.

10 Kline, *Education for the Common Good*, 79.

11 See T. J. Jackson Lears, "From Salvation to Self-Realization: Advertising and the Therapeutic Roots of the Consumer Culture, 1880–1930," in *The Culture of Consumption: Critical Essays in American History 1880–1980*, ed. Richard Wightman Fox and T. J. Jackson Lears (New York, 1983), 1–38; Warren Susman, "Culture Heroes: Ford, Barton, Ruth," in *Culture as History: The Transformation of American Society in the Twentieth Century* (New York, 1984), 122–49; and Elliot J. Gorn and Warren Goldstein, *A Brief History of American Sports* (New York, 1984), 98–182.

12 See Gorn and Goldstein, *Brief History of American Sports*, 164–69; and Richard D. Mandell, *Sport: A Cultural History* (New York, 1984), 187–95.

13 Sometimes known as the Harvard–Yale game. The Yale–Princeton game had an even longer tradition and, for a time, an equal cachet.

14   See Kline, *Education for the Common Good*, 62–85.

15   Ibid., 79.

16   Ibid., 78.

17   See Joseph B. Oxendine, *American Indian Sports Heritage* (Champaign, IL, 1988); Spotted Dog, "Baseball's Early Greats," *Many Smokes* 3 (1968): 5; and S. I. Thompson, "American Indians in the Major Leagues," *Baseball Research Journal* 13 (1983): 1–7.

18   On Indians and modernity, see P. Deloria, *Playing Indian*; and Leah Dilworth, "Imagining the Primitive: Representations of Native Americans in the Southwest, 1880–1930" (Ph.D. diss., Yale University, 1992).

19   Kline, *Education for the Common Good*, 79.

20   Grantland Rice, *The Tumult and the Shouting: My Life in Sport* (New York, 1954); see also Spotted Dog, "Baseball's Early Greats," 5–6.

21   See Richard Henry Pratt, *Battlefield and Classroom: Four Decades with the American Indian, 1867–1904*, ed. Robert Utley (New Haven, 1964), 212–338; see also the Carlisle School's various publications: *Red Man and Helper* (1880–1904); *The Arrow* (1904–17); *The Indian Craftsman* (1909–10); and *The Red Man* (1910–17).

22   See Oxendine, *American Indian Sports Heritage*, 239–55.

23   See *Indians of Today*, ed. Marion Gridley (Chicago, 1960), 10 (on Jones); 35–39 (on the Bruces); and 105 (on Key). On Johnson, see *The Arrow*, 15 September 1904, 4.

24   See Oxendine, *American Indian Sports Heritage*, 178–84, 193–201, and 199 (on Sherman); see also Maury White, "Indian Teams Had Colorful History, Great Athletes," *Des Moines Register*, 21 January 1990, 1, 9D.

25   Standing Bear, *My People, The Sioux*, 124.

26   *The Arrow*, 15 November 1907, 1. Carlisle had already beaten Penn and lost to Princeton, the other members of the "Big Four" along with Yale and Harvard.

27   See Jerry Reynolds, "Sports Is Steady Beat in the Varied Life of Moot Nelson," *Lakota Times*, 11 December 1991.

28   Ibid.

29   See "William Conquering Bear," *Indian Country Today*, 26 October 1994.

30   See Oxendine, *American Indian Sports Heritage*, 165, 224; and Sam Borowski, "Oorang Indians—One of the First NFL Teams," *Indian Country Today*, 5 January 1995.

31   Borowski, "Oorang Indians."

32   Rice, in *Tumult and Shouting*, quotes Glenn "Pop" Warner's observation that Thorpe gave 100 percent only on certain occasions: "It was difficult to know if Jim was laughing with you or at you" (233). On Tewanima, see Norm Frauenhelm, "Legends of Revered Land Are Long Running," *Lakota Times*, 7 August 1991.

33   There were, of course, exceptions: NBA player Harley Zephier, University of Washington quarterback Sonny Sixkiller, Oklahoma basketball player Etta Maytubby, and Olympic runner Billy Mills, who went on from Haskell to the University of Kansas. For a moving contemporary narrative of the problems of reservation sports, see Gary Smith, "Shadow of a Nation," *Sports Illustrated*, 18 February 1991, 60–76.

34   Vine Deloria, Sr., to John Collier, 4 February 1956, John Collier papers, pt. 3, ser. 1, recl. 34, no. 128. Manuscripts and Archives, Yale University.

Kenneth L. Parker

Never on a Sunday:
Why Sunday Afternoon Sports Transformed
Seventeenth-Century England

In the early 1980s, I was a graduate student
at Cambridge University, researching a doctoral
dissertation on early modern English Sabbatarianism—a topic so obscure and seemingly irrele-
vant that even among theologians it provoked
blank stares and, among historians, condescend-
ing platitudes. Having already researched the
theological literature of the period, I buried myself in letters and diaries, church court records,
and *Parliamentary Debates*, hunting for evidence
of the social and political impact of this doctrine on English life. By the spring of 1981, I
had reached the point that most graduate students know well—the research seemed endless
and the topic too absurd and arcane to waste
some of the best years of my life on. Then one
evening, in the midst of this existential angst, I
joined friends from my college to see the movie
Chariots of Fire. Its story had a Cambridge theme
and setting, and having witnessed some of the
filming on King's Parade the previous year, I was
keen to see the finished product. That evening
breathed new life into my work, for there on the
big screen was a twentieth-century version of the
early modern story I was seeking to tell.

The *South Atlantic Quarterly* 95:2, Spring 1996.
Copyright © 1996 by Duke University Press.
CCC 0038-2876/96/$1.50.

Eric Liddell, the great Scottish runner of the early 1920s, and later a missionary to China, had been caught in a crisis of conscience when told that his qualifying race in the 1924 Paris Olympics would take place on a Sunday afternoon. After a period of great spiritual anguish, he approached the British Olympic Committee and announced that he was withdrawing from the race because he would not break the Sabbath. The Prince of Wales summoned him and pressed Liddell to run. He refused. The prince then said, "We are appealing to your beliefs in your country and your king, and your loyalty to them." Liddell replied, "God made countries, God made kings, and the rules by which they govern; and those rules say that the Sabbath is his, and I for one intend to keep it that way." Declaring his loyalty to king and country, Liddell stated, "God knows I love my country, but I cannot make that sacrifice."[1]

Liddell was saved for the Olympics by the young Lord Lindsay, who offered to be replaced by Liddell in the 400-meter race the following Thursday. The stand taken by this zealous Scottish Presbyterian made the British papers, with a *Daily News* headline reading "Athlete: 'Won't Run on Sunday,'" and a *British Weekly* article entitled "God before King." In portraying that Sunday afternoon, the film flashed back and forth between shots of Liddell preaching to the Church of Scotland congregation in Paris and the athletes competing on the field. The runner took as his text Isaiah 40:

> Behold the nations are as a drop of a bucket, and are counted as the small dust of the balance. . . . All nations before him are as nothing; and they are counted to him less than nothing, and vanity. . . . He bringeth the princes to nothing: he maketh the judges of the earth as vanity. . . . Hast thou not known? hast thou not heard, that the everlasting God, the Lord, the Creator of the ends of the earth, fainteth not, neither is weary? . . . He giveth power to the faint; and to them that have no might he increaseth strength. . . . But they that wait upon the Lord shall renew their strength; they shall mount up with wings as eagles; they shall run and not be weary; and they shall walk, and not faint.

In our own postmodern era, when religious truth is weighed as equal (or less than equal) in merit to other ideologies, this story sounds quaint, or perhaps inspirational—a man of conviction refusing to compromise with those who wield power. Yet the force of such religious conviction is not an anachronism or a historical oddity—numerous contemporary examples illustrate how religious ideals can challenge social and political norms. When religiously minded folk feel torn between obedience to the law of God and the laws of human society, civil strife often follows. If Liddell's story is analyzed from the perspective of those who exercise political and social control, the issue becomes the threat posed by his actions to their authority and influence. Rather than a question of Sunday sports and religious observance, it becomes an issue of who has the authority to govern human affairs.

The Prince of Wales in 1924 was not the first English leader to encounter this problem, for both King James I and his son, Charles I, had already confronted the issue of sports on Sunday. For the latter, especially, the story proved neither quaint nor inspirational: its denouement was civil war and regicide. This was the story I discovered as my research on early modern Sabbatarianism progressed. What had begun as a lackluster review of theological propositions on the Sabbath became a fascinating study of authority—who has the right to exercise it, the limits on its use, and the rejection of human agents whose exercise of it violates sacred principles. That Sunday afternoon recreations proved a pivotal issue in this struggle over authority is one of the more intriguing chapters in the history of sports.

———

Richard Conder, in his youth a champion footballer and later a yeoman dairy farmer, was asked by a gathering of godly folk at Royston market in the 1650s to describe how he came to know God's saving grace. He offered the following testimony:

> When I was a young man, I was greatly addicted to football playing; and as the custom was in our parish and many others, the young men, as soon as church was over, took a football and went to play. Our minister often remonstrated against our breaking of the sabbath which however had little effect, only my conscience checked me at times, and I would sometimes steal away and hide myself from my companions. But being dexterous at the game, they would find me out, and get me again among them. This would bring on me more guilt and horror of conscience. Thus I went on sinning and repenting a long time, but had no resolution to break off from the practice; til one sabbath morn-

Boys playing football. Henry Peacham, *Minerva Britannia, or a Garden of Heroical Devises* (London, [1612]), 81 (RB 69059). Reproduced by permission of The Huntington Library, San Marino, CA.

ing, our good minister acquainted his hearers, that he was very sorry to tell them, that by the order of the King and Council, he must read them the following paper, or turn out of his living. This was the *Book of Sports* forbidding the minister or church-wardens or any other to molest or discourage the youth in their manly sports and recreations on the Lord's Day etc. When our minister was reading it, I was seized with a chill and horror not to be described. Now, thought I, iniquity is established by a law, and sinners are hardened in their sinful ways! What sore judgments are to be expected upon so wicked and guilty a nation! What must I do? Wither shall I fly? How shall I escape the wrath to come? And God set in so with it, that I thought it was high time to be in earnest about salvation. And from that time I never had the least inclination to take a football in hand, or to join my vain companions any more. So that I date my conversion from that time; and adore the grace of God in making that to be an ordinance to my salvation, which the devil and wicked governors laid as a trap for my destruction.[2]

Only a decade before Conder's Royston market testimony, England had undergone a bloody, divisive Civil War that culminated in the executions of both the leader of the church, Archbishop William Laud, and the leader of the nation, King Charles I. One major cause of England's civil strife in the 1640s was a conflict over observance of the Sabbath and the king and archbishop's endorsement of sports on Sunday afternoons. For many seventeenth-century Englishmen, nothing less than their personal salvation and England's preservation as a Christian nation was at stake. Conder's testimony reflected the convictions of these Englishmen. By the 1630s, observance of the Sabbath, and the related ban on Sunday afternoon sports, was not only an important religious issue, but one that had become a litmus test in national politics. The focal point of this controversy was the Book of Sports, which had been issued by James I in 1617 and then reissued by Charles I in 1633. While its decrees grew out of the early modern debate on the Sabbath, the controversy over Sunday afternoon sports had a much longer history.

Christian attempts to proscribe sports on Sunday date back to at least the middle of the sixth century. In an apocryphal letter from Christ that first appeared then, Sabbath abuses were condemned and violators of the Lord's day were threatened with great calamity. Among the many abuses listed were racing, shooting, and swimming, the consequences of which included tempests, sulfurous fire, flying serpents, and invading pagans.[3] While the letter was not taken seriously by Church leaders of the sixth century, it was widely circulated nonetheless and continued to be copied, translated, and distributed throughout Europe well into the fourteenth century. Interest in and concern over this issue waxed and waned with the times, but it remained a theme of European and English religious life throughout the Middle Ages. Sermons that survive from the fourteenth century condemn such Sunday desecrations as wrestling, shooting competitions, and field sports.[4]

Swimmers. Everard Digby, *De arte natandi libriduo* (London, 1587), sig. H (RB 380148). Reproduced by permission of The Huntington Library, San Marino, CA.

Political leaders during this period also discouraged the practice of certain sports on the Sabbath, but for rather different reasons. Richard II issued a statute in 1388 forbidding his subjects to play tennis, football, and similar sports on Sundays and holy days. Needing men skilled in the arts of war, he sought to promote the exclusive practice of archery on those days. Henry IV followed suit in 1409 with a statute prescribing six days' imprisonment for anyone caught playing the sports outlawed by Richard II on a Sunday.[5] These statutes provided precedents that Elizabeth I, James I, and Charles I would follow, banning as "unlawful sports" on the Sabbath all those that did not enhance physical fitness or military skills.

The Reformation did not bring about any change in the religious opposition to Sunday sports; if anything, the Protestant movement in England developed a more comprehensive and hostile position on this issue. Thomas Becon, an English theologian of the mid-sixteenth century, condemned in his *Catechism* those who misspent the day in lewd pastimes: "in dicing and carding, in dancing and bearbaiting, in bowling and shooting, in laughing and whoring, and in such like beastly and filthy pleasures of the flesh."[6] By the 1570s, a number of religious writers had published polemical works against Sabbath breakers. Humphrey Roberts, in his *Earnest Complaint of Divers Vain, Wicked, and Abused Exercises, Now Commonly Practised on the Saboth Day*, for example, condemned bearbaiting, bullbaiting, silver games, dicing, bowling, fencing, and carding on the grounds that such activities drew people away from hearing the word of God preached, which every good Protestant knew was the source of salvation.[7]

These writers were quick to find God's judgment in any disaster that occurred at Sunday sporting events. After the London earthquake of 1580, John Aylmer, Bishop of London, issued his *Godly Admonition*, a special "Order of Prayer" intended "to avert and turn God's wrath from us threatened by the terrible earthquake." Among the many corporate sins cited were spending Sunday and holy days "heathenishly, in taverning, tippling, gaming, playing, and beholding of Bear-baiting . . . to the utter dishonour of God."[8] John Field published a moralistic account of what happened on the Sunday afternoon of 13 January 1583 at Paris Garden, a well-known venue for blood sports in London. "When the dogs and Bear were in the chiefest battle," an upper gallery collapsed, crushing spectators and seriously damaging the building. While some attributed the incident to overcrowding and rotten timber, Field concluded that "it must needs be considered as an extraordinary judgement of God, both for the punishment of these present prophaners of the Lord's day that were there, and also inform and warn us that were abroad."[9]

During the last half of Elizabeth's reign, a debate arose among religiously minded Englishmen over the absolute prohibition of sports on the Sabbath versus allowing such activities after Evening Prayer on Sunday afternoon. The more radical Protestants pressed for an absolute ban on all recreations on the Lord's day, while others considered it important to give servants and other workers an opportunity to play on Sunday, which their labors prevented them from doing the rest of the week. Elizabeth, siding with the moderates, declared that no law of Parliament or injunction of

James I hunting. George Turberville, *The Noble Arte of Venerie or Hunting* (London, 1611), 108 (RB 69715). Reproduced by permission of The Huntington Library, San Marino, CA.

the bishops would prohibit sports after Evening Prayer on Sunday. When James I ascended the English throne, he brought with him from his years of ruling Scotland a great distaste for the Presbyterian rigor with which Eric Liddell would later keep faith. Yet James was confronted by the rigorist Protestants of England, who hoped to succeed with a Scottish king, nurtured in Calvinism, where they had failed with an English queen. He made a promising start in 1603 by issuing a proclamation prohibiting at any time on the Sabbath blood sports, bowling, and other activities that he styled "unlawful pastimes."[10] Had his petitioners known his views on the responsibilities and difficulties of monarchs, however, they might have been less optimistic. For example, in 1599, James observed that because subjects were prone to criticize their monarch it was important to divert them with "al honest games and exercise of armes," in which he saw no harm as long as "the Sabbothes bee kept holie, and [free of] unlawfull sportes."[11]

In the years following James's ascendance to the English throne, repeated attempts were made in Parliament to pass an act "for the better observing and keeping holy the Sabbath day or Sunday." A 1614 House of Lords bill was blocked by Bishop James Mountagu, a favorite of the king, who opposed its absolute prohibition of all recreations, lawful and unlawful, on the Sabbath. Prohibiting all sports, declared the bishop, would be "contrary to the divine rule it selfe, and the strictest and reformedest churches, for we cannot be stricter then the Jewes." Noting that even in John Calvin's Geneva tennis and other recreations were allowed after Evening Prayer on Sunday, Mountagu stated, "Those recreations that neyther breake rest nor sanctificacion . . . are lawfull and may be used."[12] As a royal confidant and the only bishop who dissented from the bill, Mountagu may be presumed to have spoken for the king on this matter. It made little difference in the end, however, because Parliament was dissolved before the bill came to a vote. But the issue was not so easily resolved.

On 11 August 1617, upon returning from a visit to Scotland, James arrived in Lancashire. Two days later, the king met with a group of laymen at Myercough who presented him with a petition on behalf of the people of Lancashire. These petitioners appealed to James to nullify orders issued by the county magistrates forbidding lawful recreations on Sunday.[13] Having recently wrangled with Scottish Presbyterians, James was all the more inclined to take exception to any local imposition of Sabbath restrictions that Parliament had failed to enact in 1614.[14] Encouraged by members of his court, including Bishop Mountagu and another royal favorite named John Williams, James received the petition and made a speech affirming that Christians were free to pipe, dance, and engage in other lawful recreations on Sundays.

The following Sunday, a group acted on this "liberty," piping and dancing outside a parish church near Houghton Tower during service time. When the king heard of these abuses from Bishop Thomas Morton, he "utterly disavowed any thoughts or intention of encouraging such prophaneness" and turned the offenders over to Morton, who punished the chief culprit—

the piper who had incited the incident. This aroused protests from some in the king's company, who complained of such a "rigorous and tyrani-call" response to what was only an "Innocent Recreation for servants and other inferiour people on the Lords day and Holy dayes, whose laborious callings deprived them of it at all other times."[15] They also claimed that such Sunday recreations were generally desired throughout the country. James conferred with Bishop Morton to determine how to satisfy his subjects on this score without running the risk of turning liberty into license. The bishop retired to his lodgings and drafted six restrictions and conditions on Sunday recreations and those who could engage in them, which James accepted, declaring that he would only "alter them from the words of a Bishop, to the words of a King." Bearbaiting, bullbaiting, interludes, and bowling continued to be prohibited, but new restrictions were placed on recusant Catholics, who were debarred from lawful recreations as well. Parish officials were required to report anyone engaging in even lawful recreations "before the endinge of all Devine service for that day."[16] All those who did participate in Sunday sports had to hear divine service first, were forbidden to wear offensive weapons while playing, and could engage in such recreations only within their own parishes.[17]

When James issued the Book of Sports several days later, he added a lengthy preface that restated concerns which had preoccupied English monarchs in previous centuries. He expressed regret at hearing "the generall complainte of the people that they weare barred from all lawfull recreacion and excersise upon the sondaie . . . after the endinge of all Devine service," noting that this prohibition might hinder the conversion of papists, render men unfit for war, and lead them to "sette upp filthie Typlinge and Drunkennes," even to making "idle and discontented speeches in theire Alehowses." He ordered that the laws of the realm and the canons of the Church be respected in Lancashire, declaring all lawful recreations permissible after Sunday Evening Prayer and encouraging such activities as piping, dancing, archery, and vaulting in particular. James directed Bishop Morton to append an order requiring all preachers to "instruct the people concerning the lawfulnes of recreacion upon Sondaies accordinge to the Limitts and restraints set downe in his majesties Declaracion." In addition, Lancashire ministers were instructed not to preach afternoon sermons exceeding "the compass of an howre least that his majesties former favourable In-tenddement and Indulgencie to his people may seeme to bee Deluded thearby."[18]

It is impossible to say why the Book of Sports became a national declaration in 1618, for nothing is known about the events leading up to its reissuing. The most significant amendment to it was in fact its broader application to the entire country, requiring that the "Declaration shall be published by order from the bishop of the diocese through all the parish churches, and that both our judges of our circuit and our justices of the peace be informed thereof." [19] James and his advisors may have hoped that a national declaration would not only specify appropriate Sunday recreations, but also preempt the imposition of overzealous local orders in the future. The result was just the opposite, however, for the Book of Sports fanned the flames of an already smoldering "culture war" between rigorist Protestants and those who advocated Sunday afternoon sports.

Shortly after the national Book of Sports was issued, local disturbances, including the disruption of divine services by rowdy behavior, occurred in many parts of England. In November 1618, for example, the parishioners of Allbriton, Staffordshire, were disturbed at Evening Prayer by "a company with a drum and guns, [who], striking up in the churchyard and under the church wall and windows, shot off their pieces, and cried, 'Come out, ye Puritans, come out.'" That same month, at Lea Marston, a group came "into the church in the fools' coats, they sat awhile ridiculously, and ere the second lesson was read, impatient of delay, they rose up and went into the churchyard . . . and at an alehouse [close] by, they tabred and danced the whole sermon time." [20]

John Williams, the courtier who had advised the king in Lancashire, found challenges of a different kind in the jurisdiction where he served as justice of the peace. There, local officials tried to enforce a stricter interpretation of the Book of Sports than he thought appropriate. When Williams challenged the local constable, he was told

> 1. that the King's declaration was a bolstering up of sin and breach of the Sabbath. 2. That his Majesty therefore ought to be prayed for, that God would give him an understanding heart. 3. That the observation of the sabbath in religious worship must be continued for twenty-four hours. [21]

Such opposition to the Book of Sports was not limited to local government officials; ministers preached against the king's declaration from the pulpit as well. The Vicar of Hominghold was reported for quoting "passages of Scripture, in opposition to the King's Book of Recreation on the

Lord's Day."[22] Gerard Prior, Vicar of Eldersfield, Worcestershire, publicly prayed for "God to turn the King's heart from profaneness, vanity, or Popery."[23] On 1 August 1619, William Clough preached against the declaration at Bramham. After reading the fourth commandment, he went on to express an attitude toward divine and human authority that Eric Liddell would echo three centuries later:

> The king of Heaven doth bid you keepe his Sabbaoth and reverence his sanctuarie. Now the king of England is a mortall man and he bids you breake it. Chuse whether of them you will followe. . . . I will tell you the reason why the king of England made Lawes against gods Lawes. . . . The reason is because he durst doe noe other for plaine feare for the saftie of his owne body in his progresse.[24]

The disorders at Allbriton and Lea Marston, the confrontation between Williams and the constable of his jurisdiction, and the sermons preached against the Book of Sports all illustrate the serious tension and cultural conflict that arose over the issue of Sunday afternoon sports. Rather than defusing tensions, James's declaration incited disorder and increased friction in communities, leading some to regard him as a maintainer of wickedness but one whose authority over his subjects was superseded by the law of God. James could not even muster the support of the leading figure in the Church of England; Archbishop Abbot forbade the reading of the Book of Sports from the pulpit in his presence on the appointed Sunday and persuaded the king to rescind the order that it be read in all parish churches. Recognizing the problems created by his declaration, James accepted the archbishop's counsel, although others in his court were not so acquiescent. One report stated that "the King was pleased to wink at [Abbot's response], not withstanding the daily endeavours that were used to irritate the King against him."[25]

The disorders provoked by his 1618 declaration surprised James, who had intended only to preserve the moderate tradition of allowing certain recreations after all the religious observances of Sunday were over—the stance taken by English rulers for centuries. He failed to appreciate the impact of Calvinist understandings of God's sovereignty and the attendant elevation of Old Testament teachings above regal decrees. The declaration polarized religious opinion and contributed to the identification of strict prohibitions of Sunday recreations with Protestant rigorism, or puritanism, despite the support for such prohibitions expressed by the Archbishop of Canterbury and most of the bishops in England. The king responded prudently and allowed the controversy to die down. He knew that forcing the issue would pit his own authority against that of God—and when governing a deeply religious people, a wise ruler does not force his subjects to choose between God and King.

In 1621 William Laud became Bishop of St. David's, an obscure diocese on the western coast of Wales. James had been reluctant to appoint him to any high ecclesiastical office, for he had misgivings about Laud's judgment. The king told Laud's patron, "The plain Truth is, that I keep Laud back from all Place of Rule and Authority, because I find he hath a restless Spirit, and cannot see when Matters are well, but loves to toss and change, and to bring Things to a pitch of Reformation floating in his own Brain, which may endanger the stead fastness of that which is in a good pass, God be praised."[26] James's assessment was amply borne out by Laud's role in the Book of Sports controversy of the 1630s. A man of strong convictions who did not hesitate to defend principles he valued, Laud opposed the rigorist Calvinism that had gained influence in the Church of England and desired a return to the moderation in teaching and practice that he believed had characterized the Elizabethan Church. And while James did not approve of Laud, his son did. After Charles ascended to the throne in 1625, Laud rose, too. Moving up from St. David's to more influential episcopal sees, he never missed an opportunity to promote and defend his principles, especially regarding ecclesiastical jurisdiction and episcopal authority. These issues sparked a conflict in 1633 that made Sunday recreations a political lightning rod once more.

Shortly after Laud became Bishop of London in 1628, the city's Lord Mayor issued a strict order against Sabbath abuses, declaring that "notwithstanding divers good Lawes provided for the keeping of the Saboth day holy according to the expresse comandment of Almightly god, divers Inhabitants . . . of this Citty and other places have noe respect of duty towards god, his Majestie or his Lawes." Laud regarded this order as a transgression of his own authority, annotating the back of his copy with the observation: "The Ld Maior of London's warrant against breakers of the Saboth—Mye jurisdiction interessed."[27] Then early in 1633, Sir Nicholas Rainton,

the new Lord Mayor of London, provided Laud with an opportunity to as-
sert his episcopal authority when he prohibited a poor woman from selling
apples in the yard of Saint Paul's Cathedral on the Sabbath. Laud rebuked
the Lord Mayor for meddling within his jurisdiction, threatened to complain to the king and council about this interference, and asserted that
the woman could continue to sell apples there "notwithstanding his [Rain-
ton's] Command to the contrary."[28]

While the Elizabethan and Jacobean eras had been marked by increasing cooperation between bishops and local officials in correcting moral
offenses, Laud sought to reverse this well-established practice, causing
consternation and concern to those in both secular and religious offices.
Yet this was only the beginning of Laud's efforts to reassert episcopal authority, for his attention soon turned to the prohibition of wakes by local
officials in Somerset. For decades, West Country justices had been issuing injunctions against wakes and punishing offenders, as these events
had long been associated with excessive drinking, dancing, and other activities prohibited on Sundays. In 1632, disturbed by reports of persons
murdering "Bastard children begotten at Wakes and Revels" and "sundry
other grand disorders occasioned by these intemperate meetings," Baron
Denham and Lord Chief Justice Richardson issued an amendment to an
earlier order, requiring every minister to "publish it yeerely in his parish
church upon the first sonday in February and two sondayes before Easter
yeerely." The first reading of this order in Somerset pulpits occurred in
February 1633 and thus coincided with Laud's conflict with the Lord Mayor
of London. Laud used this event to further his cause, complaining to the
king that the judges had infringed on Bishop Piers's jurisdiction and had
unlawfully prohibited church festivals.[29]

Charles's inquiry into the matter balanced a concern for Sabbath observance with a desire to allow his subjects appropriate recreations after
Evening Prayer. His position did not deviate from that of his father:

> Our intention in this Busines is [in] no way to give a liberty to the
> breache or prophanacon of the Lordes day, which we will to be kepte
> with that solemnity and reverence that is due to it, but that the people
> after evening prayer may use such decent and sober recreations as are
> fitt. And to that end we do heerby require you and all other . . . Justices
> of peace in your severall divisions to take speciall care, that all excesses
> in those feastes and disorders in those recreations be prevented.[30]

Nevertheless, Charles determined that the order issued by the Somerset officials had transgressed episcopal jurisdiction, so he instructed that it be revoked and that the people be allowed their wakes on the condition that these festivities not lead to excesses and abuses of the Lord's day.

Laud, by this time Archbishop of Canterbury and leader of the Church of England, suggested that Charles reissue the Book of Sports with an amendment protecting wakes. In his efforts to defend episcopal jurisdiction, Laud found the Book of Sports to be highly useful, for while it reasserted the right to recreation after Evening Prayer, justifying his position on the Somerset wakes, it also provided a basis for enforcing "conformity" to the English Church. James's 1618 declaration had established zero tolerance toward "Puritans and Precisians," requiring them either to conform or to "leave the Countrey according to the Lawes of Our Kingdome, and Canons of Our Church."[31] Concepts of orthodoxy and the definition of "puritanism" had shifted over the intervening fifteen years, and Laud, intent on suppressing Calvinism and promoting his own agenda, used this clause against those who did not share his vision of the Church of England.

Charles, with some reluctance, reissued the declaration in October 1633, appending to the 1618 Book of Sports a short preface of his own with a brief statement permitting wakes. Justices of assizes were required to see that "no man do trouble or molest any of our loyal and dutiful people, in or for their lawful recreations, having first done their duty to God." It was also stipulated that "publication of this our command be made by order from the Bishops, throughout all the parish churches of their several dioceses respectively."[32] Like his father before him, Charles sought to strike a balance between maintaining the sanctity of the Sabbath and allowing practice time in some sports for the purpose of military readiness. He also thought it prudent to permit diversion for those who might otherwise be inclined to grumble about—or even rebel against—their rulers. He failed to learn from his father's experience, however, and did not accurately read the religious signs of the times. Laud persuaded Charles to embark on a course of action that defied the prevailing current of religious opinion, a political miscalculation for which both men would pay a high price.

What followed was a disturbing clash of priorities and principles. For Laud, the primary issue was episcopal jurisdiction. Reading the Book of Sports in their parishes became a test of obedience for clergy around the country, yet for many ministers and laymen there were other, quite different issues at stake. The 1618 declaration had been unpopular among secular and church leaders because of the ensuing disorders and abuses of the Lord's day. Both parliamentary bills and theological works of the 1620s reflected a widespread concern over this issue. Many concurred with Lord Saye's view, expressed in a 1614 parliamentary speech, that even lawful recreations were "unfitt to be used on that day, for the Sabboath is as much broken by recreacions and sportes as the businesses of a mans callinge." [33] The Book of Sports troubled the conscience of good men, and many ministers struggled to obey their bishop while not violating their principles. Like the minister in Richard Conder's parish, many pastors found that obedience in this matter posed a painful dilemma.

In January 1634, Nicholas Estwick, rector at Warkton, Northamptonshire, sought the advice of Samuel Ward, master of Sidney Sussex College, Cambridge, and a man respected by the more radical Protestants of England. Estwick wrote to Ward, reporting that the Book of Sports had "caused much distraction and griefe in many honest mens hearts in our Diocese whiche have reade it; and many there be to the number at the most of three score . . . which have refused to publish it." Noting that these men were "orthodoxal, diligent preachers and conscionable practisors of what they preach," Estwick expressed concern that "if they should be deprived (which God forbid) what a losse that would be amongst us and what a blowe it would give to the power of religion your worship apprehendeth." For his own part, said Estwick, "I dare not dissent from those famous Protestants . . . which do hold a necessity that one day of seaven should be kept holy," although the issue of Sunday sports remained unresolved in his own mind. "I have laboured in the point: yet I am not satisfied, but do hange in suspense whether recreations on the Lords day be lawful or not." Because he was uncertain about whether God's moral law actually prohibited those activities, he was not willing to join those who refused to read the declaration, so "I have caused the booke to be published in my church, not looking at the Contents but at his authority which commands the publication thereof, and I hold this position to be true." Estwick was disturbed by those who refused to read the king's declaration for conscience' sake, observing that "this scrupulosity would lay the foundation of disorder and confusion both in the Church and the Comon-wealth." [34] His fears were more justified than he could possibly have known.

Ward wrote back "to signify my concurence," declaring that "a minister with safety of conscience, may publish in his church, being commanded by sovereign authority such edicts, the contents whereof he doth not approve in his owne conscience as you rightly show by sundry instances." Ward also affirmed that since some recreations on the Lord's day were lawful, not all sports violated the "law of the Sabbath." Observing that "every minister is not bound to examyne the justice of the princes action," Ward stated that "though a minister hath a speculative doubt . . . yet he knoweth it is his duty to publish it, who by lawfull authority, he is commanded." He also noted the good intentions of James, who had published the declaration to curb popery and encourage men to maintain their fitness for war. Moreover, Ward saw no harm in "honest Recreations, as pitching of the bar, ringing a pole, shooting at butts, playing at stool ball, [or] setting up a maypole." [35]

Fifteen years before, Archbishop Abbot had been in the forefront of those opposing the promulgation of the king's declaration from the pulpit. In 1633 the tables were turned, with the king reluctantly reissuing the Book of Sports and endorsing the rigorous enforcement of its publication in all parish churches at the insistence of Archbishop Laud. While Estwick, Ward, and others were able to bend their conscience to the order, many found it impossible to obey. One puritan accused Laud of attempting "to insnare, silence and root out all conscientious, preaching Ministers" through the enforcement of the declaration's pulpit promulgation. While it is impossible to determine his true motives now, this perception of the archbishop deeply wounded the nation at the time. Many ministers could not stretch their consciences and were suspended for refusing to read the Book of Sports or for preaching against its contents. In Somerset alone, twenty-four ministers were suspended by the bishop. [36]

For those who could not in conscience comply, only two options remained: to go into voluntary exile or to stand firm and face persecution. Hugh Peter, who chose exile, explained his decision as follows: "Many of my Acquaintances going for New England, had engaged me to come to them when they sent, which accordingly I did. And truly, my reason for myself and others to go, was meerly not to offend Authority in that difference of Judgment; and had not the Book for Encouragement of Sports on the Sabbath come forth, many had staid." [37] (This wave of emigration to the American colonies as a result of the Sunday afternoon sports controversy has gone unnoticed by historians.) However, many did stay to defend

Sabbath observance against the Book of Sports. George Garrard, writing to Thomas Wentworth on 6 December 1633, reported

> Much Difference in opinion about the Book; for, though it be the same verbatum that was published in King James's Time, yet it is commanded to be read in al the Churches here, and in the country. In some Churches in London it hath been read. One Dr. Denison read it, and presently after read the Ten Commandments, then said, "Dearly Beloved, you have heard now the Commandments of God and Man, obey which you please." Another in St. Giles in the Fields read it, and the same Day preached upon the Fourth Commandment; and I hear . . . Mr. Holdsworth and Dr. Gouge have refused to read it.[38]

On Easter Monday of 1634, Edward Williams of Shaftesbury, Dorset, delivered a sermon in support of strict Sunday observance. Repeating the words of the declaration that demanded "the observation of the lawes of the kingdome, and Canons of the church," he then read portions of the 1625 Lord's Day Observance Act, which forbade "certayne recreations or sportes to be used" and set out "pointes of doctrine as well out of some of the fathers, as also out of holie Scripture, to move the people to the strict observation of the Saboth day." The following Sunday he preached that if the Sabbath were free of ordinary labors, then it should not be profaned by recreations, for, as Augustine said, "Better it was to goe to plowe [than] daunce on the Saboth." He concluded his sermon with the dire warning that "it were a most dreadfull thinge and neere damnable, if not absolutely damnation to use any recreations on the Saboth or Lordes day."[39] Many other ministers similarly preached against the Book of Sports and were suppressed for their defiance of the authorities.[40]

Although the reaction of parishioners is difficult to ascertain, the testimony of Richard Conder, the "hardened" Cambridgeshire football "addict," suggests that they were keenly aware of this religious controversy. The declaration not only led some to become religious, but turned many clergy and laymen alike against both the king and the archbishop. Conder was not the only one to have counted his "conversion from that time" or to have made the Book of Sports "an ordinance to [his] salvation, which the devil and wicked governors laid as a trap for [his] destruction." In the 1630s, even the village footballer had strong convictions about Sabbath observance; for many, if not most, Englishmen considered Sabbath observance simply good Christian practice.

In the years that followed, opponents of both the Book of Sports and Laud's leadership of the English Church began to illegally publish books and pamphlets protesting Sabbath abuses. Henry Burton and William Prynne were the most prolific authors of such works. In 1636 alone they produced four defenses of Sabbath observance, one of which cited examples of God's judgment on the Book of Sports during the two years since it had been reissued. The author deplored what had befallen clergy "who now unjustly suffer through the malice of ungodly persecutors, and raging prelates, for refusing to join with others in spurring on the people to the greedy pursuite of this cryinge dangerous Syn, to the ruine of their soules, their bodies, and the shame of our religion." And it was indeed a sin, he reiterated, "a Syn, yea and a crying Syn too, as all our writers (yea and our Prelates generally), till now of late have unanimously defined, and the whole State in Parliament."[41] Fifty-five examples of God's judgment on Sabbath breakers were cited from all parts of the country, with dates, places, and often names being given, a mass of information that could not have been collected without considerable cooperation and sympathy. Some examples were more detailed than others, such as an incident that occurred on 25 January 1634: "Being the Lords day, in time of the last great Frost, 14 young men presuming to play at football upon the yce on the river Trent, neere to Ganisborrow, coming altogether in a scuffle, the yce suddainly broke, and they were all drowned." In another example, an Oxford carpenter, deciding on Sunday to finish constructing the stage for a play to be held at St. John's College on Monday, "fell backward from the Stage, being not farre from the ground, and broke his neck, and so ended his life in a fearful Tragedy."[42]

News from Ipswich, another "underground" publication, sharply criticized the established political and religious order. Lamenting the censorship of the time, the author charged that "presses formerly open only to Truth and Piety, are closed up against them both of late, and patent for the most part, to nought but error, superstition, and profanesse." He was particularly incensed by

> those many prophane, erronious, impious books, printed within these 3 yeares by the authority (point-blanke against the established doctrine of the Church of England, and his Majesties pious Declarations) . . . and which is yet more impious and detestable, against the very

morality of the Sabbath, and 4. Commandment: the devine institution, title and intire religious sanctification of the Lords day SABBATH.[43]

Recounting the changes that were being forced on the Church and re-calling Charles's promise to stand against religious innovation, the author demanded that the king reject such innovations by Laud and those who followed him.

By 1636, the strict Sunday observance "platform" had become identified with Protestants who opposed Laud's agenda for the Church of England. On 5 November, Guy Fawkes Day, Henry Burton preached two sermons against the changes introduced by the Laudians. In these sermons, later published together under the title *For God, and the King*, Burton called on Charles to put an end to what he saw as the havoc caused by Laud and his supporters. He refused to believe that the king had authorized the enforcement of the Book of Sports' promulgation from the pulpit, citing Charles's stand against religious innovation, but declared that changes had been introduced by Laud nonetheless:

> The reading of this Booke by the Ministers is to bring in . . . a mighty innovation of the unity or Doctrine concerning the Sabbath, which hath been ever since the Reformation, and so from the Raigne of Queene Elizabeth of famous memory, constantly, universally and unanimously maintayned in the church of England, untill this late faction of Anti-Sabbatarians started up, to cry downe all sanctifica-tion, all power and purity of Religion. And indeed the innovation of the Doctrine of the Sabbath bring with it an Universal innovation of all religion, as experience is an eye-witnesse.[44]

Shortly after delivering his Guy Fawkes Day sermons, Burton was sum-moned by the High Commission to answer charges of sedition. He refused to do so and appealed to the king. On 2 February 1637, the Sergeant at Arms and the Sheriff of London broke down Burton's door, arrested him, and ransacked his study. Imprisoned in the Fleet, he was soon joined by William Prynne and John Bastwick; all three were charged with producing books which slandered the ecclesiastical hierarchy. The Star Chamber trial was conducted without counsel for the defendants, for no lawyer would take their case, nor was their testimony admitted as evidence. Noted for his imposition of harsh penalties, Laud pressed for particularly severe measures to be taken against these men. Burton was deprived of his parish and defrocked, had his academic degrees annulled, and was fined £5,000. In addition, he was to be set in a pillory at Westminster, where his ears would be cut off, and imprisoned at Lancaster Castle for life. Prynne and Bastwick received similar penalties.[45] At their sentencing on 14 June 1637, Laud delivered a speech, denying the charges of innovation and defending the authority of the episcopate.[46]

Much to Laud's distress, Burton, Prynne, and Bastwick attracted a sympathetic crowd when they were pilloried at Westminster. Moreover, when Burton was transported to Lancaster Castle after his wounds had healed, he departed London (on 28 July 1637) with all the fanfare of a hero. Eyewitnesses reported a

> strange flocking of the People after Burton, when he removed from the Fleet towards Lancaster Castle. Mr. Ingram, Sub-Warden of the Fleet told the King, that there was not less than one hundred thousand People gathered together to see him pass by, betwixt Smithfield and Brown's Well, which is two miles beyond Highgate, his Wife went along in a Coach, having much Money thrown at her as she passed along.[47]

In his autobiography, Burton recalled that

> on the day appointed I passed on horseback from the Fleet through Smithfield, where for throng of people all along I could not passe, but very slowly, though the Keeper hastened all he could, who fretted to see so many all the way we went, he reckoned the number to be forty thousand. By the way so many taking me by the hand, pressed the very blood out at my finger ends. . . . I rid to St. Albans that night, being accompanied all the way with above five hundred horse of loving friends.[48]

This display of support and sympathy for Burton stood in stark contrast to the malice directed at Laud, with protests nailed to the doors of the cathedral and caricatures displayed in public places. The archbishop reported to a friend that in September 1637 a board had been "hung upon the Standard in Cheap . . . a narrow board with my speech in the Star Chamber nailed at one end of it, and singed with fire, the corners cut off instead of the ears, a pillory of ink with my name to look through it."

Below the drawing was a caption: "The man that put the saints of God into a pillory of wood, stands here in a pillory of ink. . . . The author deserves to be used thus as well as the book."[49] Laud could not have anticipated that this prophecy would be fulfilled in the not too distant future. He had not understood the power of a religious ideal, and as James I had observed, did not know when to leave well enough alone. In an effort to secure and extend episcopal authority in the name of preserving Sunday sports, he caused many to reject his authority and that of the king who followed his advice. By 1640, the power structures Laud had sought to enhance and defend were tumbling down on his head, as he was first impeached and then, the following year, arrested and imprisoned. On 10 January 1645, he was executed on Tower Hill in London. King Charles suffered the same fate after his defeat by the forces of the puritan-dominated Parliament. Both men had pressed religiously minded Englishmen to choose between temporal authority and what they understood to be the law of God. As a result, England had been changed forever.

On Sunday, 15 November 1640, three years after his imprisonment at Lancaster Castle, Henry Burton was informed that the House of Commons had dropped the charges against him and ordered that he be released. He regarded his receipt of this news on the Lord's day as a sign and a blessing, "a gracious reward of mercy from God, whose day I had formerly stood for against all the adversaries thereof." On his journey to London, Burton was met at Bagshot by his wife, "who came accompanied with many loving friends, and worthy Citizens of London." When they stopped for the night at Egham, Burton later recalled, "every house brought forth a light to light us to our lodging, where we were most nobly entertained by multitudes of friends, that from London met us there."[50] While Laud had meant to make an example of Burton and his associates, they became instead symbols of resistance to his attempt to extend his power and authority at the expense of the sanctification of Sunday.

Almost two decades before, during the Parliament of 1621, the crypto-papist Thomas Shepard had charged that supporters of the Sabbath observance bill were attempting to subvert the king's will, as set forth in the 1618 declaration on sports, and had accused them of puritanism.[51] John

Pym, later a Civil War parliamentary leader, responded with words that proved prophetic. He denounced Shepard's attempt to

> devide us amongst our selves, exasperatinge one partie by that odious and factious name of Puritans; Or at least would make the world believe we were devided, which as it may breede in the Comon adversarie boldnes to attempt soe it may nourish among us jeolosye and suspicion in defence of our selves. And it hath been often seene that small seedes of Tumult and sedition growe upp into greate dangers, even to the overthrowe of States.[52]

By 1640, England had indeed become divided over the issue of strict Sabbath observance versus Sunday afternoon sports, an issue that became one means of determining religious and political allegiances.

When Eric Liddell quoted the prophet Isaiah in 1924, he expressed the convictions not of an eccentric Highlands Sabbatarian, but of many generations of British Protestants for whom the laws of the land were superseded by the law of God: "All nations before him are as nothing; and they are counted to him less than nothing, and vanity. . . . He bringeth the princes to nothing: he maketh the judges of the earth as vanity." Divine might could empower those at the margins of society and give vision and purpose to their lives, for God "giveth power to the faint; and to them that have no might he increaseth strength." Such religious convictions also had the power to elevate a village footballer like Richard Conder and to bring down an archbishop like Laud or a king like Charles I.

In an age when many would like to ignore or discount the power of religious conviction to shape individuals and nations, we would do well to remember the seventeenth-century English conflict over Sunday afternoon recreations. Viewed through this lens, the religiously motivated controversies of our own times may appear to call for resolutions more complex than the mere appeal to the laws of the land or obedience to the dictates of the current political establishment. If God is supreme, human authority must tread with care, even on the turf of Sunday sports.

Notes

1 *Chariots of Fire*, dir. Hugh Hudson (Warner Bros., 1981).
2 Quoted in Margaret Spufford, *Contrasting Communities* (Cambridge, 1974), 231–32.

3   See J. G. O'Keeffe, "Cain Downaig," *Ériu: The Journal of the School of Irish Learning* 2 (1905): 189–214, esp. 195, 197, 201, 203, 211.

4   See Kenneth L. Parker, *The English Sabbath: A Study of Doctrine and Discipline from the Reformation to the Civil War* (Cambridge, 1988), 10–12.

5   See W. B. Whitaker, *Sunday in Tudor and Stuart Times* (London, 1933), 13; and W. Denton, *England in the Fifteenth Century* (London, 1888), 219.

6   Thomas Becon, *Catechism*, ed. J. Ayre (Cambridge, 1844 [1560]), 80.

7   Humphrey Roberts, *An Earnest Complaint of Divers Vain, Wicked, and Abused Exercises, Now Commonly Practised on the Saboth Day* (London, 1572), sig. B2V.

8   *Liturgical Services Set Form in the Reign of Queen Elizabeth*, ed. William K. Clay (Cambridge, 1847), 562, 574.

9   John Field, *A Godly Exhortation by Occasion of the Late Judgement of God, Showed at Paris-Garden* (London, 1583), n.p.

10   See E. K. Chambers, *The Elizabethan Stage* (Oxford, 1923), 4: 335.

11   James I, *Basilicon Doron* (Edinburgh, 1599), 63–64.

12   See Parker, *English Sabbath*, 128–33; quotations from 128, 131–32, 132.

13   See *Journal of Nicholas Assheton*, ed. F. R. Raines (Manchester, 1848), 41.

14   See Gordon Donaldson, "The Scottish Church 1567–1625," in *The Reign of James VI and I*, ed. Alan Smith (London, 1973), 40–56, esp. 55.

15   John Barwick, *A Summarie Account of the Holy Life of Thomas Late Lord Bishop of Dureseme* (London, 1660), 80–83.

16   Ibid. See also Raines, ed., *Journal*, 41–42; James Tait, "The Declaration of Sports for Lancashire," *English Historical Review* 32 (1917): 561–68; Lionel A. Govett, *The King's Book of Sports* (London, 1890); E. Baines, *The History of the County Palatine and the Duchy of Lancaster* (London, 1868–70), 1: 209–10; G. H. Tupling, "The Causes of the Civil War in Lancashire," *Transactions of the Lancashire and Cheshire Antiquarian Society* 65 (1955): 1–32; Robert Halley, *Lancashire: Its Puritanism and Non-Conformity* (Manchester, 1869), 1: 225–35; and John Nichols, *The Progresses, Processions and Magnificent Festivities of King James the First* (London, 1828), 3: 397. My account is based principally on Barwick's, who qualified it as follows: "All I can positively say in it, is what I have here said, and this I can positively say because I have often heard it from this reverend Bishops own mouth" (*Summarie Account*, 81).

17   See *Manchester Sessions*, ed. Ernest Axon (1901), xxv–xxvi, Manchester Central Library MS. 347.16.M2, fols. 14–15.

18   Ibid., xxiv–xxvii, M.C.L. MS. 347.96.M2, fols. 14–15.

19   *Constitutional Documents of the Reign of James I, 1603–1625*, ed. J. R. Tanner (Cambridge, 1960), 56.

20   Historical Manuscripts Commission, *Report on the Manuscripts of the Duke of Buccleuch and Queensberry, Mountagu House* (London, 1926), 3: 212–14.

21   HMC, *Report on the Manuscripts of Lord Montagu of Beaulieu* (London, 1900), 94–95.

22   Public Record Office, *Calendar of State Papers, Domestic Series, of the Reign of James [I]* (1611–1618), 1618, no. 77, p. 608.

23   PRO, *Cal. S.P. Dom.* (1619–1623), 23 Aug. 1619, no. 27, p. 72; 30 Aug. 1619, no. 39, p. 73.

24 PRO, State Papers 14/113, no. 13.

25 Nichols, *Progresses, Processions and Magnificent Festivities*, 3: 397.

26 John Hacket, *Scrinia reserata* (London, 1693), 64.

27 Lambeth Palace Library MSS. 943, 129; see also J. Rushworth, *Historical Collections* (London, 1680–1701), 2: 22–23; William Prynne, *Canterburies Doome* (London, 1646), 132; D. A. Williams, "Puritanism in the City Government," *Guildhall Miscellany* 1 (1955): 3–14, esp. 9; and Peter Heylyn, *Cyprianus Anglicus* (London, 1671), 242.

28 Prynne, *Canterburies Doome*, 132; Heylyn, *Cyprianus Anglicus*, 242.

29 Prynne, *Canterburies Doome*, 132; Heylyn, *Cyprianus Anglicus*, 242; see also T. G. Barnes, "Country Politics and a Puritan Cause Célèbre: Somerset Churchales, 1633," *Transactions of the Royal Historical Society* (London) 9 (1959): 103–22, esp. 110–11; PRO Assizes 24/20, fols. 49v–50r; and Somerset Record Office, DD/PH 222, fols. 118–19.

30 SRO, DD/PH 222, fol. 120r.

31 James I, *The Kings Majesties Declaration to His Subjects, Concerning Lawful Sports to Be Used* (London, 1618), 6.

32 S. R. Gardiner, *Constitutional Documents of the Puritan Revolution* (Oxford, 1906), 99–103.

33 HMC, *Report on the Manuscripts of the Late Reginald Rawdon Hastings, Esq.* (London, 1928), 78: 265.

34 Bodleian Library, Tanner MS. 71, fols. 186–87.

35 Bod. Lib., Tanner MS. 279, fol. 352.

36 T. H. Peake, "The Somerset Clergy and the Church Courts in the Diocese of Bath and Wells: 1625–1642" (M. Litt. thesis, University of Bristol, 1978), 456–63; quotation from 456.

37 Hugh Peter, *A Dying Fathers Last Legacy to an Onely Child* (London, 1660), 101.

38 Thomas Wentworth, *The Earl of Strafforde's Letters and Dispatches*, ed. William Knowler (London, 1739), 1: 166.

39 PRO, SP 16/267, no. 6.

40 See PRO, SP 16/267, no. 90; SP 16/278, no. 45, 45i; SP 16/294, no. 68; SP 16/280, no. 54; SP 16/287, no. 31; *Cal. S.P. Dom.* (1638–39), 362; and Prynne, *Canterburies Doome*, 149–52.

41 [Henry Burton], "To the Christian Reader,"' in *A Divine Tragedie Lately Acted* (1636), 11–12.

42 Ibid.

43 [William Prynne], *News from Ipswich* (1636), n.p.

44 Henry Burton, *For God, and the King* (1636), 56–57.

45 For accounts of Burton's arrest and trial, see Henry Burton, *A Narration of the Life of Mr. Henry Burton* (London, 1643), 10–13; William Prynne, *A New Discovery of the Prelates Tyranny* (London, 1641); and *Canterburies Doome*, 110–14; Heylyn, *Cyprianus Anglicus*, 339–43; William Laud, "The History of the Troubles and Trial of Archbishop Laud," in *Works* (Oxford, 1847–60), 4: 105–11; *Dictionary of National Biography*, s.v. Henry Burton.

46 See William Laud, "Speech at the Censure of Bastwick, Burton, and Prynne," in *Works*, 6: 42, 44.

47 Wentworth, *Earl of Strafforde's Letters*, 2: 114.

48 Burton, *Narration of the Life*, 14.

49 William Laud, *Letters*, in *Works*, 7: 371–72.

50 Burton, *Narration of the Life*, 38, 40.

51 See Parker, *English Sabbath*, 170–71.

52 *Commons Debates, 1621*, ed. Wallace Notestein, F. H. Relf, and H. Simpson (New Haven, 1935), 4: 62–65; quotation from 63.

Roberto González Echevarría

Literature, Dance, and Baseball in the Last Cuban Fin de Siècle

On 27 December 1874, the Habana Base Ball Club made its way by train to Matanzas—a trip of a little over 100 kilometers—to take on the local club in what the national mythology would later commemorate as the first baseball game between organized teams ever played in Cuba. Indeed, for the majority of Cubans today, the game played that Sunday afternoon on a field known as Palmar del Junco is the first baseball contest ever staged on the island, a contest without antecedents.[1] Despite the fact that baseball would later be proclaimed the national pastime—a status that it still enjoys even after more than thirty years of a ferociously anti-American regime—the game remains a problematic component in the Cuban nationalist narrative. It is one of our foundation myths, and a privileged one because it belongs to the domain of popular culture, which has a broader reach than most others.

Five years after that 1874 game, in that same city of Matanzas, the first *danzón*—a piece entitled "Las Alturas de Simpson" (Simpson Heights)—was composed, played, and danced. Inaugurating what would come to be known

The *South Atlantic Quarterly* 95:2, Spring 1996.
Copyright © 1996 by Duke University Press.
CCC 0038-2876/96/$1.50.

throughout the world as Cuban music, its composer was the mulatto musician Miguel Faílde, who in 1871 had founded the orchestra that bore his name.[2] The piece contained the seeds of salsa, but "Las Alturas de Simpson" was itself ripe fruit, the cultivated product of various musical strains: French (brought to Cuba by Haitian colonists fleeing Toussaint L'Ouverture's revolution), Spanish, and African. Matanzas, due to its *pleyade* of writers and its salons, journals, and cafés where the literati gathered, was by that time already known as the "Athens of Cuba." Sports, dance, and literature thus joined forces at this crucial moment in Cuban history and, along with the political developments that led to the War of Independence in 1895, helped to shape the island's nascent nationalism. There can be no doubt that since then literature, music, and baseball have become Cuba's most prestigious and internationally circulated cultural products and that they are the fundamental—and foundational—components of the national mythology. It behooves us, then, to return to that feverish time that was the last Cuban fin de siècle—when Cuba became the last Hispanic American nation to achieve independence—to see just how that cultural triad at once created and was created by the historical moment.

As Manuel Moreno Fraginals has detailed in his beautiful and thorough *El ingenio*, the decisive steps in initiating Cuba's modern era were taken by Francisco de Arango y Parreño (1765–1837) at the end of the eighteenth century, that is, during the penultimate Cuban fin de siècle.[3] Upon Haiti's collapse as the world's chief producer of sugar, due to the slave uprising, Arango y Parreño set in motion the policies that would result in Cuba's rapid rise to that position. Those policies would launch the country into a mindless "sugar race," the deleterious effects of which are still being felt today. Arango y Parreño and others not only brought Cuba into the international marketplace and into modernity, however; their policies also led to the practice of monoculture, the latifundium, economic dependency, and other unfortunate by-products. To compete in the ferocious capitalist market on a global level, the Cuban elite—sarcastically referred to by Moreno Fraginals as the "saccharocracy"—modernized the island's production of sugar by importing both steam engines and railways from England and by entering into a financial relationship with the United States which would become increasingly important. The "saccharocrats" not only advanced their country's position in the world through their acquisition of machinery and railways (at midcentury Cuba's system was the most extensive one in Latin America), but also enhanced their own status as consumers of the latest luxuries and technological devices, such as having the first water closets ever installed in the Hispanic world. In Havana and on the outskirts of the capital, they built opulent mansions, many of them on the very sugar plantations that were the source of their wealth.

The Matanzas region, east of Havana, became a prime area for the production of sugar due to its proximity to the capital, its fertile land, and its dense forests, which could both supply fuel and (when cleared) expand the available acreage for growing sugarcane. In addition to the rivers that irrigated the region and facilitated both transportation and communication, sugar producers enjoyed the added advantage of having beautiful Matanzas Bay for a port. Indeed, the port became an important piece of the navigational network that included not only the port of Havana, but also those along the North American East Coast (Baltimore, New York, Boston) and the Gulf of Mexico (Key West, Tampa, New Orleans).

With the emerging dominance of the sugar industry in this region extending from Havana to Matanzas, and beyond to Cárdenas, Sagua la Grande, and Caibarién, the culture of this particular section of Cuba underwent a marked transformation. Great numbers of slaves were imported to meet the demands of this labor-intensive industry. The area immediately surrounding Matanzas quickly attained the highest density of Blacks in the country, a demographic distinction that would persist into the twentieth century. Mulattos and freedmen who were artisans and laborers flocked to the city, where some promptly distinguished themselves as musicians. If Matanzas were indeed the "Athens of Cuba" then, it also became a Rome or a Jerusalem for Afro-Cuban religions and, subsequently, a Bayreuth in the development of Cuban music. To this day, Matanzas retains its preeminence in these areas.

With the opening of U.S. trade relations in 1817 and the increasing North American involvement in the Cuban sugar industry, a considerable number of Americans took up residence in the areas surrounding Matanzas. Some owned plantations and refineries, while others were employed as mechanics or machinists or in related trades; still others opened a variety of businesses.[4] Who was the Simpson to whom the title of Faílde's song referred? An American living in Matanzas. Apparently, the neighborhood called "Simpson Heights" developed on what then was or had been

Simpson's property, suggesting that this particular American community in Matanzas experienced some growth during the 1870s. Certainly, the amount of Cuban property purchased by Americans increased then as a result of the Ten Years War (1868–78) ending with the defeat of the Cuban insurrectionists and the so-called Truce of Zanjón. A number of powerful Creole families were financially ruined during the war not only as a result of the conflict itself, but also due to the downward trend in sugar prices that would continue through the fin de siècle. Numerous bankruptcies occurred, leaving many plantations and refineries in the hands of the North American banks to which the Cubans were heavily indebted. The Matanzas region, while barely affected by the actual fighting (which was largely confined to the central and eastern regions), nevertheless underwent a considerable transformation. To the conditions just enumerated, one significant development must be added—the creation of enormous sugar factories (*centrales*) that would grind the cane grown by smaller plantation owners (*colonos*), whose outdated mills could no longer process sufficient amounts of the crop. The large centrales effectively *centralized* both capital and production by making previously independent plantation owners dependent on them for sugar-processing. It is not difficult to imagine how these American landlords, in frequent contact with their own country where baseball had evolved and was quickly catching on, would play the game in Cuba and teach it to their friends and neighbors.[5]

In Havana, the sugar boom enabled the construction of private mansions and small palaces, the widening of avenues, the proliferation of parks, and the general growth of the city beyond the western wall that had protected it for years against the incursions of pirates and corsairs. Indeed, shortly after midcentury (c. 1863) the wall was demolished. The districts to the south, southeast, and west of the city—those at the highest elevations, which enjoy the most refreshing sea breezes—were taken over as recreation areas by the saccharocracy. Havana spread out in these directions, slowly absorbing the leisure spaces and incorporating them into its expanded urban grid. An effort was made to set aside land for the purposes of amusement and play within the original city limits as well. The Paseo del Prado—the famous thoroughfare that runs perpendicular to the sea—became a gathering place not only for the numerous carriages that effectively showcased the nouveau riche in all their finery, but also for the crowds of pedestrians who collected to witness the display and pursue their

Figure 1. The Prado, Havana (c. 1898). Reproduced from *Picturesque Cuba and Our Navy: Reproductions of Photographs with Graphic Descriptive Text* (Chicago: Belford, Middlebrook, 1898), n.p.

own social agendas (Figure 1). Havana theater flourished with the con-struction or renovation of such playhouses as the Tacón, the Albisu, and the Irajoa, where the most prominent European troupes would later play, including several French companies whose productions were performed in that language (Figure 2). Opera and musical theater also enjoyed great popularity during the nineteenth century. A number of new cafés and res-taurants with such names as The Louvre and The Tullerías revealed the source from which Cubans were taking their cultural cues and a model eti-quette to imitate. The Louvre Portals became the preferred gathering place not only for the Cuban literati, but for all who would abandon themselves to decadent worldly pleasures, baseball players and fans included. Many of these youths were also fans and practitioners of the danzón, the lewdness of which had provoked a series of polemical editorials in the capital city's press. The danzón, baseball, and literature shared a set of characteristics, emblematic of the fin de siècle, that made their alliance possible at the his-toric moment of Cuban independence, an alliance that left a visible and durable impression on national culture.

Figure 2. Central Park, the Tacón Theater, and the Inglaterra Hotel, Havana (c. 1898). Reproduced from *Picturesque Cuba and Our Navy: Reproductions of Photographs with Graphic Descriptive Text* (Chicago: Belford, Middlebrook, 1898), n.p.

The first of these common characteristics was exoticism; late-nineteenth-century Cubans had a predilection not only for whatever was foreign—and, above all, French—but for whatever was not Spanish, which was viewed as backward and demodé. The effects of the French influence on late-nineteenth-century Latin American literature are well documented and require no further elaboration here. That influence extended from the names of cafés to the title of one of Cuba's leading cultural journals, *El Fígaro* (to which I will return). Touring French theatrical companies, including that of the famed Sarah Bernhardt, played in Havana en route to Mexico City or New Orleans. Anyone who is familiar with Cuban publications of that era cannot help but notice the degree to which their readership was attuned, "à la page," to the latest Parisian trends. The influential French poets were models for Cuban authors, not only in literary matters but also in lifestyle. A neurasthenic, a homosexual, and an alcoholic, Julián del Casal practiced his decadence in the French fashion, whether ensconced in his Havana atelier, where he experimented with drugs, or as a flaneur strutting through the city's parks, boulevards, and cafés.[6]

The danzón, as has already been noted, was Afro-French in origin. In his elegant and insightful *La música en Cuba*, Alejo Carpentier described how the English "country dance" developed into the French *contredance*, which evolved in turn into the *contradanza*, the *habanera*, and, finally, the danzón. As is well known, the habanera was incorporated into *Carmen* by Bizet, indicating that the musical and cultural "traffic" between France and Cuba ran in both directions. The habanera thus circulated throughout the world and was the first Cuban music to achieve international diffusion, while the contradanza, after finding its way to Spain, reached Buenos Aires in variations that would contribute to the creation of the tango. What is most striking about the danzón, however, is that despite a strong African component it became the preferred dance music of Cuban high society, successfully competing with the internationally fashionable mazurkas, polkas, and waltzes and prevailing over the scandalized reaction of Cuba's moral watchdogs to the suggestive rhythms and lyrics of some danzones. These often had provocative titles, such as "Negra, dame tu amor" (Black Baby, Give Me Your Love). But the danzón was far less sexually explicit than the music to which Cubans danced the *arroz con picadillo* (rice with chopped meat), *empinar el papalote* (hoist the kite), or *matar la culebra* (kill the snake) in halls such as the one on The Louvre's second floor. Havanans could also cross the bay to Regla and Guanabacoa—then as now centers of Santería and African culture—and hear pieces daringly (it seems) called "Cochino" (Swine), "Oso" (Bear), and "Baja la pata" (Lower Your Leg). But not the danzón. From our perspective, the danzón seems rather decorous, almost chaste: a dance in which partners embrace lightly and at arm's length, never dancing cheek-to-cheek. While the synchronized "quadrilles" of the contradanza did indeed give way to the couple dancing of the danzón, the latter remained as formally stylized as *modernista* poetry, marked by pauses, ritualized openings of a fan by the woman, and a light hold at a proper distance. What the danzón also included, however, was a suggestive swaying of the hips, especially during the piece's final movement (perhaps already anticipating the *sones* and *guarachas* that were to come), and a series of feints and thrusts reminiscent of the ritual persecution of the female enacted in some Afro-Cuban dances. In the context of the Spanish-influenced prudishness that prevailed in the 1890s, the danzón seemed dangerous, exotic, decadent, and altogether too Cuban. It represented nothing less than the blatant incorporation of African culture into the social life of the Cuban upper classes, an incipient "mulattoization" of the privileged.

The danzón's exoticism was reinforced by its capacity to incorporate foreign elements into its melodic framework. While we may find it surprising
today to hear in a danzón like "El cadete constitucional" (The Cadet of
the Constitutional Army) passages from a John Philip Sousa march ("Stars
and Stripes Forever," no less), this tendency—analogous to the French and
Oriental allusions found in Latin American modernista poetry—was inherent to the danzón from the very beginning. Zoila Lapique Becali quotes
a Cuban who was present at the premiere of "Las Alturas de Simpson" as
remarking that "these danzones, based on melancholic African music, in
an artistic mix—very pleasant to the ear—regaled us with bits of Italian
opera, Spanish zarzuelas, French operetta, and Cuban songs, with a unique
cadence and harmony."[7] It is significant that baseball, too, was influenced
by Italian opera, with various Cuban teams of that era taking their names
from operas (the Bocaccio and Fattinitza teams, for example). The cult of
the foreign was a generalized phenomenon that involved, as one might expect, the appropriation of foreign words, which in music and baseball was
virtually inevitable.

The Cuban saccharocracy soon realized that a North American education would prove more useful to their children than a European one, and
they began to send their sons (and sometimes their daughters) to the universities *del norte*. In the United States, these young Cubans learned to play
baseball and, upon their return to the island, would find Spanish social
mores backward, arbitrarily restrictive, or simply barbaric in comparison
to American customs. Among these Spanish mores, none was more dis-
tasteful than bullfights, which were then quite popular in Cuba. Indeed,
the most famous Spanish bullfighters of the era would often exhibit their
skills in Havana's bullring en route to exhibitions in Mexico (Figure 3).[8]
Baseball soon came to be seen as an antidote to Spanish primitivism. The
game rapidly caught on in Havana and Matanzas not only with the sons of
well-to-do families but also among the lower classes, including the many
Blacks who had become freedmen with the abolition of slavery in 1886.
The so-called *emigración*—the exile of numerous Cuban families following the Truce of Zanjón in 1878—contributed in no small measure to the
popularization of the game, as Cuban communities in port cities like Key
West, Tampa, Jacksonville, and as far north as New York and its environs,
grew considerably larger in this period.

Of course, baseball had been played by Cubans on the island long be-

Figure 3. Plaza de Toros, Havana (c. 1898). Reproduced from *Picturesque Cuba and Our Navy: Reproductions of Photographs with Graphic Descriptive Text* (Chicago: Belford, Middle-brook, 1898), n.p.

fore then, and there were already organized clubs by the 1870s, beginning with the Habana Base Ball Club, which, as we already know, traveled to the "Athens of Cuba" in 1874 to play (and defeat) the local team. By the 1880s, hundreds of clubs dotted the island, as did the dozens of journals and newspapers that covered the game. Indeed, we owe much of our extensive knowledge of Cuban baseball's early days to its close relationship with literature, to accounts and references in contemporary journals, chronicles, novels, and poems. The aforementioned literary journal *El Fígaro* proclaimed itself, in its very first issue of 23 July 1885, "a Weekly devoted to Sport and Literature" and the "Organ of Baseball" (Figure 4). Manuel Serafín Pichardo was one of the journal's founders and its chief creative force. *El Fígaro* published summaries of games and feature articles on famous players. Its content was an intriguing combination of literary, musical, and social gossip, with pieces by some of the era's most prominent writers (Julián del Casal, for one). The first history of Cuban baseball, published in 1889, was written by a novelist, Wenceslao Gálvez y Delmonte, who, not coincidentally, played shortstop for the Almendares Base Ball Club and is

Figure 4. Front page of the first issue of *El Fígaro*, 23 July 1885.

enshrined in the Cuban Baseball Hall of Fame.[9] Gálvez, a friend of Casal's, also published a soporific novel (albeit under the promising and decadent title of *Nicotina*) and a collection of essays, chronicles, and vignettes, *Esto, lo otro, y lo de más allá (mosaico literario)*, in which he displayed a great familiarity with current trends in European, Spanish, and Latin American literature. For these and other writers, baseball was exotic and decadent, diametrically opposed to Spanish prissiness, hypocrisy, and (literally) bullish savagery; therefore, a love of baseball was understood to be compatible with both the new modernista literature and the struggle for Cuban independence.

Gálvez's *El baseball en Cuba: Historia del baseball en la Isla de Cuba* could very well be the first history of the sport ever written. It is certainly noteworthy that a history of Cuban baseball had already been written by 1889, when organized baseball was only a little over thirty years old in its country of origin. At Gálvez's urging, Dr. Benjamín de Céspedes wrote a preface to the book, a brilliant and lighthearted analysis that extolled the sport's therapeutic physical and moral effects. The doctor, like Gálvez, was a Darwinist and an agnostic, somewhat cynical but a believer in the ability of both medicine and sports to enhance one's sense of physical well-being. He subscribed to the theories regarding physical fitness then current in both the United States and Europe and maintained that playing baseball would produce a more robust—and sexually potent—individual. Dr. de Céspedes contrasted the vigorous health of young baseball players with the endemic flaccidity of his own, mostly sedentary patients. His view of the relationship between sports and medicine was not idiosyncratic but part of the decadent cult of the frivolous: good health was to be cultivated for the sake of pleasure, not productivity. Decadence involved an intense pre-occupation with the physical that was manifested in the contrasting figures of the neurasthenic or sickly poet, who reveled in his infirmities, and the athlete, who was primarily concerned with his strength, agility, and grace-fulness. On one side of this equation, then, we have the poet Casal; on the other, his friend Gálvez.

Like Dr. de Céspedes's preface to it, Gálvez's book extolled baseball's therapeutic and civilizing effects in addition to tracing the history of the many clubs then playing in the capital and the provinces. Casal wrote a laudatory review of the book, which, he acknowledged, was by "one of [his] best friends." Emphasizing the work's vigor and optimism, Casal declared,

> There is nothing more rare in these times than the publication of an unpretentious book, exuding a healthy joy and written as quickly as the pen would allow, whose pages serve to undo the most austere frowns, to part the most serious lips [as in a smile], and to lift the melancholic mists that lie over our spirits and extend the miseries that are paraded in their disgusting nakedness in page after page of modern pessimistic literature.[10]

Two years before, another notable writer—none other than the prominent philosopher Enrique José Varona—had written an article on baseball in which he took up the question of its moral benefits, concluding that base-ball would be highly beneficial even if all it taught Cubans was how to compete, and lose, in a civilized manner.[11] The game had clearly evolved into a social activity of great importance not simply in terms of encoun-ters between competing teams, but also because these teams functioned as social clubs in which other activities were pursued, as we shall see.

While it is true that the U.S. presence in Cuba quickly threatened the island's sense of nationality, it is ironic that things American at first represented for Cubans of the fin de siècle a rejection of decrepit Spanish domination. This is precisely why baseball became so readily incorporated into a patriotic anti-Spanish ideology that led to the War of Independence. There were baseball teams in Key West, for example, that donated their earnings from games to the revolutionary cause. Moreover, the Florida teams were largely composed of tobacco workers, and it was from among their ranks (in both Key West and Tampa) that José Martí promoted and organized the war. Many of these ballplayers joined the insurrectionist troops when war broke out. One such ballplayer–turned–patriot, Emilio Sabourín, was subsequently detained for conspiring against the colonial government and incarcerated in the notoriously harsh prison at Ceuta, where he died, a martyr to the cause.

Baseball, like the danzón, held a considerable erotic charge, and, also like dancing, it brought young people together, functioning as a kind of prenuptial ritual. The first baseball uniforms, in the context of the conservative fashions of the time, were extremely provocative. It is surprising to see in old photographs of Cuba many Havanans wearing black coats and bowler hats despite the oppressive Antillean heat. The ballplayers, in contrast, typically wore tight white knickers, colorful knee-high stockings, loose flowing shirts that usually featured a team's emblem or initials (in gothic script) across the chest, color-coordinated bandanas, and caps. Such an outfit was clearly designed to display the athlete's physique (Figure 5). Dressed in this manner, players would take to the field and brandish potent sticks, the symbolism of which is too obvious to require further comment.[12] Performing feats of athleticism that showcased their strength, agility, and conditioning, these rugged youths displayed themselves to crowds filled with young women who would cheer their favorites and even reward outstanding players by presenting them with colored ribbons. Such exchanges were evidently part of a symbolic ritual that led to further erotic play in and outside of socially prescribed channels.

It takes no stretch of the imagination to see in early baseball uniforms, with their gothic script emblazoned across the chest, their tight-fitting knickers, and their colorful hosiery, a modernista quality. Indeed, baseball, by virtue of its exquisite aestheticism, reflected an undeniably modernista sensibility. One cannot help but see ballplayers as male counterparts to the various ballerinas described with such sensual dynamism in the poetry of Casal and even in that of Martí.[13] Furthermore, the game is free of the crude

Figure 5. Players from the Habana Base Ball Club. Reproduced from *El Fígaro*, 9 September 1900, 558.

war symbolism of basketball and football, sports that emphasize the conquest of territory to score goals or points and thus to vanquish an enemy. Baseball operates in a way that is both more oblique and more metaphoric. A player runs in a circle around a square to score a run, all the while avoiding being tagged with the ball by his opponents. (Baseball may be the only sport in which the defense controls the ball.) Propelled by the bat, the ball may either fly in a broad parabola through the sky or roll rapidly along the ground until it is caught by a player, who then throws it a great distance to a teammate in order to make an out in an utterly symbolic way. (Often, the runner need not even be tagged with the ball to be declared out.) Baseball thus proceeds as a series of quite indirect associations, with a rule structure so subtle and contingent as to render the game almost incomprehensible to anyone who has not grown up playing or watching it. The appeal that baseball had for young Cuban intellectuals and patriots was doubtlessly rooted in those characteristics of the game—elegant stylization, inherent aestheticism, and elaborate artifice—that also characterized modernista poetry.

But baseball's popularity was due above all to its ability to incorporate into its ritual Sunday performances other forms of expression, most notably, dance. From the very beginning, baseball clubs (in the United States as well as in Cuba) sponsored a host of activities, not all of which occurred in conjunction with scheduled matches against rival clubs. Each club comprised several teams with different levels of ability. The "first team" would represent the club in inter-club games, but many intra-club games were also played between the club's other teams. Both inter-club and intra-club games would be followed by elaborate dinners featuring extravagant toasts, laudatory speeches, readings from various literary texts, and so forth. In Cuba, a dance was added to the traditional dinner, with an orchestra hired first and foremost to play danzones. A philosopher to the very end, Varona preferred sport to dance and wrote that Cuba's "progress will be indisputably assured the day that the accomplished sportsman dethrones the accomplished dancer"[14]—a maxim as lapidary as it was powerless to arrest the forces that joined these two activities.

Toward the end of the century, the most celebrated of all the orchestras regularly hired to play for the postgame dances was that of Raimundo Valenzuela, a famous and distinguished mulatto musician from Matanzas, who elevated the danzón to its highest form. Publications from that era often advertised upcoming postgame dances in baseball jargon, such as referring to the celebrated orchestra as "Raimundo Valenzuela's first team." I think we can safely assume that at these dances the prenuptial ritual launched by that day's match became less ritualistic and more (re)productive. The interaction between a young man and woman on these occasions constituted a public consummation of sorts, a collective recognition of a bond. What began with the flirting facilitated by the baseball game would be subsequently advanced by literary means (writing poems in each other's albums, exchanging favorite poems, etc.) before reaching the physical stage with the intoxicating movements of the danzón, during which, as if to confirm the fulfillment of the evening's purpose, the couple became visible as such to all. (An 1885 piece in *El Fígaro* even informed its readers that after one particular game there had been much dancing, due to "the presence of many Eves, many Adams, and of Valenzuela, who played the part of the serpent."[15]) If I am emphasizing baseball's ability, like that of dancing, to pair couples (i.e., its "distributive" quality), it is because I believe that its early incorporation into Cuban culture had much to do with this capacity to channel erotic desire into socially acceptable expressions

Figure 6. Almendares Park, Havana, 1909. The field did not change substantially until 1919. Reproduced from *El Fígaro*, 28 November 1909, foldout.

through the complex Sunday rituals that were performed both as part of the game itself and in its associated activities. Cuban society largely (and often literally) reproduced itself as a result of these rituals, these activities that ritualized and organized the collective use of leisure time in urban areas, particularly Havana, and that evolved specifically for that purpose.

The *glorieta*, or pavilion, was the place where the activities and drives that I have been discussing converged. The two most important clubs on the island—the Habana Base Ball Club and particularly the Almendares Base Ball Club—had their own grounds in those sections of Havana that the saccharocracy had taken over and converted into summer recreation areas. What had once been uncultivated or productive fields, then, were transformed into parks or gardens, sites for summer homes, and hunting grounds. The original Almendares Club field was in the neighborhood of Cerro or Tulipán, southwest of the city and accessible by Carlos III Avenue, one of the first roads to have been extended beyond the city walls during Havana's westward expansion. That rudimentary field soon gave way to the celebrated Almendares Park, which would survive (with renovations) into the 1920s (Figure 6). The Habana Club field was in the Vedado district, an area west of Havana that the Spanish authorities had made off-limits (hence its name) because its wilderness provided a kind of natural defense for the coastline.

When they traveled to the outskirts of Havana, young ballplayers were not plunged into the wilds or the bush, but rather ushered onto fields that had been carefully cleared and prepared by gardeners after having been planned and laid out by surveyors and landscape architects. The very field on which baseball is played reflects the mixed character of this intermediate urban space of the faubourg or *faux bourg*, the "false city" that John M. Merriman has described so magisterially.[16] There is grass, to be sure, but it is a carpetlike lawn that recalls the English origins of the game. Meadows suitable for baseball are not natural to tropical Cuba, so fields must be worked over intensively in order to transform them into baseball diamonds. Indeed, as that term suggests, a ballfield has a precise geometrical form, a kind of enigmatic mandala: a square surrounded by a circle that itself contains another circle (the pitcher's "box" or "mound," which at one time had a rectangular shape). The "foul" lines separate the playing area from that other, uncultivated space where the ball is "out of bounds" or "foul" (for which the batter is penalized). The ball that lands within the foul lines is *buena*, or "good," the one that lands just outside is *mala*, or "bad," in baseball parlance, as reproduced in Cuban Spanish.

The glorieta was erected in such a way that the spectators, especially the female ones, could watch and admire the players in action while remaining protected from the implacable tropical sun. Like the field itself, the glorieta was an intermediate construction between the undeveloped countryside and the man-made city, between nature and art. The word "glorieta," according to Joan Corominas, was derived from the French and has been in use as a Spanish term since the twelfth century.[17] It originally referred to a building that was separate from the main house and set within a garden, a gazebo or summerhouse where one could hold a feast and enjoy other fine pleasures as if one were *en la gloria*, in heaven. Baseball's glorieta, like its precursor, was set aside entirely for pleasure, not for any practical purpose, and was always part of a garden, never of a domestic or utilitarian space. The glorieta's isolation or self-contained autonomy—in accordance with the aestheticism of modernista poetry and its decadent tendencies—contradicted its openness to its context, the field. It was as if the structure were simultaneously denying and affirming its separation from the countryside. The walls of the glorieta, a latticework of wood and mesh, allowed in not only the breeze, which was essential in the tropical heat, but also the smell of the grass and the sounds of the game. From the glorieta, young women could watch the game almost outdoors, in an enclosure with false walls. Banners and pennants of the various clubs, hanging from rooftop masts, fluttered in the wind. (From far away, the glorieta would have resembled a large paddleboat adorned with colorful streamers. Close up, it would have looked like the stands at a racetrack, and, in fact, some glorietas—Almendares's, for example—were used by spectators during horse races and other equestrian events.) After the game, in a transformation that recalled its origins, the glorieta became a dining hall. Once dinner was over it would be transformed again, this time into a dance hall. The glorieta often served in another capacity, like theaters and halls hired for such occasions, as the site of literary competitions in which poets and orators ostentatiously displayed their talents and essentially competed in a manner not unlike that of baseball players. Indeed, poet and player were often one and the same person. Toward the end of the century, the glorietas were wired for electricity, allowing the night to be banished by an artificial day, a protracted day of recreation, love, and pleasure upon which nature could impose no limits.

But literature, baseball, and dance were not only mutually reinforcing expressions of decadence; they were also components of an emerging nationalism. Bound by a common social effect—bringing young people together—and by their ability to channel desire through a stylized aesthetic, they were also jointly associated with a wholesale rejection of all that was Spanish and a yearning for whatever seemed to be more modern and democratic. Gálvez and others stressed baseball's capacity to move young men of modest means up the social ladder and allow them to rub elbows with the upper classes. Baseball, like everything else that had North American origins, was considered exempt from aristocratic pretensions, an agent of social equality. Dancing the danzón, delighting in a French-influenced literature that was aesthetic and erotic, and participating in baseball (whether as player or spectator) were all modern activities and contrary to the spirit of the colonial order. Indeed, it was precisely because they were foreign that all three could be reconfigured as expressions of nationalism, paradoxically transformed into essential components of Cuban national life. The inherent and manifest artificiality of these three "national pastimes" distinguish them as not only modern but modernista. *Modernismo*, as Cathy L. Jrade has argued, by virtue of its extravagant artificiality, constituted an assault upon the status quo. Having been handed down or inherited, the Spanish tradition seemed to flow "naturally" from some ancient source. Consequently, and conversely, all that was artistic, innovative, or even unique would be oppositional by definition—and therefore essentially Cuban.[18] Or, as Jorge Olivares observed about the decadent impulse in Latin American literature: "The cultured and the artificial are simultaneously an escape and a rebellion against established norms and through them the desire to go 'à rebours' becomes an inviolable law for these writers."[19] While the other Latin American nations had been forged in the crucible of Romanticism, then, Cuban nationalism was essentially modernista: an artful construct, consciously fabricated from foreign components that were capable of sublimating desire. Gustavo Pérez Firmat would say that anything Cuban is always the product of translation.[20] These, then, are the reasons why baseball, dance, and literature—regardless of the "higher" expressions of nationality that often seek to exclude them—remain essential to the Cuban people.

Beyond the context of Cuba and its last fin de siècle, what seems most remarkable about the fusion of baseball, dance, and literature with the formation of nationalism is the fact that the first two are physical and essentially playful activities. I believe that this is precisely what makes the Cuban case so instructive, enabling it to productively inform our approach to the emergence of other modern nationalisms. Our historical narratives are almost always written in terms of political and intellectual forces at the expense of more physical or material agencies, such as games, dances, collective rituals, and even cuisine. All of these activities constitute discourses that lend themselves, like literature, to a kind of anthropological analysis that we are probably incapable of formulating without grounding it in literature itself, which contains all of them.

—Translated by Gaspar González

Notes

1 The field was actually called Palmar *de* Junco, meaning that it belonged to someone named Junco. (The Junco family had initially established itself in St. Augustine, Florida, and later moved to Matanzas.) But because "del Junco" is more evocative ("junco" sig-

nifying a kind of reed), the famous field has always been known as Palmar del Junco. Given that the palm tree is a fundamental symbol in the Cuban national imagination, it is easy to understand why the name resonates with patriotic significance. ("I am a sincere man / from where the palm tree grows," as José Martí would say.) According to contemporary accounts of the game, however, there were no palm trees on the Palmar de Junco. What does appear to be certain is that the baseball game played there was the first to be chronicled. The account, by the aspiring writer Enrique Fontanils (publishing under the name "Henry"), appeared in the 31 December 1874 issue of *El Artista*, a satirical paper devoted to the theater that was published in Havana.

2 Alejo Carpentier maintained that the piece was one of four composed by Faílde in 1877, while Helio Orovio argues that "Las Alturas de Simpson" was first played in 1879; see Carpentier, *La música en Cuba* (Mexico City, 1972 [1946]), 237; and Orovio, *Diccionario de la música cubana: Biográfico y técnico* (Havana, 1992 [1981]), 161. According to Zoila Lapique Becali, "On January 1, 1879, in the city of Matanzas, a development was taking place that would prove to be of crucial importance in the history of Cuban music. Miguelito Faílde, appearing with his popular dance orchestra, was unveiling in the dance hall of the Club Matanzas—later the Lyceum—his danzón 'Las Alturas de Simpson'"; see *Música colonial cubana, Tomo I (1812–1902)* (Havana, 1979), 46–47.

3 Manuel Moreno Fraginals, *El ingenio: Complejo económico social cubano del azúcar* (Havana, 1978), 1: 47.

4 For details, see Laird W. Bergard, *Cuban Rural Society in the Nineteenth Century: The Social and Economic History of Monoculture in Matanzas* (Princeton, 1990).

5 The best general history of baseball is still Harold Seymour's *Baseball: The Early Years* (New York, 1960).

6 See Oscar Montero, "Translating Decadence: Julián del Casal's Reading of Huysmans and Moreau," *Revista de Estudios Hispánicos* 26 (1992): 368–89; and Jorge Olivares, "La recepción del decadentismo en Hispanoamérica," *Hispanic Review* 48 (1980): 57–76.

7 Lapique Becali, *Música colonial cubana*, 47.

8 Bullfighting was permanently abolished in Cuba by decree of military governor Leonard Wood in 1900, during the U.S. occupation following the Spanish–American War. Today, few Cubans even realize that bullfights were once staged in Havana, nor do they appear to be interested in such sports.

9 Wenceslao (Wen) Gálvez y Delmonte, *El baseball en Cuba: Historia del baseball en la Isla de Cuba, sin retratos de los principales jugadores y personas más caracterizadas—en el juego citado, ni de ninguna otra* (Havana, 1889). I have been unable to discover much about Gálvez except that he was born in Matanzas, studied law at the University of Havana, and spent several years in Tampa, Florida. His brother, José María Gálvez y Delmonte (1835–1906), was a famous nineteenth-century jurist who collaborated with Carlos Manuel de Céspedes in the revolutionary cause. He was also a ballplayer and, after retiring from competitive play, became a respected and much sought after umpire.

10 Julián del Casal, "El Base Ball en Cuba," *La Discusión*, 28 November 1889; reprinted in *Prosas, Tomo II* (Havana, 1963), 11.

11 Enrique José Varona, "El base ball en La Habana," *Revista Cubana* 4 (1887): 84–88.

12   The perverse Gálvez, however, could not resist asking, "Isn't this business about a 'bat' and balls very masculine?" (*El baseball en Cuba*, 23).

13   I am thinking specifically of Martí's "La bailarina española," and of Casal's *Salomé*. I made use of Esperanza Figueroa's recent edition of the latter's poetry, *Julián del Casal: Poesías completas y pequeños poemas en prosa en orden cronológico* (Miami, 1993).

14   Varona, "El base ball en La Habana," 87.

15   *El Fígaro*, 29 October 1885, 7.

16   John M. Merriman, *The Margins of City Life: Explorations of the French Urban Frontier, 1851–1951* (New York, 1991).

17   Joan Corominas, *Breve diccionario etimológico de la lengua castellana*, 3d ed. (Madrid, 1987).

18   Cathy L. Jrade, "Modernism, Modernity, and the Development of Spanish American Literature" (unpublished manuscript).

19   Olivares, "La recepción del decadentismo en Hispanoamérica," 59.

20   Gustavo Pérez Firmat, *The Cuban Condition: Translation and Identity in Modern Cuban Literature* (Cambridge, 1989).

Patrick Allitt

English Cricket and Literature

Class, race, gender, hegemony, imperialism, ritual, liminality, sex, and discourse! Everyone's favorite analytical instruments—and never more useful than in the interpretation of England's national game, cricket. Played since the Middle Ages by men and women and written about since the early eighteenth century, it developed out of rough, ancient folk sports like Knurr-and-Spell in Yorkshire and Dab-and-Billet in Nottingham-shire to become a refined, precise, and etiquette-bound game. It changed as English society changed, traveled abroad with the Empire, and became one of the main avenues of trans-class encounter every English summer. Cricket at once muted class distinctions by holding all players to the same rules and intensified them by drawing sharp dividing lines between gentle-men and professionals on the field of play. It held the British Empire together in the same way by giving Indian and West Indian elites some-thing in common with their White overlords, but cricket also helped to condemn imperialism by showing the great gulf between English ideals of good sportsmanship and the gritty reality of the

The *South Atlantic Quarterly* 95:2, Spring 1996.
Copyright © 1996 by Duke University Press.
CCC 0038-2876/96/$1.50.

Empire's military and economic domination. Industrialization, democracy, subdivision of labor, mechanization, advertising—all the great forces of modernization—have found their counterparts in cricket, and writers have used the game extensively as an illustration of, and a metaphor for, social changes.

=====

Anyone who loves baseball will love cricket too, but it will not be love at first sight. Americans getting their first glimpse of cricket are typically baffled: the players on both teams wear not different uniforms but identical outfits—white "flannels." And the umpires, far from ejecting players who tamper with the ball, watch unconcerned as the bowler (pitcher) carefully polishes up one side of the ball to help it curve through the air on its way to the batsman. There are only two innings to a cricket game, not nine, but each innings (not "inning") lasts for ten wickets (outs) rather than three. And if it's an international match, it goes on not for a mere three or four hours but for *five days*. The spirit of amiable boredom sacred to America's national summer pastime is here raised to heroic dimensions. Television commentators have to ramble along with the game, providing anecdotes about the players, their families, the weather, the pitch, and the crowd, not just for an evening but for up to thirty-three hours. Only fans with lots of money and a week to spare can witness a whole game.

The vexation is a two-way affair, of course, and Limeys think Yanks are crazy when they first see the uncricket-like aspects of baseball. For a start, what about those wimpy mitts? Cricket is a bare-hands game for every fielder except the wicket-keeper (catcher), and when you catch the hard red ball you expect it to hurt. English observers regard fielding gloves as unmanly. And why hit out of one corner of the field, a paltry ninety-degree radius, instead of standing sensibly in the middle and hitting freely in every direction to score runs, as cricketers do? Finally, an innings in cricket often yields hundreds of runs, so after watching inning upon inning of baseball in which there are no runs at all a Briton feels half-starved.

And yet the two games have much in common. They are both bat-and-ball games played on big, beautiful green fields in summertime. Both offer players long stretches of indolence punctuated by bursts of intense concentration and excitement, when a split second or a quarter-inch makes the difference between success and disaster. Both games appeal to citizens of all social classes and are played at the fanciest private schools as well as in industrial slums. Fans of both games have an unreasonable love of statistics, and they can remember achievements not merely from this season and the last but from games and seasons further back in time than their own years of birth. Both games give rise to heroes of supernatural dimensions, idols to adults and children alike, around whom a divine aura glows. Both have been played with no major rule changes for more than a century, making it possible to compare the feats of this year directly with those of 1896 and to speculate on which decade would contribute the most players to the all-time dream team. The games share another feature too: their essentials can be explained and grasped in half an hour, yet even a lifetime is not enough to educate the player or devotee in every refinement. Far from being limited or repetitive, cricket and baseball are infinitely variable, and each just gets more intricate the longer you play or watch.

Here are the basic rules of cricket: The side that is batting sends two men, rather than one, onto the field, and they each stand beside a set of three "stumps" or "wickets"—vertical wooden bars, twenty-two inches high, which are stuck in the ground and topped by small wooden cross-pieces called "bails." The two sets of stumps are twenty-two yards apart, and the closely mown stretch of grass between them is called "the wicket" (Figure 1). The bowler, leading the attack against these batsmen for the fielding team, is not allowed to bend his elbow during delivery of the ball, but he is allowed a run-up (as opposed to the baseball pitcher's wind-up) before he bowls. He runs from behind one set of stumps and, on reaching it, bowls the ball in an over-the-head windmill motion, keeping his arm straight. (The fastest bowlers can deliver the ball at ninety miles per hour.) If he has bowled well, the ball bounces once and rises as it approaches the batsman, who is standing in front of the other set of stumps. He bowls six times (eight in Australia) to complete an "over," then another bowler delivers another "over" from the opposite set of stumps. A bowler can be relieved and brought back at the captain's pleasure; unlike a baseball pitcher, he does not leave the game.

The batsman's first job is to prevent the ball from hitting his stumps. If he fails, he is "bowled out." If he hits the ball with his flat-faced bat and it is caught in the air by the bowler or any of the other ten fielders, he is "caught out." If the ball hits his leg and would otherwise have hit the wicket, he is out "leg before wicket" (LBW). Assuming that he hits the ball safely along

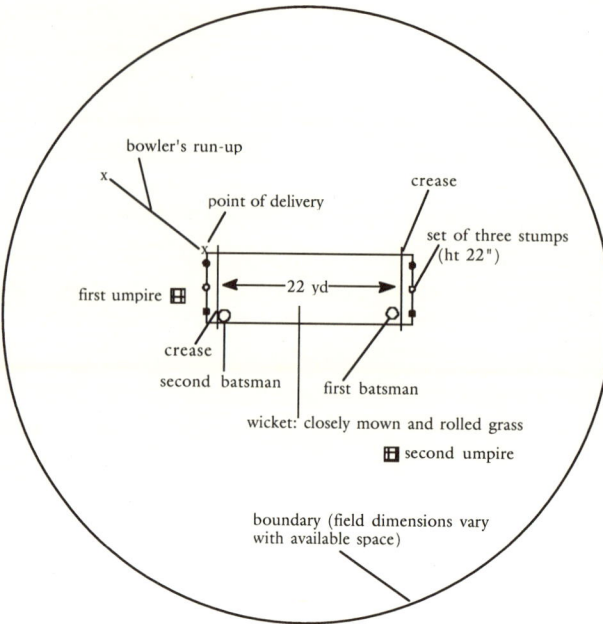

Figure 1. Cricket field.

the ground or into the air and away from any fielder, he can then decide whether to run. If the batsman is confident that he can get to the other set of stumps, twenty-two yards away, before the ball is returned to the bowler, he shouts "run." He and the other batsman, who has been waiting beside the opposite stumps, then set off toward one another, passing halfway down the wicket. If he has hit the ball hard enough, he will shout "two" or "three," meaning that he thinks they can safely get back to their respective stumps again once or twice more. Meanwhile, the fielder chasing the ball has to throw it back to the bowler or the wicket-keeper, each of whom is guarding a set of stumps, as quickly as possible. If one of them catches the ball and then hits the stumps with it before the batsman crosses a "safe" line beside them called "the crease," the batsman is "run out." If the ball reaches the boundary of the field before being intercepted, the batsman scores an automatic four runs, and if it reaches the boundary without touching the ground, like a baseball home run, he scores an automatic six.

The batsman does not *have* to run when he has hit the ball, nor does he

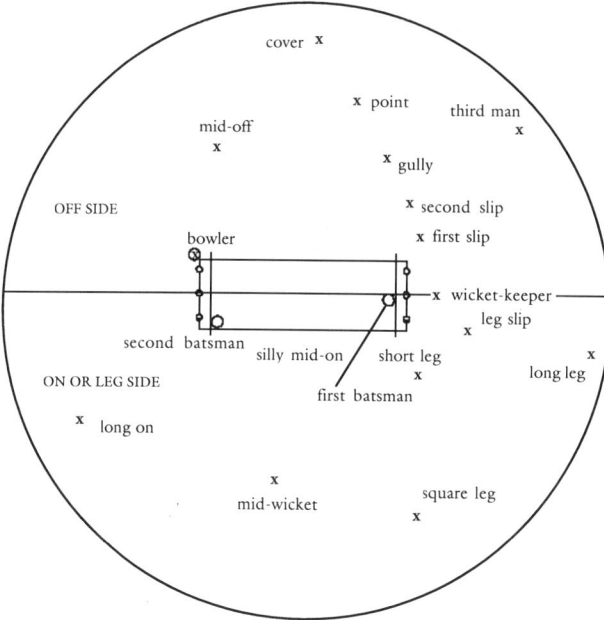

Figure 2. Characteristic fielding positions relative to a right-handed batsman. (With a left-hander everything is reversed; the "leg" side is always the side of the stumps on which the batsman stands.) More positions are shown here than can be filled at any one time. In general, as the batsman gains confidence in hitting, the fielding team moves away from the wicket.

even have to try to hit it if he's sure it will miss the stumps. And unlike a baseball batter, whose turn "at bat" always comes to a crisis quickly, a skillful batsman, good at deflecting dangerous balls and hitting them along the ground, can stay "in" for hours at a time. His teammates wait in the pavilion or on the sidelines until he is out and then the next batsman enters the arena. The greatest batting feat is to score a "century" of 100 runs. If the batsman gets out without making any run, on the other hand, he scores a "duck," and an out on his very first ball earns him a "golden duck." New batsmen replace those who have gotten out until ten of the eleven players on the team are out. Since this leaves the last man with no partner, he is obliged to give up too, and the innings comes to a close.

Then the team that has been bowling bats in its turn and the process is repeated. Each team bats twice, and the winner is the team with the highest score after two innings. However, if one team has scored fewer runs but still has men batting at the end of the game's previously agreed upon time limit, the game is a draw. Captains therefore have to "declare" (i.e., give up batting before all their men are out) if they fear that they will otherwise draw, despite having more runs than the opposition. There is plenty of scope for strategy and gamesmanship in deciding when to declare because a premature declaration can turn an apparent victory into a defeat, while a declaration too long delayed turns an apparent triumph into an ignominious draw. (Incidentally, when a team begins its second innings, it starts again at the top of its batting order. This sometimes means that the best men bat twice, while the "tail-enders," who are on the team for their bowling skills, do not bat at all.)

Cricket has different time limits for games at different levels. School and village matches are one-day affairs, often abbreviated from two innings per team to one each. The County Championship—equivalent to the major leagues—entails a series of three-day games, while international matches last for five days. As the quality of the players increases, their ability to bat for long periods tends to increase too, even in the face of the very finest bowling.

The fielders in cricket have to cover a much greater territory than their counterparts in baseball because the batsman can run after hitting the ball in any direction. The usual field has a wicket-keeper (catcher), one or two "slips" hoping to catch an "edge" shot from the bat, and several fielders scattered among the places where a particular batsman is known to hit (Figure 2). All those on the same side of the field as the batsman's legs when he prepares to hit are on the "leg" or "on" side, while all those on the same side as his bat are on the "off" side. Fielders standing close to the batsman, in an "aggressive" field setting, are positioned for quick catches but risk being injured by a well-hit ball; these positions are called, aptly enough, "silly mid-on" and "silly mid-off." To learn that a man is "short square leg" tells you nothing about his anatomy or build, only where he is standing on the cricket field (Figures 3, 4, 5).

Cricket is a team sport in which individual skills are at a premium. The batsman and the bowler are involved in a succession of one-on-one confrontations, but the batsman may be either playing cautiously to help his team stay in for as long as possible or hitting hard, risky strokes in an attempt to make quick runs for the team. The boundary fielder, like the

Figure 3. The batsman, wearing protective pads, gloves, and helmet, prepares to hit the ball as it rises off the bounce. The wicket-keeper waits to catch the ball if it is missed or hit with the edge of the bat, while a "forward" fielder is aggressively placed for a catch off the face of the bat. Photograph courtesy of *The Guardian*.

outfielder in baseball, may endure half an hour of uneventful solitude before being abruptly called upon for a catch or throw which can change the fortunes of the entire team. His own innings may last for as little as one ball or as much as an entire day, depending on his luck and skill, but in either event it will have repercussions on the team as a whole. There is little physical contact among team members (although in recent decades there has been some hugging of the bowler when he claims a victim)—no huddling, chanting, or butt-slapping—and, unlike baseball, cricket teams are not named after beasts of prey or fighting men (e.g., "Tigers," "Braves," "Pirates," or "Indians"). In fact, just as the teams have no colors (except on their caps), they usually have no names other than their places of origin. The game's traditions and etiquette put a premium on restraint and understatement, so aficionados have to learn where to look for the drama.

Cricket is a rich source of metaphors, and the English use them as freely

Figure 4. The batsman has hit a fast bowler's delivery backwards. The wicket-keeper jumps, but cannot catch the ball. If it reaches the boundary of the field, the batsman will score four runs. Photograph courtesy of *The Guardian*.

in everyday life as Americans use baseball talk. "That's just not cricket" is a forceful way of condemning conduct as disgraceful, although the expression has a dated quality now and is more likely to be used ironically. "A good innings" means a full opportunity to do something pleasurable and is quite often applied to a long and successful life. To be stumped in cricket is to be given out in a particularly annoying way, so to say that one is "stumped" by a knotty problem conveys the same sense of baffled dismay. Since a ball that reaches the boundary without bouncing adds six runs to the score, "hit for six," used metaphorically, means being hit extremely hard (as in a car accident, for example) or being soundly defeated in verbal combat. Children playing street cricket often devise makeshift rules, such as that hitting the ball over a hostile neighbor's fence or through a window gets the player six runs, but also gets him out. Hence, "six and you're out" is a metaphoric way of apportioning praise and blame simultaneously. "Batting on a sticky wicket" literally means finding the ball bouncing in unpredictable ways and metaphorically means encountering awkward problems which seem likely to get the better of you. Freudians will be interested to learn that when a bowler delivers the ball six times (an "over") without the

Figure 5. The batsman has hit the ball sideways and backwards from the edge of the bat, and the fielder at "second slip" has dived to his right to catch it. Photograph courtesy of *The Guardian.*

batsman hitting any runs, the feat is called a "maiden over" because, in effect, the "maidenhead" of the "over" has remained intact. There is room for ribaldry and double entendre here, of course, and the news that a man has seduced a woman is often reported as "he's bowled a maiden over!"

———

Cricket's origins, much debated in the last 100 years, lie somewhere in the folk sports of the Middle Ages. A thirteenth-century illuminated manuscript at Oxford's Bodleian Library shows a group of gowned men and women playing a bat-and-ball game which could as easily be rounders or baseball as cricket. Scattered literary references and court records indicate that several types of cricket, largely varied by region, were played in the sixteenth and seventeenth centuries, sometimes by big groups of men whose ill grace in defeat led to brawls and even deaths. In 1622, three townsmen were prosecuted in Chichester not merely "for playing at Cricket in the Churchyard," but because they "used to break the Church windows with the balls" and "little children had like to have their braynes beaten out with the cricket batt."[1] Puritan legislation during the Interregnum of the 1650s aimed to suppress the sport on Sabbatarian grounds, but was unable to make much of a dent in this venerable folk tradition.

After the Glorious Revolution of 1688, the nobility and some members of the rising merchant classes took to the game and began to write down rudimentary sets of rules. Among the leisured elite, who enjoyed playing before crowds of London artisans and laborers, matches became occasions for large bets, which made agreement on ground rules all the more important. But villagers in the southern counties of Kent, Surrey, Sussex, and Hampshire continued to play solely for pleasure or small stakes. John Dance, a mid-eighteenth-century poet, described the pleasures of the game in "Cricket: An Heroic Poem," which begins with a tribute to the onset of summer, the cricket season:

> When the returning sun begins to smile
> And shed its glories round this sea-girt isle;
> When newborn nature, decked in vivid green,
> Chases dull winter from the charming scene
> High-panting with delight, the jovial swain
> Trips it exulting o'er the flow'r strewed plain.
> Thy pleasures, Cricket! all his heart control;
> Thy eager transports dwell upon his soul.[2]

By Dance's day, odes to cricket were already being written in Latin and Greek as well—further evidence that members of the classically educated elite were taking an interest in the game. In 1748 the Court of King's Bench declared for the first time that cricket was not illegal, finding it "a very manly game, not bad in itself, but only in the ill use made of it by betting more than ten pounds on it."[3] Lord Chesterfield, a master of eighteenth-century good manners and social accomplishments, remarked to his son that "you will desire to excel all boys of your age at cricket," a sure sign of the game's high social standing.[4] A cricket incident changed the course of history in 1751, when Frederick, Prince of Wales, a keen player and a patron of the game, was hit in the head by a fast-moving ball and died soon after; the throne to which he would have ascended was taken instead by George III, with fateful consequences for England's American colonies.

The first team to stimulate a cricket prose literature, a genre which has flourished ever since, played on Broadhalfpenny Down in Hampshire, at the village of Hambledon, in the 1770s and 1780s. Its captain was Richard

Nyren, and his son John's 1833 book about the team described cricket more clearly than any predecessor. The millers, blacksmiths, and yeoman farmers of Hambledon, enjoying aristocratic patronage, were skillful enough to take on and beat teams made up from the best players in the rest of England. John Nyren (1764–1837), striking the combined heroic and elegiac note which has characterized cricket literature ever since, lamented that men so fine as his father's generation would never again grace English fields. His character portraits are all vivid and always larger than life:

> Tom Walker's hard, ungainly, scrag-of-mutton frame; wilted apple john face . . . his long, spider legs, as thick at the ankles as at the hips, and perfectly straight all the way down—for the embellishment of a calf in Tom's leg, Dame Nature had considered would be a wanton superfluity. Tom was the driest and most rigid-limbed chap I ever knew; his skin was like the rind of an old oak, and as sapless. . . . He moved like the rude machinery of a steam-engine in the infancy of construction, and when he ran, every member seemed ready to fly to the four winds. He toiled like a tar on horseback.[5]

Nyren also realized that describing the events of the games alone would soon weary the reader, so he added a colorful account of the crowd's vivid characters—and their favorite beverages:

> How those fine brawn-faced fellows of farmers would drink to our success! And what stuff they had to drink! Punch! and not your Ponche a la Romaine, or Ponche a la Grosseille, or your modern cat-lap milk punch—punch bedevilled; but good unsophisticated John Bull stuff—stark!—that would stand on end—punch that would make a cat speak! Sixpence a bottle! . . . The ale too—not the modern horror under the same name, that drives as many men melancholy mad as the hypocrites; not the beastliness of these days, that will make a fellow's inside like a shaking bog—and as rotten; but barley-corn such as would put the souls of three butchers into one weaver: Ale that would flare like turpentine.[6]

Among Hambledon's greatest players was John Small (1737–1826), whose death prompted a verse elegy from Pierce Egan that was packed with cricket metaphors and puns:

Here lies, bowled out by Death's unerring ball,
A cricketer renowned, by name John Small,
But though his name was Small yet great his fame,
For nobly did he play the noble game;
His life was like his innings, long and good,
Full ninety summers he had death withstood
At length the ninetieth winter came, when (fate
Not leaving him one solitary mate)
This last of Hambledonians, Old John Small,
Gave up his bat and ball, his leather, wax, and all.[7]

Hambledon dominated English cricket through the 1770s and 1780s, but the remoteness of the village and the demise of the team's local patrons led to its decline by 1800.

Schoolboys at England's elite private academies began to play the game during the Hambledon era. By 1800, the annual match between Eton and Harrow, the two most renowned of these schools, had begun. Lord Byron played for Harrow in 1805, even though he was lame and had to have a substitute runner, and got roaring drunk after Harrow's defeat. He boasted in a letter to a friend that he had scored eleven runs in the first innings and seven in the second, but the official score shows him hitting seven in the first and just two in the second. In a later poem to his friend "Alonzo," he invoked cricket as a symbol of school life:

Our sport, our studies, and our souls were one:
Together we impell'd the flying ball;
Together waited in our tutor's hall;
Together join'd in cricket's manly toil.[8]

Keats, like Byron, enjoyed the rough and tumble cricket of the early nineteenth century. Writing to his family from London in March 1819, he reported that he had just suffered a black eye playing cricket—his second one since leaving school—but added that it was all in fun and that he had found the appropriate remedy: "Brown, who is always one's friend in disaster, applied a leech to the eyelid, and there is no inflammation this morning though the ball hit me directly on the sight."[9]

A fictional contemporary of Byron and Keats, Catherine Morland in Jane Austen's *Northanger Abbey*, also loved the game. A plain and boisterous tomboy, Catherine "was fond of all boys' plays and greatly preferred cricket not merely to dolls, but to the more heroic enjoyments of infancy, nursing a dormous[e], feeding a canary bird, or watering a rose bush." Austen adds that Catherine was still running wild at fourteen, playing "cricket, base ball, riding on horseback, and running about the country," instead of turning to the ladylike arts.[10]

Among Austen's contemporaries was Mary R. Mitford (1787–1855), who revived her family's exhausted fortune when she won £20,000 with a lottery ticket at the age of ten. Mitford lived in a small Berkshire village, which she commemorated in an affectionate account of life there, *Our Village*. Among the village boys she singled out two cricket lovers. Joe Kirby, aged twelve, was helpful to everyone, hardworking, and poor; after fourteen hours of farmwork, he would "work still harder, under the name of play— batting, bowling, and fielding, as if for life." His bowling went "straight to the mark like a bullet," and he was "king of the cricketers from eight to sixteen." Jem Eusden, by contrast, was "a stunted lad of thirteen . . . of extraordinary ugliness, colourless, withered, haggard, with a look of extreme age." He would rush "into the field at night . . . ripe for action, to scold and brawl, and storm and bluster." In showing these very different boys at play, Mitford made the earliest known reference to what has remained a great hazard of children's cricket. If the boy who owns the bat and ball becomes unhappy, he may go off in a sulk, taking his vital belongings with him![11] In a short story, "Lost and Won," she told the tale of a village lad whose sweetheart, a local farm girl, rejects him when he causes the village team to lose an annual cricket match against a neighboring village. Only when his cricket has improved a few years later and he turns up again, playing triumphantly for the other village, does her heart melt and the wedding bells ring.[12] (A comical yokels' game of the Mitford type between All Muggleton and Dingly Dell features in Dickens's *Pickwick Papers* and is perhaps the most widely known cricket episode in the canon of English literature.[13])

Since the 1830s the annual Eton–Harrow game has been played at Lord's, the London headquarters of the Marylebone Cricket Club (MCC), which became the governing body for English cricket in the early decades of the nineteenth century. The gentry of the MCC played in tall hats and silk shirts for high stakes at Lord's then, and many of them, aiming to ensure victory, imported and paid "professionals" (usually talented villagers from the provinces) to strengthen their teams. Thomas Lord himself, after whom the ground was named, was a sharp-eyed entrepreneur who looked at the potential cricket audience, beheld big profits, and began the advertising and commercializing of the game which eventually dominated first-class cricket. Bookmakers were a fixture at Lord's until an 1852 regulation banned them, and cricket was as much an occasion for gambling then as horse racing. The size of the bets made the game deadly earnest. As early as 1835, one enthusiast, the Reverend Charles Townsend, complained that both the high stakes and the high level of the play were taking some of the fun out of what was meant to be a game. "The play there [at Lord's] seems to partake too much of the cold character of science, and to have something of the insensibility and hardness of mechanism about it . . . which shows how much the wary understanding and how little the promptness of the heart is engaged."[14]

The sharp division between "gentlemen" and "players" (i.e., paid professionals) persisted throughout the nineteenth century and well into the twentieth. The annual Lord's match between the Gentlemen of England and the Players, beginning in 1806, was not finally abandoned until 1963, long after the distinction had begun to lose its force. During the nineteenth century, however, the Gentlemen, who could afford to play without payment, enjoyed a far higher status than the Players, even though the latter nearly always won. The Gentlemen took advantage of the Players' skills but condescended to them and treated them as hardly better than servants or mercenaries, thus keeping a sharp class distinction at the heart of the game. Aristocratic patrons sometimes gave poor but talented cricketers permanent jobs on their estates in order to have a squad ready to meet every challenge. H. G. Wells's father, Joseph Wells (1827–1910), was one such retainer–professional in his youth and made a name for himself in an 1862 Sussex–Kent game by bowling four batsmen out with four consecutive balls, the only time this feat had ever been accomplished in a first-class match.[15]

As in most elements of British life, class has been paramount in cricket, the history and literature of which are brimming with class implications. It is also possible to see how ideas about class, and ideas about cricket, changed with the maturing of Britain as an industrial society. When boys at the elite schools began to adopt the game, their masters' first response was to suppress a sport so closely associated with gambling and metropolitan vice. Rugby School's Dr. Thomas Arnold (headmaster from 1827 to 1842) was the first great educational reformer of his era and a towering Victorian moralist who had no patience with games. A little later, however, head-masters abandoned their efforts to suppress cricket and instead tried to give it a new meaning. Dr. Frederick Temple, Arnold's successor at Rugby, and Dr. John Percival, headmaster of Clifton College, Bristol, both believed that cricket (when detached from betting) was the perfect medium for the training of Christian gentlemen because it promoted cooperation, team-work, courage, self-discipline, and selflessness. Played keenly and soberly, though with a dash of chivalric flair and romance, the game required ad-herence not just to the explicit rules but to an elaborate code of sporting etiquette; it was, above all, to be taken absolutely seriously. Fifty years later George Bernard Shaw had this style of Victorian high-mindedness in his sights when he wrote that "the well-fed Englishman, though he lives and dies a schoolboy, cannot play. He cannot even play cricket or football: he has to work at them."[16]

Rugby School is the scene of "old boy" Thomas Hughes's *Tom Brown's Schooldays*, the great didactic public school novel of its day. Its climactic last chapter depicts a cricket match between the Rugby boys and a team of tough, businesslike "players" from the MCC. For Tom, captain of the school team, the game is a coming-of-age ritual. It is striking to see that in narrating this match, Hughes scarcely mentions Tom as either batting or bowling. Instead, he concentrates on Tom's judicious leadership of the team and on the sense of sportsmanlike decency which prompts his one rather rash decision. The passage emphasizes that while other members of his team can bat, Tom can also chat easily about Aristophanes with his favorite Greek master. The school loses the game, but Tom's team-mates, recognizing him as a true sportsman and scholar—a real young gentleman—hoist him to their shoulders and sing "For He's a Jolly Good Fellow."[17] The book and its ideals remained fixtures of English public (i.e., private) school life for nearly a century. Hughes later emigrated to America and founded a community for the younger sons of English nobility, named (perhaps inevitably) Rugby, Tennessee.

In the English school system of the late nineteenth century, the autumn and winter terms were devoted to football (i.e., soccer) or rugby, and the spring term to cricket. Hundreds of schoolboy novels since *Tom Brown's Schooldays* have followed its convention of climaxing with a cricket match that, for its senior players, also serves as a valedictory to the school itself.

While football was played in a season of cold, rain, and mud, after which students would always be back for the next term, cricket's place in the school year gave it a glow of golden finality.

Several historians in recent decades have shown that organized cricket could be used by the rising commercial and industrial elite to instill a sense of order in unruly working-class players, potentially making the game an instrument of social control. Whereas it had once been boozy and lawless, it acquired increasingly precise written rules along with an unwritten etiquette of sportsmanship and self-restraint. By 1864, a royal commission was arguing in its report that cricket helped "to form some of the most valuable social qualities and manly virtues."[18] H. B. Philpott, a London educator, made the same point two decades later and remarked with pleasure on the ethos of the game having spread through the "lower orders." Poor schoolchildren, after undergoing "a period of friendly supervision," learned good cricketing manners:

> No one quarrels with the placing of the field. . . . The young captain does not bawl "butter fingers" or "silly fathead" whenever a catch is missed. . . . The batsman bowled for a duck neither shouts "it ain't fair" nor punches the umpire. . . . No, they have learned to "play the game."[19]

And, he added sententiously, "the change is not a matter of cricket only; in becoming better cricketers they have become better boys." James Walvin, a historian of leisure, has concluded that such changes in the players' approach to the game "reflected the more fundamental changes in society at large, for by the last quarter of the nineteenth century the working population had itself become disciplined and attuned to the rigours of a clock- and machine-dominated life. The games they turned to . . . were in keeping with that discipline."[20] The cricket "missionaries" of the late nineteenth century certainly regarded the game as a source of cross-class goodwill. George Trevelyan, England's first great social historian, claimed that "if the French *noblesse* had been capable of playing cricket with their peasants their chateaux would never have been burnt."[21]

The maturing of English industrial society also facilitated the spread of cricket as a leisure activity. With the completion of a nationwide railway network by the mid-1860s, it became possible for teams from distant parts of the country to play one another easily and punctually. It is no coincidence that the County Championship began in that decade, nor that it was matched throughout the nation by the flowering of local clubs and leagues, many of which played cricket in the summer and football in the winter. Municipalities and farsighted employers began to provide cricket and football grounds for working-class men, while urban parks throughout England were leveled and closely mown to prepare them for the game.

The emergence of an anti-cricket literature coincided with these changes. One Rugby School alumnus who disagreed with the *Tom Brown's Schooldays* ideal was Charles Dodgson (Lewis Carroll). He went to Rugby in 1846, at the age of fourteen, and found school life a misery because he was bullied for his stammer and his ineptness at games. His academic successes, which led to his becoming an Oxford mathematics don, did nothing to allay his schoolmates' unkindness. In 1867 he wrote a witty parody of Oliver Goldsmith's "Deserted Village," claiming that the transformation of Oxford's University Parks by cricketers was as damaging then as the enclosure movement's usurpation of old English villages had been a century earlier. In each case a thrusting, overly organized commercial society was displacing the old ways. Addressing the park in mock-heroic style, Dodgson declaims:

> Amidst thy bowers the tyrant's hand is seen
> And rude pavilions sadden all thy green.
> One selfish pastime grasps the whole domain,
> And half a faction swallows up the plain;
> Adown thy glades, all sacrificed to cricket,
> The hollow sounding bat now guards the wicket;
> Sunk are thy mounds in shapeless level all,
> Lest aught impede the swiftly rolling ball.
> And trembling, shrinking from the fatal blow
> Far, far away thy hapless children go.[22]

When Dodgson wrote that "in barren splendour flits the russet ball" he was joking, but the poem's bitterness lends a serious edge to his parody— part of a growing literary protest against the modern, highly organized society that was displacing an older, less orderly rusticity.

As industry advanced, so did the British Empire. Until the late Victorian era, the Empire had been a makeshift affair, formed (according to an old saw) in a fit of absentmindedness. Then, facing trade competition from other European nations and fearing American and German power, Disraeli's Conservative Party aimed to make the Empire the foundation of Britain's world dominance. Along with pots and pans, textiles, opium, and Anglicanism, the British exported cricket to the peoples they had vanquished. Cricket, says historian Benny Green, "seems to have been a typically English compromise between a religious manifestation and an instrument of policy, occupying a misty hinterland in which ethics and biceps merged into a third entity, an exquisite refinement of that other imperial concept, the White Man's Burden."[23] The rising public schools found an additional role for themselves in the training of imperial soldiers and administrators who then took the game to India, Australia, Ceylon (Sri Lanka), South Africa, the West Indies, and the Pacific Islands. One of the most popular poems of the imperial era was Henry Newbolt's "Vitae Lampada" (1898), which made an explicit connection between the chivalric cricketing schoolboy and the fearless imperial soldier:

> There's a breathless hush in the Close tonight—
> Ten to make and the match to win
> A bumping pitch and a blinding light
> An hour to play and the last man in.
> And it's not for the sake of a ribboned coat,
> Or the selfish hope of a season's fame,
> But his Captain's hand on his shoulder smote:
> "Play up! play up! and play the game!"
>
> The sand of the desert is sodden red,
> Red with the wreck of a square that broke;
> The Gatling's jammed and the Colonel's dead,
> And the regiment blind with dust and smoke.
> The river of death has brimmed his banks,
> And England's far, and Honour a name,
> But the voice of a schoolboy rallies the ranks:
> "Play up! play up! and play the game!"[24]

Despatches from colonial wars often used cricket analogies unselfconsciously in describing the fortunes of battle, and medal citations for conspicuous gallantry used the same vocabulary as commendations of fine batsmen.[25]

The first international cricket rivalry, between England and Australia, began in 1876, and this contest, now reenacted regularly, is fought for an unusual trophy called "the Ashes." The name originated from a satirical advertisement placed in the *Sporting Times* after Australia won a surprise victory over the complacent England team in August 1882. The ad announced that "English Cricket died at the Oval" (a London cricket ground) and was "deeply lamented by a large circle of sorrowing friends and acquaintances. . . . The body will be cremated and the ashes taken to Australia."[26] Picking up on the joke, a group of Australian ladies burned the bails which topped the wickets in a subsequent game between the two countries. The England players then put these ashes in an urn and placed it in the Imperial War Memorial Gallery at Lord's, where it has stayed ever since. Even when the Australians win "the Ashes" (i.e., win a series of "test matches" against England), which they usually do, they never actually take possession of the urn/trophy.[27]

Cricket was popular even in America, an ex-colony, in the mid- and late nineteenth century, especially among English immigrants to New England and the Philadelphia area, before it was eclipsed by the rise of baseball.[28] When English touring teams visited the United States in the 1870s, they allowed the Americans to play with twenty-two men, against their own eleven, and still managed to win, which suggests a rather marked disparity of skill levels.[29] But by 1900 the Americans could compete on almost equal terms, and one player, "Mr. King of Philadelphia," was famous on both sides of the Atlantic. Philadelphia alone produced two monthly cricket magazines, while well-organized leagues played on regular schedules and some U.S. colleges sent their own cricket teams on English tours. (Haverford College sent five cricket teams to England between 1896 and 1914.[30]) By the turn of the century, Australian, American, Indian, and West Indian cricketers had all served notice on England that its teams could not be assured of winning against English-speaking cricketers abroad. A little later, the same would also hold for tennis and golf—both British inventions at which the importing nations soon outshone the exporter.

The most famous cricketer in English history, W. G. Grace (1848–1915), was a Gentleman who, from mid-Victorian to Edwardian times, led England's teams on tour to the colonies. Ironically, as recent historians have revealed, he was sometimes paid to take part in English tours of Australia, but only covertly, and, like his fellow Gentlemen, he was ostentatious about playing solely for love of the game. A true sporting prodigy, Grace played his first first-class game in 1862 at the age of fourteen. He went on to lead English teams to some of their greatest victories and did not retire from his county team, Gloucestershire, until he was almost sixty. In the middle of his career, his batting average was far higher than any rival's, he bowled extremely well, and his 250-pound figure, topped by a regal head with a huge beard, made him instantly recognizable—and easily caricatured. Parodies of popular verse, such as the following lines, celebrated his fame:

> The champion Grace to the match has gone,
> In the British ranks you'll find him,
> His magic bat he has girded on,
> And his pads are slung behind him.[31]

Grace's father, brother, and several other relations were Gentlemen too. One cousin, W. R. Gilbert, who played alongside Grace on the Gloucestershire team, was so impoverished that he contemplated taking the dreadful step of turning "professional," which would have dishonored him in his own eyes and those of his friends and family. He chose a drastic alternative. In 1886, several Gloucestershire men reported that their street clothes, hanging in the pavilion while they played on the field, had been rifled and money removed. After a detective stood watch and discovered that Gilbert was the thief, his family ordered him not only to give up cricket, but to emigrate to the colonies and never come back. Gilbert obeyed, spending the rest of his life in Canada and dying (in 1924) in Calgary, Alberta, where he had lived a blameless life and worked in the land-titles office. The scandal itself was hushed up—so successfully that it was not revealed until a curious cricket historian, Roland Bowen, finally unraveled the story and published it in 1970.[32] The incident starkly illustrates the lengths to which Gentlemen would go to avoid being touched by the dread hand of "professionalism."

Cricket historians consider the late nineteenth and early twentieth century its golden age, when superbly talented amateurs like Grace could hold their own with the professionals. A doctor by training, Grace practiced medicine only during the off-seasons, hiring a locum for the duration of every cricket season. There are several tales of how he gave first aid on the cricket pitch to wounded players, including one A. C. Crome, who was impaled by the throat on the boundary railings at Old Trafford, Manchester, in 1887 while trying to catch a ball hit by Grace. "They had to send out for a needle and thread to sew it up and for nearly half an hour W. G. held the edges of the wound together," Crome wrote later, in a grateful tribute to Grace. "It was of vital importance that the injured part should be kept absolutely still, and his hand never shook all that time."[33]

One of Grace's most brilliant teammates was an Indian prince, Colonel His Highness Kumar Shri Sir Ranjitsinhji Vibhaji, Jam Sahib of Nawanagar (1872–1933). Like the Indian Independence leaders Gandhi and Jinnah, he was born in Gujurat, and, like Gandhi at least, he seemed frail and delicate yet displayed immense stamina and willpower. Ranjitsinhji (whose name meant "the lion that conquers in battle") was a schoolmate of Gandhi's at the Rajkot College, but went on to finish his education at Cambridge. Snubbed at first for his dark skin, he was finally given a place on the university cricket team in 1893, his third year, and played with such distinction that the county team of Sussex recruited him. He played with Sussex for the next ten years, rising to captain in 1899. Beginning in 1895, he also played for the England team, the first Asian ever to do so, and scored 175 during his first overseas test match (in Australia in 1897), at that time the highest score ever made by an England player in a test match. "Australia," says one biographer, "went Ranji mad with Ranji bats, Ranji bars, Ranji sandwiches, Ranji matchboxes and even a Ranji hair-restorer."[34] That same year, in honor of Queen Victoria's sixty years on the throne, Ranjitsinhji published *The Jubilee Book*, in which he argued that "cricket brings the most opposite characters and the most diverse lives together. Anything that puts very many different kinds of people on a common ground must promote sympathy and kindly feelings."[35]

Immensely rich, in 1907 he ascended the throne of Nawanagar, where he proved, unlike Gandhi, to be a staunch supporter of the British Raj. The pressure of political business at home allowed him to make only occasional visits to England after that, but his play in these rare later appearances delighted his English admirers, as did his volunteering to fight on the western front in the First World War. The figure of Krishna Ram in John Masters's novel *The Ravi Lancers*, a thinly fictionalized version of Ranjitsinhji, gives a taste of the excitement and exoticism he provoked in English fans.[36] Among the many English authors to rhapsodize over him, the best known was the *Manchester Guardian*'s cricket and music writer Neville Cardus (1889–1975), who said that Ranjitsinhji was "unique; he was not biologically accountable; he was a case of a complete and magical divergence from type." In a vein which Edward Said would have cherished as an illustration for *Orientalism*, Cardus elaborated:

> A strange light from the East flickered in the English sunshine when he was at the wicket. . . . When he turned approved science upside down and changed the geometry of batsmanship to an esoteric leger-demain, we were bewitched to the realms of rope-dancers and snake-charmers; this was a cricket of Oriental sorcery, glowing with a dark beauty of its own. . . . It was like a shooting star, all wrong in our astronomy, but right and splendid in some other and more dazzling stellar universe.[37]

A lesser cricket writer, Ted Wainwright, added that Ranji "had never made a Christian stroke in his life!"[38]

Indian authors too, then and since, have eulogized Ranjitsinhji for his role in forcing Britons to reckon with Indian cricket. In *The Tao of Cricket*, Ashis Nandy explains its deep appeal to various castes in India and the way in which the game, learned from the conquerors, could be applied as a critique of their motives:

> To the Brahminic, the posture of moral superiority and self-control of the gentleman cricketer was bound to be attractive. The Kshatriyas and the Kshatriya-like found him attractive for his defiance of fate, empha-sis on style and honour. Both appreciated the gentleman cricketer's emphasis on rituals or forms over substance and his overt defiance of the professional cricketer's profit motive and performance principle, which were associated not only with the Bania and some of the "low" cultures of India but also with the colonial rulers. This was the first sense in which cricket was a criticism of colonialism. . . . It allowed Indians to assess their colonial rulers by western values reflected in the official philosophy of cricket, and to find the rulers wanting.[39]

But Nandy adds that cricket occasionally brought out the worst in Indian princes, as they tried to emulate British habits while taking advantage of their local subjects' servility. The Maharaja Pratap Singh of Jammu and Kashmir, for example, cheated shamelessly. He tolerated only the slowest and most inaccurate bowling from his subjects, and whenever he hit the ball the fielders, rather than trying to throw it back quickly to the wicket-keeper, deliberately kicked it toward the boundary so that he could score more runs and further inflate his self-image as a great cricketer. Since the maharaja thought that fielding was servile work, he always sent a servant out to deputize for him when his team was bowling.[40]

Other colonized peoples likewise took both the game and its etiquette to heart. In the West Indies, for example, cricket soon became popular among all classes, and the island colonies began a regular competition against one another in 1893. An all-Trinidad team defeated the first touring side from England in 1895, and in 1900 the first united West Indies team, made up equally of Black and White players, toured England. For poor villagers, according to Trinidad historian Ivar Oxaal, "the stem of one palm tree branch provided a bat, and three more propped up against each other supplied a wicket for the plebeians, who had observed the British gentlemen engaged in their favorite sport."[41] The 1900 touring team was utterly thrashed by England. A Black bowler named Woods pleaded with his White captain to be allowed to bowl barefoot, as he had always done at home. The captain, Aucher Warner, stiffly denied the request, but after a few more massive hits from the English star G. L. Jessop, Woods renewed his plea, though offering to compromise: "Mr Warner, let me take off one [shoe]—just one and I could get him—just one, sir." Warner was indignant: "Out of the question. You can't do that here, Woods," he replied, preferring defeat to the disgrace of a barefoot (or one-shoed) bowler.[42] The West Indians soon improved, however, and a Trinidad player, Learie Constantine, touring England with an all–West Indies team just after the First World War, played so well that, like Ranjitsinhji, he was invited to stay on and play for an English league team. Constantine, wrote Oxaal, was "a sportsman of legendary prowess and one of the early heralds of the phenomenal ability that West Indians were to bring to the game."[43] Indeed, the world's greatest players in recent years, by consensus, have been West Indians.

Among the gifted English Gentlemen of the late-Victorian and Edwardian eras was Arthur Conan Doyle (1859–1930). Born and raised a Catholic, Conan Doyle attended Stonyhurst, the premier Catholic boys' boarding school, where an irregular version of cricket was played on a gravel pitch with a homemade wooden ball and a curved alderwood bat. He was a champion player there, later adapting to the standard grass-pitch, willow-bat, and leather-ball game well enough to play for England's premier team, the Marylebone Cricket Club. Conan Doyle scored a century in his very first game at Lord's and once managed to bowl out W. G. Grace, which pleased him so much that he wrote a poem about it.[44] Batting for the MCC against Kent in another game, he was hit on the thigh by a fast ball:

> A little occasional pain is one of the chances of cricket, and one takes it as cheerfully as one can, but on this occasion it suddenly became sharp to an unbearable degree. I clapped my hand to the spot and found to my amazement that I was on fire. The ball had landed straight on a small tin vesta box in my trousers, had splintered the box, and set the matches ablaze. . . . W. G. Grace was greatly amused. "Couldn't get you out—had to set you on fire!" he cried in the high voice which seemed so queer for so big a body.[45]

When Conan Doyle was on an England touring team to the Netherlands in 1892, he saved a seemingly lost match by bowling out the last four Dutch batsmen. In later life he took time out from his medical practice and his writing to play for the Allahakbarries, a team of literary and theatrical celebrities captained by the prolific cricket writer J. M. Barrie. Press accounts of their games imply that Conan Doyle was the team's best player by far.[46]

Barrie, a Scot, began his London journalism career by writing newspaper articles on cricket in the 1880s and 1890s. One recent biographer argues that cricket was the key to Barrie's entire life and that, like his creation Peter Pan, he was unable to leave boyish things behind.[47] Much of his cricket journalism is labored and dull because he made the mistake of focusing too much on the details of particular matches (most of the players' names mean nothing to us now) and too little on the wider context and social implications of the game. But there are good moments: Barrie had a sharp eye for the way in which success at cricket could inflate egos, and failure deflate them. Of one boy who hit forty-four runs in the annual Eton–Harrow match, Barrie wrote: "No victorious General entering Rome in triumph could strut more magnificently, or gather a more loyal crowd of worshippers."[48] He also wrote some early descriptions of working-class children's street cricket. In "Urchins at Play" (1889), he contrasted two groups of boys, one poor and the other rich, showing how, despite all their differences of appearance, dress, accent, and equipment, they could share a passion for cricket. But Barrie found "the ragamuffins . . . more interesting than the velveteens" because they were not coddled by governesses: if their game got slow, "they [would] dance in a puddle"; if they broke "a window, they [would] give a cheer, and bolt"; and they lived in constant fear of the patrolling policeman.[49]

Urban street cricket, with rules to suit that environment, was also the subject of "Six and Out," a poem by Barrie's contemporary G. D. Martineau (1835–1919):

> It was a keen determined school
> Unorthodox and free
> Harsh circumstance oft made the rule
> And not the MCC.

The narrator enjoys watching the players until a powerful hit produces disaster:

> So standing, musing on the scene,
> I let the moments pass.
> How well he drove it to the screen
> And then—the crash of glass!
> I watched the players as they ran
> And heard while yet they fled,
> The loud voice of an angry man
> The law's majestic tread.[50]

It was in street games like these that most of the men who grew up to play professional cricket began their sporting lives.

Barrie's patronizing accounts of ladies' games also offer a glimpse of late-Victorian women at play and their enjoyment at temporarily upsetting gender conventions. The first recorded women's cricket match took place in 1745, and the game had been sporadically pursued by women ever since. When two wealthy ladies' teams played for high stakes in 1811, the scene was recorded in Thomas Rowlandson's (1756–1827) satirical cartoon "Cricket Match Extraordinary." According to one, perhaps apocryphal tale, overarm bowling, which is now universal in the men's game, was first developed in the early nineteenth century by a woman named Christina Willes whose bulky crinolines made the old style of underarm bowling impossible. At any rate, we do know that her brother, John Willes, was the first man to introduce overarm bowling to the MCC, playing for Kent against the club in 1806 and occasioning outrage at first—but emulation soon thereafter![51] By the late nineteenth century, women's cricket had become a club sport, and a team of "Original English Lady Cricketers" (all using assumed names) toured England, accepting all challenges. Male writers found it hard to resist the ironic mode when they reported such games. Barrie made fun of female players, depicting them as distracted by flowers in the outfield and more attentive to matters of dress, deportment, and hairstyle than to the game itself. In the 1890s, Norman Gale, an ex–Rugby School boy and minor cricket poet, wrote "A Tomboy," describing a twelve-year-old girl who recalls Austen's Catherine Morland:

> That long-legged darling, Alice James,
> Plays cricket with the Johnson boys;
> A dozen engines could not make
> So shrill a noise.
>   She's only twelve and so, unfrocked,
> Beyond her sometimes shameless knee;
> And never maiden longed so much
> A boy to be. . . .
>   So, riding roughshod over rules,
> This long-legged Darling has her will;
> And when she's twenty, I expect,
> She will do so still.[52]

Despite smirking accounts by men, women's cricket persisted, becoming popular in girls' private schools in the interwar years and leading to the creation of a women's cricket World Cup in 1973. In their study of English schoolgirl literature, *You're a Brick, Angela,* Mary Cadogan and Patricia Craig note that the emphasis on games in girls' fiction of the early twentieth century was almost comparable to that in boys' stories of the same era because, they suggest, games served as a useful metaphor for other desirable qualities: "An enthusiasm for games implies an attitude of fairness, self-effacement and loyalty which is far more to be applauded than any intellectual achievement."[53] Female writers of adult fiction, however, showed little interest in cricket, unlike their male counterparts, whose works and letters of the late nineteenth and early twentieth century contain numerous scattered references to the game.[54]

P. G. Wodehouse, a cricketing contemporary of Conan Doyle and Barrie, said that "cricket is a great safety valve. If you like the game, and are in a position to play it at least twice a week, life can never be entirely grey."[55] But Wodehouse could see the game's subversive possibilities as well as its gentlemanly character-building side. In *Mike and Psmith*, for example, a schoolboy, Mike Jackson, uses his excellent cricketing skills to thwart a master, Mr. Downing, whose excessive "keenness" for the game as well as his goading remarks have annoyed him. Mike bats so well that the opposition is unable to get him out, and he scores over 200 runs in one innings. The opposition, like Mr. Downing, expects him to declare (i.e., quit batting voluntarily) and give them a chance to bat. The game's etiquette requires a declaration and so indeed does his team, if it is to win. But Mike gaily bats on to the end of the allotted game time, with the result that his team has scored 471 runs, the opposition has not batted, and the game is a draw. Wodehouse designed this scene artfully, showing that Downing is powerless to complain because Mike has outwitted him by doing exactly what Downing wanted — playing his very best at the game. Downing loses both ways because the reader infers that it was unsporting of him to nag Mike in the first place, so Mike's unsporting conduct becomes a pardonable deviation from the conventions.[56] (Mike shows up again in later Wodehouse novels where, as a member of the faded gentry, he too has to face the dilemma of whether to demean himself and turn professional — which, by subterfuge, he avoids.)

Still more subversive was the gentleman–rogue of the *Raffles* novels written at the turn of the century by E. W. Hornung, Conan Doyle's brother-in-law. Raffles is a jewel thief who draws a former school chum, Bunny, into his life of crime. Less imaginative and brilliant than Raffles, Bunny is the narrator of these novels, and the two men in some ways mirror Sherlock Holmes and Dr. Watson, but as master thief and apprentice rather than master detective and student. Raffles is a great cricketer with a superb sense of sportsmanship, which includes a willingness to accept dares and take calculated risks, in life as on the field. Playing for the Gentlemen of England against the Players at Lord's, Raffles takes the game very seriously, although he observes the convention of pretending not to care for it too much. "Cricket, like everything else, is a good enough sport until you discover a better," he tells Bunny, extolling crime as a more exciting alternative. "What's the satisfaction of taking a man's wicket when you want his spoons?"[57] But Bunny knows better; he sees Raffles practicing his batsmanship in the nets (i.e., the batting cage),

> with his pockets full of sovereigns, which he put on the stumps instead of bails. It was a sight to see the professionals bowling like demons for the hard cash, for whenever a stump was hit a pound was tossed to the bowler and another balanced in its stead. . . . Raffles's practice cost him eight or nine sovereigns; but he had absolutely first class bowling all the time; and he made fifty seven runs next day.[58]

Together, Raffles and Bunny lead a sporting life of crime. Like their real-life counterpart W. R. Gilbert, they are hard up but regard turning professional as more dishonorable than stealing. "Nothing riles me more than being asked about for my cricket as though I were a pro. myself," says Raffles, after being invited to play in a countryhouse weekend party match.[59] (He avenges himself by robbing the richest female guest.)

Raffles and Bunny have an absolute trust in one another because they bonded as schoolboys. "Everybody knows," recalls Bunny, "how largely the tone of a . . . school depends on that of the eleven, and on the character of the captain of cricket in particular, and I have never heard it denied that in A. J. Raffles's time our tone was good, or that such influence as he troubled to exert was on the side of the angels."[60] Gentlemen like Raffles did not admit to taking their cricket too seriously, but gentlemen-in-training, while still at school, certainly did. Leonard Woolf, for example, writing of his schooling in the 1890s, recalled a master named Woolley who would line up the whole school on the playing fields every summer day for a quarter of an hour's "bat drill." Every boy had a bat, and Woolley,

> a handsome, dark, lean, graceful man, [faced] us with a bat in his hand, like a conductor before his orchestra. "Forward" or "off drive," he would say making the stroke perfectly himself, and the whole school would play forward or off drive, and he, like the great conductor, would spot even the smallest boy in the back row if he did not come perfectly straight forward or did not follow through with the drive in perfect style.[61]

From Woolley, says Woolf, without apparent irony, "I learned . . . the seriousness of games, the importance of style, the duty when you go in to bat of making every stroke with a concentration which an artist puts into every stroke of his brush in painting a masterpiece." The obverse side of this intense seriousness about games, he adds, was being "taught to take all other lessons not seriously." Since the academic subjects bored both the masters and the boys, "to take lessons at all seriously, was entirely despicable."[62] Woolf describes how carefully he had to conceal his intellectual interests, or present them as harmless eccentricity, and recalls the relief and delight with which, as a Cambridge undergraduate, he met a handful of other young men who had genuine intellectual curiosity and were willing, after cautious preliminaries, to admit it. Woolf was Jewish, but his cricketing prowess more than offset the other boys' latent anti-Semitism and gave him a much easier time in school than his anti-games Bloomsbury contemporary Lytton Strachey experienced.

Cricket at the big public schools was compulsory, and, in the nature of things, some boys were good at it and others were not. The ones who were bad at cricket hated being shown up, day after day, and sometimes got a belated literary revenge. For example, Rudyard Kipling, who was so nearsighted and had to wear such thick lenses that he was exempted from all games at his Devonshire boarding school, had to stand humiliated on the sidelines, bored and resentful. In his novel about school life, *Stalky and Co.*, his heroes are three boys who avoid cricket and spend their leisure time taking adventurous rambles on the sea cliffs and into the surrounding countryside, befriending the local gentry and outwitting conformist busybodies like their master Mr. Prout. "If you order us to go down [to watch cricket], sir, of course we'll go," says Stalky, "with maddening politeness. But Prout knew better than that. . . . He had tried the experiment once at a big match, when the three [friends], self-isolated, stood to attention for half an hour in full view of all the visitors, to whom [junior boys], subsidized for that end, pointed them out as victims of Prout's tyranny."[63] Kipling shows that Stalky's irregular conduct and avoidance of games (he calls cricketers "flannelled fools") are ideal preparation for his later life as a soldier. In the last scenes of the book, Stalky is shown outwitting England's tribal enemies on the northwest frontier of India by undertaking just the kind of daring high jinks that he had learned at school, while his commanding officers, ex-cricketers devoid of initiative, appear to be facing certain defeat and death. (Kipling's novel, which was almost exactly contemporaneous with Newbolt's "Vitae Lampada," makes almost exactly the opposite point! For Newbolt cricket made the soldier, whereas for Kipling it was evasion of cricket that made him.)

Criticism of compulsory games—and of the anti-intellectualism that often went with it—was intensifying by the time of the First World War. Precocious seventeen-year-old Alec Waugh (brother of Evelyn) made the point forcefully in *The Loom of Youth*.[64] Waugh, having been expelled from Sherborne School after his masters caught him in the midst of a homosexual tryst, was an officer cadet preparing to go to the western front when he published this thinly fictionalized account of his school years. It caused a terrific scandal and split English society into defenders and detractors because it was the first work to speak candidly about the homosexual romances, the bullying, and the hypocrisy of the English public school and its vulgar contempt for intellectual life by comparison with sports. In a climactic scene the hero, Gordon Caruthers, argues that Germany has caught Britain unprepared for this Great War after several decades during which the young English elite have neglected their studies and devoted far too much energy to sports. And yet, ironically, as Waugh showed, Caruthers's argument is persuasive only because he is himself a good athlete: "Gordon's speech really made an impression. After all, he was a blood, one of the best all-round athletes in the school, and if he thought like that, there must be something in what so many people were saying who ran down games."[65] To emphasize the point that prowess in games was all-important even to those who would deny it, Waugh's book closes with Caruthers neglecting his schoolwork, giving frivolous answers to questions on his final exams, and then scoring eighty-five runs (lovingly detailed by the narrator) in his last school cricket match.[66]

Another bitter anti-cricketer who had been made miserable by the sport at boarding school was C. S. Lewis. Describing its horrors in his autobiography *Surprised by Joy*, Lewis used cricket as part of a clever inversion of a modern literary tradition.[67] At the place he called "Wyvern" (actually Malvern) in the years just before the First World War, Lewis had been bullied and maltreated by older, stronger boys until he felt continuously exhausted:

> Oh the implacable day, the horror of waking, the endless desert of hours that separated one from bedtime! And remember that . . . a

school day contains hardly any leisure for a boy who does not like games. For him, to pass from the form room to the playing field is simply to exchange work in which he can take some interest for work in which he can take none, in which failure is more severely punished, and in which (worst of all) he must feign an interest.[68]

Any boy who wanted to become a "blood," to cut a figure in the school, had to succeed at cricket. As a result, his schoolmates "went to the playing fields not as men go to the tennis club but as stage-struck girls go to an audition; tense and anxious, racked with dazzling hopes and sickening fears, never in peace of mind till they had won some notice which would set their feet on the first rung of the social ladder."[69] After his long, harrowing, joyless years of school and compulsory cricket, Lewis graduated into the wartime army and arrived at the western front on his nineteenth birthday. As he wrote his autobiography almost forty years later, knowing that in postwar literature the western front of World War I had become a metaphor for all that was destructive, futile, and cruel, Lewis made a point of favorably comparing the trenches to life in an English public school: "Straight tribulation is easier to bear than tribulation that advertises itself as pleasure. The one breeds camaraderie and even (when intense) a kind of love between the fellow-sufferers; the other, mutual distrust, cynicism, concealed and fretting resentment."[70]

Lewis's contemporary Robert Graves, who also went straight from boarding school to the trenches, had run an anti-cricket campaign in the Charterhouse School newspaper, the *Carthusian*, which he edited. Describing cricket as a game "in which the selfishness of the few [does] not excuse the boredom of the many," Graves also contributed "pro-cricket letters" signed "Judas Iscariot."[71] But unlike Lewis, Graves was quite a good player—it was the compulsion he deplored, not so much the game itself. In *Goodbye to All That*, his classic account of the war, he fondly recalled makeshift cricket matches on the western front:

> June 24, 1915 . . . This afternoon we had a cricket match, officers versus sergeants, in an enclosure between some houses out of observation from the enemy. Our front line is perhaps three quarters of a mile away. I made top score, twenty four; the bat was a bit of rafter; the ball, a piece of rag tied round with string; and the wicket, a parrot cage with the clean, dry corpse of a parrot inside. It had evidently

died of starvation when the French evacuated the town. . . . Machine gun fire broke up the match.[72]

By the end of the war, Graves, wounded and neurasthenic, had become embittered over the political folly that permitted such slaughter to continue and the pointless snobbery and class bias of his army regiment, which had worsened an already horrible situation. After the war he lived for a while at Islip, Oxfordshire, where he played soccer in the winter and cricket in the summer with the villagers. But he later "resigned because the team seldom consisted of the best eleven men available; regular players would be dropped to make room for visiting gentry," part of the same class prejudice Graves had found so intolerable in the army.[73] He eventually left England altogether to live first in Egypt, then in Majorca.

Graves's fellow infantry officer Siegfried Sassoon also used cricket to dramatic effect in his trilogy of novels about the western front, *The Memoirs of George Sherston*. In the first volume, *Memoirs of a Fox-Hunting Man*, George Sherston describes his coming of age as a rider and huntsman—and his triumphant scoring of the winning run in a village cricket match. *Memoirs of an Infantry Officer*, its sequel, places Sherston at the western front, where he tries desperately to keep despair at bay by talking of happier days with his comrades. Recalling the grueling route march to the Battle of Arras at Easter 1917, Sherston mentions that "our second-in-command (a gentle middle-aged country solicitor) was walking beside me, consoling himself with reminiscences of cricket and hunting."[74] When the battalion reached its billet, a dilapidated chateau, they found "Ormand and Dunning and one or two others . . . playing cricket with a stump and a wooden ball, using an old brazier as a wicket." For two days they waited anxiously to be sent into a battle whose overwhelming noise already surrounded them:

> In the middle of Wednesday afternoon we were having an eleven-a-side single-brazier cricket match on a flat piece of ground in the chateau garden. The sun was shining between snow showers, and most of the men were watching from the grassy bank above. One of the company Sergeant-Majors was playing a lively innings, though the ball was beginning to split badly. Then a whistle blew and the match ended abruptly. Less than an hour later the Battalion marched away from Basseux.[75]

Like his prose of the war, Sassoon's poetry often uses the image of cricket for contrast to the horrors of the fighting, as in these lines from "Dreamers":

> I see them in foul dug-outs gnawed by rats,
> And in the ruined trenches, lashed with rain,
> Dreaming of things they did with balls and bats. . . .[76]

Similarly, in *Memoirs of an Infantry Officer*, George Sherston and his company pass through the "shattered relic" of a village called St. Martin and a desolate landscape of mutilated bodies during the springtime, a season that evokes "April evenings in England and the Butley cricket field where a few of us had been having our first knock at the nets. The cricket season had begun." But here they are plunged into a "life-denying region . . . stumbling along a deep ditch to the place appointed for us in that zone of inhuman havoc."[77]

During the 1920s, a new style of nostalgic cricket fiction emerged, with novels devoted entirely to the game. These usually had rustic settings and aimed to demonstrate the organic wholesomeness of village life, with a colorful cast of golden-hearted yokels living happily under the guardianship of the benevolent local gentry. The cricket field may be partly overgrown with wildflowers, but the game itself is pure Olde England. Novels such as Hugh de Selincourt's 1924 *Cricket Match* and its 1931 sequel, *The Game of the Season*, seem self-consciously archaic in their depictions of teams that smoothly blend gentlemen and commoners, with all social distinctions forgotten for the duration of the game and all individuality merged in the team's collective identity. The rhetoric is nearly biblical in its prelapsarian tone and imagery:

> And each man, as he came on to the ground, got slowly caught up in the spirit of the game, emerging, each in his own way, from the habits of worry and care; as each man was given the chance not too frequently offered in modern life of living for a time outside himself, with a common purpose, in which he took genuine interest; and nearly every man, each in his own way, availed himself of this great, good thing, unconsciously of course, for the most part, but eagerly.[78]

In 1933, A. G. Macdonell, a Scottish writer, produced a telling satire on the game and the clichés of its literary representation. *England, Their En-*

gland follows the fortunes of a Scottish innocent, Donald Cameron, as he tries to understand and write about the English way of life, but finds each of his preconceptions affronted by the reality of postwar England. His editor, a Welshman, warns Cameron: "I've found out something about the English . . . you must never, never rag them about . . . the team spirit in cricket. You must never suggest in any sort of way that there are any individuals in cricket. It's the highest embodiment on earth of the Team."[79] However, Cameron soon discovers when he goes to a village match—played on a field of "daisies, buttercups, dandelions, vetches, thistle-down, and clumps of dark red sorrel"—that everyone is a rabid individualist and teammates never cooperate with one another; through drink, carelessness, and ineptitude, the game ends in a shambles.[80]

By coincidence, evidence of the less than wholesome reality of the first-class game emerged at the same time as Macdonell's book. A notorious series of matches between England and Australia that winter (1932–33) showed that the code of gentlemanliness was getting frayed around the edges. England's captain, D. R. Jardine, encouraged his bowler Harold Larwood to bowl fast, accurate, early-bouncing balls which would reach the batsman at head height and intimidate him into hitting easy catches to the surrounding fielders. After several Australian batsmen had been hit, and hurt, by this aggressive "bodyline" bowling—and the great Australian virtuoso of the day, Donald Bradman, had been rendered less effective than usual—the Australian Board of Control (counterpart of the MCC) sent a cable to London officially accusing the English of unsportsman-like conduct. Since there was no written rule against aiming for the batsman's head, the MCC was outraged by the accusation. The rights and wrongs of the incident—and of bodyline bowling—are still being hotly debated over sixty years later, with some writers maintaining that the English had the better team and would have won anyway, while others argue that Jardine could not bear to lose to a colonial upstart like Bradman and would have done anything, even in breach of etiquette, to defeat him.[81]

Bradman himself was a demigod to Australian cricket fans. An aspiring Australian writer then living in London, Philip Lindsay, wrote a book about Bradman and about his own reactions to the great one, whom he had never met. Recalling the desperate months in 1930 when, hoping to become a writer, he was broke and starving, Lindsay credited his survival to Bradman:

That during those months of misery I did not lose faith in myself and abandon all hope of success by writing I must thank Don Bradman. That I never made that final desperate choice between hunger and ambition and pawned my typewriter, as often the devil gnawing in my empty belly prompted me to pawn it, I must thank Don Bradman. . . . He helped to keep my faith alight, and this association of myself with him as nearly of an age and of the same country made me feel somehow that I must not let him down as he had not let me down.[82]

Australians took a zealous pride in their own expertise and style of play. The hard, hot, dry fields on which they learned cricket made the ball behave differently than it did on the soft, damp fields of England. Edmund Blunden, a leading cricket eulogist of the mid-twentieth century, noted in 1944 that "Australia once produced poets who were English poets a little out of touch," but had since perfected her own idiom. Of an eminent Australian bowler, he remarked, "O'Reilly, with ball in hand is quite the parallel of an Australian poet, territorially distinct in rhythm, passion, scheme, and transition. Within him, an experience decidedly different from even the dales or the hills of Yorkshire is for ever prompting and proposing."[83] The idea that each country's cricketers reflect the national character has since become a commonplace of cricket literature.

The Australians were not the only ones who took cricket seriously during this period. The interwar years produced a generation of superb players in New Zealand, South Africa, India, and the West Indies, while less developed British colonies, such as the Trobriand Islands, also began to take up cricket at the urging of missionaries, who encouraged them to adopt Western dress and embrace good sportsmanship along with the Gospel. They saw the game as a welcome substitute for intertribal warfare. The BBC documentary *Trobriand Cricket* (1967) has become a minor anthropological classic, showing cricket teams of up to 100 men and with such names as "The Aeroplanes" dancing their arm-waving aircraft dance before starting to bat. In *A Pattern of Islands*, Arthur Grimble, a colonial district commissioner on the Gilbert and Ellice Islands of the South Pacific, described how tribes there adapted the game to local conditions and played out intertribal feuds on the cricket field with bats and balls instead of spears and clubs.[84]

The detective fiction that Conan Doyle had popularized continued to flourish in the interwar years, reinforcing a link between cricket and murder which has remained strong up to the present.[85] Dorothy Sayers's detective, Lord Peter Wimsey, is a great cricketer who, among his many other accomplishments, once scored 200 in Oxford's first innings against Cambridge and another 200 in the second innings of the same game, just prior to World War I. In *Murder Must Advertise* (1933), Lord Peter is working at an advertising agency under the assumed name "Death Bredon" (though retaining his own Balliol College, Oxford, affiliation), secretly investigating the mysterious death (suspected murder) of an agency employee. When the agency has a summer cricket match against another company, Lord Peter reminds himself that he must play cautiously. "A quiet and unobtrusive mediocrity, he decided, must be his aim."[86] But when he is struck by a wildly bowled ball, it makes him so angry that he hits out in his old style to win the match. His batting style having betrayed his identity, Lord Peter is accosted at the end of the game by the head of the opposition's company, Mr. Brotherhood: "Pardon me—the name has just come to my recollection. Aren't you Wimsey of Balliol?" Although he denies it, only the timely arrival of Lord Peter's brother-in-law, "Parker of the Yard," prevents the detective from being exposed and his plan to foil the villains from unraveling.[87]

One of the conventions of cricket, as of baseball, is that the game means as much (or more) to its fans as it does to the players themselves. The single-mindedness of two cricket fans, Charters and Caldicott (nicely acted by Naunton Wayne and Basil Redford), plays a key role in Alfred Hitchcock's Depression-era film *The Lady Vanishes* (1938). An apparently harmless old woman (but actually a British spy) disappears from a train crossing Central Europe. The young heroine, who has been talking with her, finds that none of the other passengers will admit to having seen the old woman. Each character has a motive for denying her disappearance; the cricket fans fear that if the train is stopped, they will miss their connection and thus miss the last day of an exciting test match. They sit in the dining car reconstructing great games from the past, with a milk jug as the wicket and sugar lumps as the players, and quoting old cricket statistics to one another from *Wisden's Cricket Almanac*. When they get hold of an English-language newspaper, it is the *New York Herald–Tribune*. Charters searches the sporting columns, then tosses the paper aside in disgust: "Nothing but baseball: these Americans have got no sense of proportion!" When the heroine finally proves that the old woman has been the victim of political foul play, Charters and Caldicott stump up, showing that they are true-blue English gentlemen after all by bravely holding off a group of attacking soldiers and enabling their fellow passengers to escape with their lives. Hitchcock adds an ironic twist to the end of the film: as the two fans finally alight from the train back in England, a newsboy walks past wearing a sandwich board that reads "Test Match Canceled Due to Flooding."

Cricket's class-bound character persisted into the mid-twentieth century, but some observers felt that, by its nature, the game tended to alleviate rather than intensify class antagonisms. George Orwell, for example, who often found himself at odds with other members of the British Left, commended cricket, arguing that it was far less class-bound than tennis or golf, which "causes whole stretches of countryside to be turned into carefully guarded class preserves."[88] By contrast, said Orwell in 1944, "since [cricket] needs about twenty five people to make up a game it necessarily leads to a good deal of social mixing." Orwell loved village cricket, where the dress was informal, "where the blacksmith [was] liable to be called away in mid-innings on an urgent job, and sometimes, about the time when the light [began] to fail, a ball driven for four [would kill] a rabbit on the boundary." This moderate view was a judicious compromise between de Selincourt's sentimentalizing and Macdonell's debunking in the 1930s. Orwell, like Graves, Lewis, and other public school old boys, particularly deplored the compulsoriness of cricket (to which he too had been subjected at Eton) and regretted that "for a long period cricket was treated as though it were a kind of religious ritual incumbent on every Englishman."[89]

Orwell made these observations in the course of reviewing a tribute to the game by a man who had always loved it. As a traumatized literary survivor of the First World War, it seemed to Edmund Blunden afterward that cricket itself "had been dismayed; it did not guess in the golden days at things like world wars, or that the score-books should be splashed with the blood of the quiet men its votaries."[90] But Blunden's enthusiasm for the game soon revived as England faced the crisis of an even mightier war. Writing in the middle of World War II, when an Allied victory was still far from certain, Blunden declared that

> for the average Englishman this cricket and football and all the games and sports are the finest preparation for such military life as he may be suddenly required to lead. Mentally and physically they keep him young when those of equal years begin to age; and they help to nour-

ish in him that religious simplicity which prevails no matter how empty the churches are.[91]

He explained both the successful British military campaign against Rommel in the African desert and the Tommies' ability to accept temporary defeats (of which there were plenty) as the fruits of boyhoods devoted to cricket. The cricketer's landscape once again became what it had been for Blunden and his fellow soldiers in the Great War—both a symbol of peacetime England and a metaphor for the human condition:

> The game itself, if it is found in its natural bearings, is only the agreeable wicket-gate to a landscape of human joys and sorrows, and is greatest where it fades away most imperceptibly into their wider horizon. Glance from your post in the field, young cricketer . . . away to those farms and woods, spires and hills about you; rest your high spirits a moment on the composure of that young mother with the sleeping baby, on the old white horse as still as if he was carved in chalk on the down. One day you will seek in your mind for the scores of the match which are now so important and definite, and they will not be there—only, in place of them, the assurance of an eternal summer.[92]

Another friend of Orwell's who covered the cricket pitch was a Trotskyite from Trinidad named C. L. R. James. After arriving in England in 1932, he spent each summer of that decade writing brilliant newspaper articles about county cricket matches—and each winter agitating for West Indian independence and a world revolution. James persuaded Virginia and Leonard Woolf to publish *The Case for West Indian Self-Government*, which their Hogarth Press brought out in 1933, and he made passionate anticolonialist speeches at meetings of the Independent Labour Party. Frederic Warburg, founder of Secker and Warburg and publisher of James's 1937 Trotskyite manifesto, *World Revolution*, recalled the young writer (and cricketer) in his autobiography:

> He wrote splendid articles on county matches for the *Manchester Guardian* during the summer. Indeed, it was only between April and October that he was in funds. Sometimes he came for the weekend to our cottage near West Hoathly in Sussex and turned out for the local team. He was a demon bowler, and a powerful if erratic batsman. The

village loved him, referring to him affectionately as the "black bastard."[93]

James's own autobiography, *Beyond a Boundary*, which I believe to be
the finest cricket book ever written, shows how important the game was
to him. As a boy growing up in Trinidad at the beginning of the century,
he had loved cricket, only later recognizing its links to the racism and imperialism he so deplored. In Trinidad there was a hierarchy of first-class
teams based on class and skin color. "Here began my personal calvary,"
says James, recalling his dilemma over which team to join. "The British tradition soaked deep into me was that when you entered the sporting arena
you left behind you the sordid compromises of everyday existence. Yet for
us to do that we would have had to divest ourselves of our skins."[94] The
British code of fair play and impartiality which he had learned as a cricketer, James added, enabled him to recognize that British imperialism and
its adjuncts were unjust. Cricket thus remained for him a source of liberation, and he explicitly criticized Marx and Trotsky (whom he otherwise
revered) for seeing sports as opiates rather than as resources that could be
deployed against oppression.[95]

Cricket was an art of the first order for James, and he did not hesitate to
draw analogies between champion cricketers and the greatest musicians
or dancers, nor to fortify his arguments with references to Bernard Beren-
son's theories of aesthetics. Like John Nyren and Edmund Blunden before
him, however, James believed that he lived in an age of lesser mortals
than the great cricketers of yesteryear. Thus his chapter on W. G. Grace
is pure hagiography, while his treatment of the "bodyline bowling" controversy of the 1930s casts the English cricketers as counterparts of the
totalitarian rulers whose shadow fell across the world in that same decade.
Like all the best Marxists, he applied an unsparing analytical rigor to every
issue he took up, linking each of them to the general crisis of society. The
unsportsman-like first-class cricket of the 1930s seemed to him a harbinger of the world war that would ensue, and he warned of what it boded for
the future: "It cannot get much darker without becoming night impene-
trable."[96]

English first-class cricket was suspended during the Second World War but
resumed in its aftermath. Cricket literature resumed too, with many of its

old motifs intact, but it also began to reflect the dramatic social changes occurring in English life. A cross-class cricket match plays a central role in *The Go-Between*, L. P. Hartley's popular postwar novel in which class prejudice figures powerfully.[97] Its narrator recalls in 1952 events that occurred during the Boer War era fifty years before, when beautiful Miriam Maudsley, a nouveau riche banker's daughter, became engaged to Lord Trimingham while having a passionate, clandestine love affair with Ted Burgess, a local farmer. Narrated by Leo Colston, a thirteen-year-old guest at the Trimingham estate who becomes the lovers' confidant and go-between, the affair is filtered through the postwar lens that Colston has acquired in the intervening fifty years. He depicts himself back then as a young prig, sharing the upper-class values of his hosts.

When a cricket match is arranged between the Trimingham estate and the local village, whose star player is Ted Burgess, young Leo's support at first goes entirely to the Trimingham team, a loyalty to the estate that others, ironically, share: "I remember how class distinctions melted away and how the butler, the footman, the coachman, the gardener and the pantry boy seemed completely on an equality with us."[98] Seeing how shabby the villagers look beside the smartly flanneled estate team, Leo is "distressed by their nondescript appearance" and concludes that those who are not properly dressed for a game cannot possibly win it. But the villagers play well, and, suddenly recalling how the ragtag Boers have been humiliating English regulars in South Africa, Leo imagines that he is witnessing a symbolic replay of the war, making this cricket match an augury of social revolution, with the lower classes overturning their betters. "It was shocking—these Boers, in their motley raiment, triumphantly throwing the ball into the air after each kill! How I disliked them! The spectators on the boundary, standing, sitting, lying, or propped against trees, I imagined to be animated by a revolutionary spirit and reveling in the downfall of their betters."[99] The only estate batsman to do well is Mr. Maudsley, Miriam's banker-father, "a wizened individual with a stringy neck and creaking joints," over fifty years old, who "by dint of headwork and superior cunning" scores fifty runs and saves the estate team from disaster. When the village team bats and Ted Burgess also scores fifty runs, Leo again attaches symbolic importance to the display:

> It was a very different fifty from Mr. Maudsley's, a triumph of luck, not of cunning. . . . Dimly I felt that the contrast represented some-

thing more than the conflict between Hall and village. It was that, but it was also a struggle between order and lawlessness, between obedience to tradition and defiance of it, between social stability and revolution, between one attitude to life and another. I knew which side I was on, yet the traitor within my gates was not so sure.[100]

By an ironic turn of events, Leo has to substitute for an injured estate fielder, and at the decisive moment he catches a ball hit by Ted Burgess, achieving a last-minute victory for the Trimingham team. He is exuberant, flattered by the adults' praise, "but I was uneasily aware of one separate element that had not quite fused in the general concourse of passions; the pang of sharp regret, sharp as a sword-thrust, that had accompanied the catch."[101] The novel ends with farmer Ted's suicide after he and Miriam have been caught making love near the Hall, an event that the older Leo relates to the unfulfilled promise of the twentieth century, of which he had had such high hopes at its outset when he was thirteen. (A terrific film version of *The Go-Between* was made in 1971, in which Alan Bates smolders with earthy vitality as Ted Burgess and Julie Christie dazzles him as the ambitious, lustful Miriam. The cricket scene, very well made, captures the spirit of the village-level game as well as the class tensions of the novel and of turn-of-the-century England.)

Imagine the tensions of this cricket scene made all the more acute not just by an illicit cross-class love affair, but by a cross-class homosexual relationship, and you have E. M. Forster's *Maurice* (written in 1913 but not published until 1971). Although Forster had been bullied at school and disliked games, here he tried to show that cricket could become a bridge across the gulf created by repressive social and sexual conventions. Maurice, a Cambridge undergraduate, falls in love with a more highborn fellow student, Clive Durham, and for three years they enjoy a chastely homosexual romance. Then Clive decides that, having matured beyond homosexuality, he will marry and become a conventional pillar of society. When Maurice later goes to Clive's estate, he finds that his former lover has become a conservative country squire, determined to forget his early indiscretions and eager to enter local politics. Maurice is himself a young snob, but even so he falls in love with Alec Scudder, a gamekeeper on Clive's estate (in a kind of gay foreshadowing of *Lady Chatterley's Lover*). While the combined forces of class prejudice and homosexual taboo seem certain to keep Maurice and Alec apart, after a night of passion they find themselves together again on the cricket field. But "Maurice hated cricket. It demanded a snickety neatness he could not supply; and . . . he disliked playing with his social inferiors. . . . In cricket he might be bowled or punished by some lout, and he felt it unsuitable."[102] Finding himself secretly allied with exactly the kind of man he once deplored, then, Maurice's batting partnership with Alec takes on an acute erotic charge and becomes a symbol of their dilemma in the world:

> Abandoning caution [Alec] swiped the ball into the fern. Lifting his eyes he met Maurice's and smiled. Lost ball. Next time he hit a boundary. . . . Maurice's mind had cleared, and he felt that they were against the whole world, that not only Mr. Borenius [the interfering village vicar] and the field, but the audience in the shed and all England were closing round the wickets. They played for the sake of each other and of their fragile relationship—if one fell the other would follow. They intended no harm to the world but so long as it attacked they must punish, they must stand wary, then hit with full strength, they must show that when two are gathered together majorities shall not triumph.[103]

Forster gave the novel an unexpectedly happy ending, with Alec and Maurice achieving the partnership promised by their alliance on the field of play. Ironically, though, Forster knew that *Maurice* could not possibly be published in the intolerant England of 1913, and it was not released until after his death, in 1971—a delay which seemed to make the successful union it posits all the more improbable.

The emergence of the working-class novel in the 1950s changed the character of English fiction. Although England's Angry Young Men were less inclined than their middle-class elders to dwell upon the game as an exhibition of manliness and character, cricket nevertheless played an occasional role in the scene-setting and mood of their work. In William Cooper's *Scenes from Provincial Life*, for example (which some critics now see as the harbinger of the working-class novel), the cynical narrator, Joe Lunn, recounts his duties as a schoolmaster in a poor, urban, provincial neighborhood: "In a feeble effort to compensate for deficiency of social cachet, the headmaster insisted on the boys wearing white flannels whenever they went to the field in the summer term. It was about the only rule they kept, and they looked surprisingly presentable as a consequence." Only from a distance, however—as one boy approaches Lunn, he sees that "the green of his blazer was echoed in the greyish colour of his skin" and that "his hair was dripping with brilliantine."[104] Four years later, Kingsley Amis published *Lucky Jim*, the story of Jim Dixon, a history professor in petty rebellion against his way of life and the tradition of "Merrie Olde England" he is expected to sustain. Dixon is far too lazy and unhealthy to play games of any kind, but at one point, driving along with his hated boss, Professor Welch, he witnesses a telling pair of scenes: first, a grossly overweight barber leers at two young girls, then "another big fat man," playing cricket, is hit by the ball and doubles over in pain. "Uncertain whether this pair of vignettes was designed to illustrate the swiftness of divine retribution or its tendency to mistake its target," says the narrator, "Dixon was quite sure that he felt in some way overwhelmed."[105] The etiquette of cricket hardly applies in Dixon's dismal world—only its power to hit, and hurt.

The class rigidities of the game relaxed at about the same rate as the class rigidities in English society as a whole, which is to say very slowly indeed. At the end of the Second World War, "gentlemen" and "players" on the same county teams still had separate dressing rooms and left the ground through different exits. In a short story from the 1950s, "Not 'Arf a Blooming Game," John Arlott (himself a fine player) describes the dilemma of George Kennett, an aging cricket professional in imminent danger of being dropped from his team after a run of bad luck. Kennett thinks of his gentleman-captain, K. E. Tallis, as a "blasted snob" with "a Napoleonic air which each of the pros, in his different way, resented."[106] For his part, Tallis ("Mr. Tallis" to the professionals) finds Kennett too crude to understand the finer points of the game: "The trouble with these fellows was that they could never appreciate the decent tradition in the game. Look at him [Kennett] now, gulping cold tea like a navvy: and why didn't the scruffy devil change his socks when he came in after a day's fielding?"[107] As the story develops, each man finds the other's contribution to the team indispensable, but their truce across class lines is always grudging and tenuous. William Godfrey's *Friendly Game*, on the other hand, links class tensions to the rural–urban antagonisms of the 1950s. A country village has had a large factory built at its edge, along with an ugly public housing estate (adjacent to the village's old rustic dwellings) to accommodate the unwelcome urban workers imported for the factory. The village cricket team, led by Colonel "Squire" Holt, represents the old order of the Tory countryside and bitterly resents the proletarian ways of the newcomers, led by an argumentative Socialist councilman, Ron Bates. But Bates and his factory lads are good cricketers too, and the novel's climax is a "friendly" match between the two teams which brings the antagonism into sharp focus. As each team plays its best, it comes reluctantly to respect the other. A foreign visitor, seeing cricket for the first time, asks his friend the vicar, "The cricket match— it has brought unity where there was strife?" "Hardly that," answers the clergyman, "but it's forced them to look each other in the face. And, wonderful to relate, each finds the other human."[108] *The Friendly Game* is clearly biased toward the old order, and it draws to a bittersweet close, drenched in nostalgia for great days never to be seen again. Colonel Holt, the mouthpiece for this order, sees the cricket field not only as a force that binds the villagers, but also as one that binds the present to the past: "The field belonged not only to him, and to the village. It belonged to the past, to the ghosts who had played and watched here in summers long dead."[109]

By the 1960s most of the English county teams were impoverished. In order to meet expenses, they reluctantly accepted sponsorship from tobacco and insurance companies. They also boosted their leisurely three-day game schedule with a series of fast-scoring, crowd-pleasing, one-innings games on Sundays. For the first time ordinary working people could watch an entire first-class game rather than just the Saturday segment of it. The last Gentlemen–Players game took place in 1962. Cricket's commercialization has progressed, seemingly irrevocably, since then, although the players are still far less well paid than their American counterparts in major league baseball. Most teams today wear commercial logos on their flannels, and international "test matches" in England have "Cornhill Insurance" painted right onto the turf behind the wickets. The gentleman/player dichotomy is still not quite extinct, although all first-class players are now paid. Among the recent captains of the England team, for example, were David Gower, alumnus of one of the most prestigious public schools—Kings, Canterbury—and Ian Botham, from a working-class family in Somerset. But, to honor another old tradition, Botham, a prodigy to rival or even exceed W. G. Grace, turned out to be the greater player.

While the standard of play remains exceedingly high, the genteel code which restrained cricket's potential violence has continued to erode. Bodyline bowling persisted, and the repertoire of all fast bowlers now includes "bouncers" or "bumpers"—to which the alert batsman reacts by ducking and letting it sail over his helmeted head. (The batting helmet accordingly became necessary two decades ago.) As Dennis Lillee, a swaggering Australian fast bowler of the 1970s, revealingly stated, "I try to hit a batsman in the rib-cage when I bowl a purposeful bouncer and I want it to hurt so much that the batsman doesn't want to face me any more."[110]

Cricket has proved a potent scene-setter and symbolic device in English literature of many different genres for over a century, and it can even be found in science fiction now. Douglas Adams made cricket central to *Life, the Universe, and Everything*, his comic SF novel of 1982, and cleared up, at least to his own satisfaction, the mystery of the game's origins. Here, the sports-loving inhabitants of the planet Krikkit, far out on the galactic perimeter, discover by chance that they are not alone in the universe. Unable to accept the presence of other beings, they set about building a race of lethal, all-white robots armed with laser bats, with which they hit round, red nuclear bombs that can annihilate entire solar systems. The galaxy fights back, and after millions of deaths Krikkit is quarantined, permanently surrounded by a "slo-time" lock that can be opened only with a key shaped like three wickets and two bails. Chance historical circumstances lead to the war's commemoration billions of miles and millions of years later:

> "The game you know as cricket," Slartibartfast said, and his voice still seemed to be wandering, lost in subterranean passages, "is just one of those curious freaks of racial memory that can keep images alive in the mind eons after their true significance has been lost in the mists of time. Of all the races in the Galaxy, only the English could possibly revive the memory of the most horrific wars ever to sunder the Universe and transform it into what I'm afraid is generally regarded as an incomprehensibly dull and pointless game."[111]

More to the point, however, the Krikkit robots have escaped and are in the process of gathering the steel wicket, the wooden wicket, the plastic wicket, the "Golden bail of prosperity and the Silver Bail of Peace" that will set their planet free.[112] But due to the extremely inaccurate bowling of geeky Arthur Dent, the novel's hero, when he faces one of the batting robots at Lord's in the novel's climactic scene, the universe is saved. Here, as in Kipling's *Stalky and Co.*, the anti-cricket forces win the day.

Cricket writing still flourishes in England, most of it beset by a nagging sense of nostalgia that makes Adams's satire all the more refreshing. Ever since John Nyren established the cricket lament over 150 years ago, English writers have bemoaned the great days of yore—and nevermore—linking the irretrievable past to a lost England of sterling character in a golden summer. Anyone who sat through Ken Burns's great baseball elegy will be familiar with an American version of this idiom. So let me conclude my own piece of cricket writing by declaring that the golden age of cricket is right now. The quality of play is as high as, or higher than, ever, for it was only in 1994 that a West Indian batsman, Brian Lara of Trinidad, pulled off two of the greatest accomplishments in the entire history of the game. That spring, in the final game of the England team's West Indies tour, at Antigua, Lara scored 375 runs in one innings, the highest score ever achieved in an international match. He then crossed the Atlantic, having already agreed to spend that summer playing for the English county team of Warwickshire. With them, from the fifth to the sixth of June at the Edgbaston ground in Birmingham, Lara became the first man ever to score over 500 runs in a single innings. Hitting at a rate of over one run per minute, he scored 62 fours, 10 sixes, and 390 runs, all on the second day, enabling his team to declare with a total of 810 runs. Lara achieved these dazzling feats at the age of only twenty-five, and judging by the lives and careers of the game's other "greats," he can look forward to perhaps another twenty years of first-class play, well into the twenty-first century. Here surely is cause to think that the game's greatest days are by no means lost and gone—and that its literary possibilities are far from exhausted.

Notes

Thanks to the friends and colleagues who suggested likely sources, read drafts, and helped me with picture research: Catherine Bennett, Jim Fisher, Fraser Harbutt, Kate Joyce, Harry Rusche, Randall Strahan, and Tom Lancaster.

 1 Christopher Brookes, *English Cricket: The Game and Its Players Through the Ages* (London, 1978), 21.

 2 John Dance, "Cricket: An Heroic Poem," in *Sporting Literature: An Anthology*, ed. Vernon Scannell (Oxford, 1987), 227.

 3 See Christopher Hibbert, *The English: A Social History, 1066–1945* (New York, 1987), 370–71.

 4 Quoted in Roy Porter, *English Society in the Eighteenth Century* (London, 1982), 254.

 5 John Nyren, *The Young Cricketer's Tutor*; quoted in Edmund Blunden, *Cricket Country* (London, 1944), 114.

 6 Nyren, *Young Cricketer's Tutor*; quoted in Brookes, *English Cricket*, 57.

7   Pierce Egan, "John Small, 1737–1826"; quoted in Scannell, ed., *Sporting Literature*, 229.

8   George Gordon, Lord Byron, "Childish Recollections," in *The Complete Poetical Works*, ed. Jerome McGann (Oxford, 1980), 1: 166.

9   *The Letters of John Keats*, ed. Hyder Rollins (Cambridge, 1958), 2: 78.

10 Jane Austen, *Northanger Abbey* (London, 1978 [1818]), 37, 39. The reference to "base ball" may provide a clue to the English origins of the American game, but Austen does not elaborate.

11 Mary Russell Mitford, *Our Village* (London, 1893 [1824]), 168–71.

12 Mary Mitford, "A Country Cricket Match," in *Sketches of English Life and Character* (Edinburgh, 1909 [c. 1830]), 18–34.

13 Charles Dickens, *The Posthumous Papers of the Pickwick Club* (New York, 1952 [1837]), 87–95.

14 Quoted in Blunden, *Cricket Country*, 77.

15 See Norman Mackenzie and Jeanne Mackenzie, *H. G. Wells: A Biography* (New York, 1973), 6–14. Later in life, Joseph Wells became a small and unsuccessful shopkeeper who sold cricket bats and balls.

16 G. B. Shaw, *Three Plays for Puritans* (London, 1930), x.

17 [Thomas Hughes], *Tom Brown's Schooldays* "by An Old Boy" (London, 1896 [1857]), 281–300.

18 James Walvin, *Leisure and Society, 1830–1950* (London, 1978), 85.

19 Quoted in Peter Bailey, *Leisure and Class in Victorian England: Rational Recreation and the Contest for Control, 1830–1885* (London, 1978), 128.

20 Walvin, *Leisure and Society*, 87.

21 George M. Trevelyan, *English Social History: A Survey of Six Centuries, Chaucer to Queen Victoria* (London, 1942), 408.

22 Lewis Carroll, "The Deserted Parks," in *The Nonesuch Lewis Carroll*, ed. Alexander Woollcott (London, 1989), 823–24.

23 Benny Green, *A History of Cricket* (London, 1988), 193.

24 Henry Newbolt, "Vitae Lampada," in Scannell, ed., *Sporting Literature*, 243–44.

25 Sir Henry Newbolt (1862–1938) wrote his poem just before the ugly Boer War knocked some of the romance out of colonial soldiering, and well before the First World War extinguished the remainder. Newbolt himself came to regret having penned this, his most famous, poem; see Vanessa Furse Jackson, *The Poetry of Henry Newbolt* (Greensboro, NC, 1994), 79–85. To the generation disillusioned by World War I, Newbolt symbolized all the sham of Victorianism; see Paul Fussell, *The Great War and Modern Memory* (New York, 1975), 25–26.

26 Quoted in Green, *History of Cricket*, 121.

27 Legends of the origin of the Ashes tradition vary; see Roland Bowen, *Cricket: A History of Its Growth and Development Throughout the World* (London, 1970), 125–27.

28 See George B. Kirsch, *The Creation of American Team Sports: Baseball and Cricket, 1838–1872* (Urbana, 1989).

29 See R. A. Fitzgerald, *Wickets in the West, or The Twelve in America* (London, 1873). This weird book, written by one of the England players, is an account of the team's 1872 tour of the United States and Canada.

30 See Bowen, *Cricket*, 159.

31 Norman Gale, "England v. Australia," in *Cricket Songs* (London, 1894), 59. (The poem is a parody of "The Minstrel Boy to the Wars Is Gone.")

32 Bowen, *Cricket*, 123; see also Robert Brooke, *The Tragedy of W. R. Gilbert* (London, 1984).

33 Quoted in Green, *History of Cricket*, 80.

34 T. G. Vaidyanathan, "The Batting Prince," *Deccan Herald*, 14 September 1983; quoted in Ashis Nandy, *The Tao of Cricket* (New Delhi, 1989), 66.

35 Quoted in Green, *History of Cricket*, 161.

36 John Masters, *The Ravi Lancers* (Garden City, NY, 1972).

37 Neville Cardus, *English Cricket* (London, 1948), 36–37.

38 Quoted in Nandy, *Tao of Cricket*, 62.

39 Ibid., 7.

40 Ibid., 74–76.

41 Ivar Oxaal, *Black Intellectuals Come to Power: The Rise of Creole Nationalism in Trinidad and Tobago* (Cambridge, MA, 1968), 62.

42 See C. L. R. James, *Beyond a Boundary* (New York, 1983 [1963]), 78–79.

43 Oxaal, *Black Intellectuals Come to Power*, 63.

44 See Arthur Conan Doyle, "A Reminiscence of Cricket" (1895), in Scannell, ed., *Sporting Literature*, 239–41.

45 Arthur Conan Doyle, *Memories and Adventures* (Garden City, NY, 1930), 314–15.

46 See Charles Higham, *The Adventures of Conan Doyle* (New York, 1976), 29–30, 98, 105.

47 David Rayvern Allen, *Peter Pan and Cricket* (London, 1988).

48 Ibid., 69.

49 Ibid., 63–67.

50 G. D. Martineau, "Six and Out," in Scannell, ed., *Sporting Literature*, 244. As a boy in the 1960s, I played on a steeply sloping street, Hardwick Drive, in my home village of Mickleover, Derbyshire. In place of three wooden stumps we used the grass-box of a lawn mower standing on end, bowled with a tennis ball, and tried not to hit it into un-friendly neighbors' front yards. Every time a car turned into the street (about once every five minutes), we had to scatter to the sides, scooping up our mower box along the way.

51 See H. S. Altham and E. W. Swanton, *A History of Cricket*, 3d ed. (London, 1947), 66.

52 Norman Gale, "A Tomboy," in *Cricket Songs*, 23–24.

53 Mary Cadogan and Patricia Craig, *You're a Brick, Angela: A New Look at Girls' Fiction from 1839 to 1975* (London, 1976), 198.

54 See "Women's Cricket," in *The Oxford Companion to World Sports and Games*, ed. John Arlott (London, 1975), 213–14; and Green, *History of Cricket*, 32.

55 P. G. Wodehouse, *Mike and Psmith* (1908), in *The World of Psmith* (London, 1974), 37.

56 Ibid., 52.

57 E. W. Hornung, *The Amateur Cracksman* (New York, 1899), 77–78.

58 Ibid., 79.

59 Ibid., 87.

60 Ibid., 13.

61 Leonard Woolf, *Sowing: An Autobiography of the Years 1880 to 1904* (New York, 1960), 64.

62 Ibid., 65.

63 Rudyard Kipling, *Stalky and Co.* (Garden City, NY, 1922 [1899]), 76.

64 Alec Waugh, *The Loom of Youth* (New York, 1916).

65 Ibid., 320. The controversy surrounding the book is described by Martin Stannard, *Evelyn Waugh: The Early Years, 1903–1939* (London, 1986), 41–46.

66 Ibid., 334.

67 C. S. Lewis, *Surprised by Joy: The Shape of My Early Life* (New York, 1955).

68 Ibid., 96.

69 Ibid., 97–98.

70 Ibid., 188.

71 Robert Graves, *Goodbye to All That* (Garden City, NY, 1957 [1929]), 55. Graves was a foe of school tradition in general, but realized that a position opposing all sports would win him no support. Instead, he campaigned for tennis as an alternative to cricket not because he cared for tennis, but because it seemed more likely to carry the day, especially after world tennis champion Anthony Wilding, a Charterhouse old boy, wrote a letter in support of Graves's campaign.

72 Ibid., 116. On the trustworthiness of Graves as a historian, however, see Fussell, *Great War and Modern Memory*, 203–20.

73 Graves, *Goodbye to All That*, 313.

74 Siegfried Sassoon, *Memoirs of an Infantry Officer*, in *The Memoirs of George Sherston* (New York, 1937), 193.

75 Ibid., 198–99.

76 Siegfried Sassoon, "Dreamers," in *Collected Poems: 1908–1956* (London, 1961), 71–72; quotation from 72.

77 Sassoon, *Memoirs of an Infantry Officer*, 207, 209.

78 Hugh de Selincourt, *The Cricket Match* (London, 1924), 94.

79 A. G. Macdonell, *England, Their England* (London, 1933), 48. The novel was dedicated to a London editor, J. C. Squire, who led a team of enthusiastic authors in amateur cricket matches every summer of the interwar years. On Squire's life, work, and cricket, see Alec Waugh, "Two Poet Cricketers," in *My Brother Evelyn and Other Profiles* (London, 1967), 141–61.

80 Macdonell, *England*, 104–24.

81 See, for example, Altham and Swanton, *History of Cricket*, 336–37, defending the England team; and Green, *History of Cricket*, 237–38, criticizing them.

82 Philip Lindsay, *I'd Live the Same Life Over* (Melbourne, 1941); quoted in James, *Beyond a Boundary*, 99.

83 Blunden, *Cricket Country*, 80.

84 Arthur Grimble, *A Pattern of Islands* (London, 1952). The U.S. edition (New York, 1952) was retitled *We Chose the Islands*. I read and enjoyed this book as a boy. Returning to it for the first time in twenty-five years, and on a different continent, I was dismayed to discover that the American edition omits the chapter on cricket altogether. This omission was presumably made because the tribes' modifications of cricket, humorously described by Grimble and startling to English readers familiar with the game, would have needed too much explanation to remain entertaining on this side of the Atlantic. Films, too, are sometimes cut in different versions for British and American audiences.

For example, when I first saw *Chariots of Fire* in England, it included a scene in which the Olympic athletes played cricket on the cross-channel ferry as they traveled to Paris for the games, but when I later saw the American version, I found that the scene had been deleted and other scenes inserted to emphasize the friendly rivalry between the English and American athletes.

Perhaps this is the place to mention the difficulties of researching and writing about cricket with only the resources of an American university library, even a good one like Emory's. After having combed the library and interlibrary loan for biographical information on English authors, trying to find out which of the "greats" had played or enjoyed cricket, I concluded that today a large percentage of these biographies are written by Americans who often mention an author's interest in cricket, but, not knowing the game themselves, skim over it hastily rather than savoring it!

85 See, for example, Denzil Batchelor, *The Test Match Murder* (Sydney, 1936); Vicars Bell, *Death Has Two Doors* (London, 1950); Douglas Clark, *The Libertines* (London, 1978); Ted Dexter and Clifford Makins, *Testkill* (London, 1976); and Elizabeth George, *Playing for the Ashes* (New York, 1994).

86 Dorothy Sayers, *Murder Must Advertise* (New York, 1967 [1933]), 253–54.

87 Ibid., 257, 260.

88 George Orwell, review of Edmund Blunden's *Cricket Country*, in *As I Please*, Vol. 3 of *The Collected Essays, Journalism and Letters of George Orwell*, ed. Sonia Orwell and Ian Angus (London, 1968), 47–50; quotation from 48.

89 Ibid., 47, 49.

90 Blunden, *Cricket Country*, 82.

91 Ibid.

92 Ibid., 20.

93 Frederic Warburg, *An Occupation for Gentlemen* (London, 1959), 215.

94 James, *Beyond a Boundary*, 72.

95 Ibid., 149–56 ("What Do Men Live By?").

96 Ibid., 190.

97 L. P. Hartley, *The Go-Between* (New York, 1954 [1953]).

98 Ibid., 135–36.

99 Ibid., 141–42.

100 Ibid., 147.

101 Ibid., 152.

102 E. M. Forster, *Maurice* (London, 1971), 186.

103 Ibid., 186–87. The "new" Forster novel was a literary event much discussed in London at the time, but most reviewers found it unsatisfactory from a literary point of view. "The cricket match at Clive's country house," wrote C. P. Snow, "is the most absurd and incomprehensible since [Dickens's] Dingley Dell"; see *E. M. Forster: The Critical Heritage*, ed. Philip Gardner (London, 1973), 435.

104 William Cooper, *Scenes from Provincial Life* (New York, 1984 [1950]), 53–54.

105 Kingsley Amis, *Lucky Jim* (New York, 1979 [1954]), 177.

106 John Arlott, "Not 'Arf a Blooming Game" (1953), in *Best Cricket Stories*, ed. Denzil Batchelor (London, 1967), 21–44; quotation from 25.

107 Ibid., 39.

108 William Godfrey, *The Friendly Game* (London, 1957), 92.

109 Ibid., 239.

110 Quoted in Nandy, *Tao of Cricket*, 38–39.

111 Douglas Adams, *Life, the Universe, and Everything* (New York, 1982), 86. Thanks to Nick Proctor for alerting me to this novel.

112 Ibid., 62.

Stephen Rachman

It Isn't Easy Being Green

I came to the Midwest knowing of it mainly through the names and shapes of places on the map or the novels of Cather, Garland, and Fitzgerald, through the Kansas of Dorothy and the Minnesota of *Prairie Home Companion*, through the Midwestern cities where the old *Bob Newhart* and *Mary Tyler Moore* TV shows were set. I was too small when we moved away to remember much about Minneapolis, and, after my family settled in Massachusetts, the Midwest basically became a region that I flew over or drove through on my way to someplace else. But experience has a way of disabusing us of the insidious assumptions we make about places we have never really seen or lived in, about jobs we are about to begin, about journeys we are about to take—about who we are—and so it was when I got my first job at Michigan State University. My Middle West proved to be neither amber waves of grain nor windy prairies, neither remote Scandinavian enclaves nor the quaint and frosty holiday towns of Wisconsin that Nick Carraway celebrated; my Middle West rises out of the swamps of central Michigan, the strips of convenient shopping centers, and the Spartan green of the Big Ten.

The *South Atlantic Quarterly* 95:2, Spring 1996.
Copyright © 1996 by Duke University Press.
CCC 0038-2876/96/$1.50.

The land around East Lansing is low, green, lush, and muddy, parceled into farms and little lakes and lots of northern trees—beech, maple, oak, and pine. A ten-minute bike ride from town in any direction brings you into the eccentric countryside. Here, tract housing neighbors on an oddball ranch with cow skulls on its gate. Hunters convene to shoot skeet and game next to an arts-and-crafts commune. A stretch of trailers, ticky-tacky yard sales, Christian lawn statuary, and rusting automotive projects is punctuated by a druidical arrangement of half-buried tires. A monotonous vista of golden-brown fields and well-maintained silos is sometimes disturbed by the bobbing heads of a flock of emu, the practical whimsy of a farmer–poet. The landscape veers between the semirural and the semisuburban, with dirt roads leading to ranch houses that sport patios and swimming pools. There are pockets of hidden wealth and pockets of hidden poverty, satellite dishes and deer that come out of the mist like lost patrols of Confederate soldiers.

A small shopping center, a post office, and a superette at a crossroads make a little town. On Sunday afternoons the cars steadily pull in and out of the sandy parking lot of the superette every two minutes or so. It sells soft drinks, beer and wine, convenience food, quarts of milk, vegetables, some fruit, a wide selection of gum and candy, and videos. The magazine rack carries the usual national ones plus UFO rags, *Muscle & Fitness, Car & Driver, Guns & Ammo, Weapons & Guns* (for law-enforcement officers). There are business cards on the counter: "deer skinned and ground." An enormous woman buys two six-packs of Bud talls, throws one into the back of her station wagon, and puts the other on the front seat for the ride home. Her tires and fenders are coated with a reddish sand. The land is green and lovely even in late October, but the earth is brown and there are many unpaved roads. Michigan has more unpaved roads than you might imagine—they thrive between its highways. There is an abundance of nature here, much hard water (and, consequently, a good many Culligan men), millions of frogs, slightly fewer intelligent-looking black squirrels, and too much roadkill. Still, it is a pleasure to breathe in the smell of pine needles and decomposing leaves and to look into woodland pools of blue and green.

Out in the country you would scarcely know that you were ten minutes from the strip of Little Caesar's, Subway, and other fast-food joints catering to the throngs of students in East Lansing; or that East Lansing is a suburb of Lansing, the state capital, which is itself a suburb of the universe.

Lansing has an eerie, existential quality that makes the natural world, in all its luxuriance, seem remote and insupportable. Like Hartford, Albany, Trenton, or any other small urban capital, Lansing abides in its diminished stature, the seat of government alone, no longer a center of industry, culture, or life (if it ever was). Like an ashtray you might empty at 3:00 A.M. after a party, Lansing seems all too real. It feels deserted. The onion dome of the capitol building, the cigarette-like smokestacks of the power plant, and a few towers form the skeleton of a skyline. With little or no verticality, the city sprawls like a large parking lot; it meanders like the Grand River that runs through it. While it is probably not all that dirty, it has the gritty integrity of pollution.

East Lansing is, as the signs welcoming us to town say, the home of Michigan State University and the Michigan State Spartans. It sits poised between the underpopulated parking lot of Lansing and the teeming fields of the outlying area. Founded in 1855 as the Michigan Agricultural College and made a land-grant college by the Morrill Act of 1863, the school became Michigan State College in the 1920s and in 1955 acquired its present name in recognition of how John Hannah, a chicken farmer and the college's president, had transformed the place after World War II into a big-time state university. The campus still reflects this agrarian legacy and the natural beauty of the farms of Michigan. Bounded by roads—not walls or buildings—it is laid out like a series of farms or a park. The smell of manure wafts from its fields, gracing all. While there is hardly a quadrangle to be found, there is a dairy store, as well as canola research fields and impressive horticultural gardens. The campus is all curving roads, roundabouts, bike paths, and fields. People are friendly here, but they find it difficult to give directions with everything so diffuse. A friend of mine once suggested that parts of the Midwest lack focus, and one look at Lansing or the MSU campus confirms this. There may very well be a relationship between friendliness and this lack of focus. It is a commonplace that people are friendlier in the Midwest, and my experience tells me this is more or less true. The people here are superficially friendlier: they smile more; they wave more; they are more likely to make eye contact without mugging you. In New York, to prove by counterexample, there is a superabundance of focus and the people are superficially unfriendly.

A few campus buildings echo Oxonian architecture, but many others have the brick-and-green-glass functionalism of the 1950s and 1960s.

Figure 1. Sparty statue. Photograph by Bruce A. Fox, courtesy of Michigan State University.

Figure 2. Sparty logo. Courtesy of Michigan State University.

Beaumont Tower, which decorates a slope in the center of the north side of campus, is in the Yale Gothic style. A freestanding bell tower that rings out on the quarter hour, it has its own society to preserve and maintain it. It is a pleasant-looking structure, but its purpose remains elusive. It is a timepiece without a fob or a campanile that seems to have lost its church. Perhaps the whole campus—the whole institution—is intended to be its church, but this is obscure because there is another, more potent cathedral that dominates the campus: Spartan Stadium. As in most Big Ten institutions, as in most of America, sports are at the heart of everything, and at the heart of this campus stands a golden idol of sports, Sparty (Figure 1), a crewcut idealization of the male MSU athlete. Jutting his smooth, hairless chest and proud Aryan features (though oddly emasculated by his bronze gym shorts), Sparty is a beloved embarrassment, a prime piece of Third Reich artwork around which alumnae wedding parties still gather for photo opps. The cartoon version of Sparty (Figure 2) is more interesting: his bulging eye and three-day growth of stubble evoke the heartiness of a GI. The stadium over which Sparty presides can hold more than 70,000 spectators, and on Saturday afternoons in the fall when the Spartans are at home it usually does, testifying to either the power of football or the fact that there is nothing else to do. The faithful, wearing their green and white school colors, tailgate in the parking lots, eating bratwurst and wieners, drinking beer and pop, until, at the appointed hour, they stream into their Saturday church, armed with their foam seat cushions and stadium blankets, to pray and wail and roar for victory. "Go State!" they cheer. How odd to hear that generic term "State." Wally Cleaver went to State—the non-brand-name higher education experience—and here, too, they root for the genre. "Goah Staaaate!" the flat Midwestern accent drawing it out. "Go Green! Go White!"

Or "Red" or "Maroon" or "Crimson" or "Blue," or any monolithic school color that stands for God and Country. In this respect MSU is no different than any other Big Ten university, and the Spartans are like any big-time college football team/cult. I have been in Madison, Wisconsin, on a homecoming weekend and seen the same blanket of colors. Badgers versus Golden Gophers, Spartans versus Wolverines—the same mighty contests of rodents, weasels, and ancient warriors. The same Golden Horde of hired students parades through the same streets atop a fire engine painted black and gold, urging all in sight to celebrate the annual rivalry with Miller Genuine Draft. The same alumni stand around on the patchy lawns of the same fraternities while the current brotherhood paints their faces with the school colors or tosses a ball around. The same wild men go shirtless in the chilly autumn air perfumed with piss and beer, body odor and grilling meat, and no sooner do the games begin than the human scavengers descend on the great harvest of returnable cans and bottles discarded by the faithful. Sunday is a day of mess, with cleanup crews and herring gulls swarming over the tailgate remains, eyed by displaced crows from their perches atop the stadium. It is all a great boon to the local economy.

These spectacles are at once impressive and off-putting, powerful and mindless, products of a residual culture that has lost its pathos. The annual games, the pride of spectatorship, the beer, the hot dogs, and the cold, fall Saturday afternoons do not elevate but bloat. Go Red! Go Green! Go White! Go Blue! I am not saying that I am immune to the power of football or of big events. We all need big events. The pull to align oneself with states and state universities and with mighty masses is strong, but there is too much goddamned school spirit around here. The corporate blankness, the insipidity of institutionalized high spirits, gets to me.

Of course, football may only *appear* to comprise the totality of human existence on Saturdays in October. Obviously, not everyone in the Midwest is a football enthusiast. Some take to raising emu. Others take up vast, solitary projects like ultramarathoning or long-distance cycling, organizing their lives according to an arduous regimen. For most people around here, the drive to lose themselves in the mass spectacle is counterbalanced by a firm belief in their own rugged individualism. There are hunters like Ted Nugent and those who believe it is their natural right to defend themselves and their property at forty rounds per second. There is even a paramilitary group, the now infamous Michigan Militia, who protested the raising of the UN flag over the statehouse as a seditious act impinging on the sovereignty of the United States. They excoriated a group of schoolchildren who came to the flag-raising ceremony to sing for world peace. And, of course, Michigan still produces that great vehicle of individualism, the automobile, without which there would be no tailgate party.

If you are looking, you can perceive all of this inside Spartan Stadium. It is overwhelmingly green (and the fans are overwhelmingly White), but it is not a green found in nature. On the scoreboard and walls, it is the green of dumpsters and waste-management equipment. On the field, it is Astroturf green. In the stands, it is windbreak green. Beneath the stands, it is hospital green. And no matter what surface it tints, you can almost see nylon in it. Staring at all the artificial green during a game makes you realize that, in a curious way, it is MSU itself, a simulacrum of the school's agricultural past. It is an official kind of green, the green of institutions. Although gray is the institutional color par excellence—the nondescript color of flannel suits—here it is green, and it isn't easy being green.

There is surely a connection between the oppressively artificial verdancy and the quality of the football played here. The linemen are ponderously massive, the linebackers stoked with murderous brawn, the backs fleet; the cheerleaders are peppy and athletic in more human proportions, the band is nothing if not uniform; and the coach (back in 1993), paunchy and unadventurous—sort of likable or detestable, depending on what you admire in football coaches—had his own local television show. His 1993 squad was tough, not outstanding but capable of knocking an unprepared team on its butt. Football has been played here for nearly 100 seasons. Michigan State has an excellent overall record which obscures the early drubbings suffered by the old Aggies of Michigan Agricultural College. Since the de-

cades after World War II, when Clarence L. "Biggie" Munn and his disciple
Duffy Daugherty did for the football program what John Hannah had done
for the school at large—transformed it into a Big Ten power—MSU has
moved up to the top twenty-five all-time Division 1-A percentage of games
won, with national championships in 1952 and 1965, and a near miss in
1966 (which included an epic 10–10 tie with Notre Dame). But there was,
is, and likely always will be a Michigan, a Notre Dame, and an Ohio State
whose fabled teams cast long, long shadows over all who place second.

In terms of national reputation, Michigan's Wolverines occupy more of
the psychic landscape of football glory. Ann Arbor is the gridiron mecca
around here, and you can catch more than a whiff of sour grapes from the
Spartan faithful. "Go Blow!" sneers a bumper sticker, mocking the Wol-
verine cheer "Go Blue!" It doesn't show a lot of class, but it expresses an
authentic bird-flipping defiance. Unlike the homoerotic put-downs of the
Ivy League (e.g., "Harvard Sucks," "Princeton Swallows"), Big Ten kiss-offs
convey less parity, less reciprocity, and a more restive craving for victory.
When the Spartans knocked off the Wolverines in 1993, the joy on campus was palpable. A holiday atmosphere pervaded; the students were truly
grateful. But the 1994 team had a mediocre season: a few middling victories, a few promising halves, a near miss against a less-than-spectacular
Notre Dame team—and a crushing defeat by Michigan. The new president
of MSU, in his first official declaration, had demanded an "extraordinary
season," but it was, alas, an ordinary season, and the school has a new
coach now. And so the quest for glory goes on. It is tempting to view MSU
as labor and U of M as management in their rivalry, as if the corporate
politics of GM were being played out in the public universities of Michigan: flagship versus land-grant, national powerhouse versus plucky state
underdog, "Moo U" versus "the U." But it is more likely that the rivalry engages the phony elitism of Ann Arbor and the equally phony populism of
East Lansing, pitting one big corporation against another, slightly smaller
corporation. Football runs on big money, and, of course, Michigan will
generally outperform Michigan State because the U of M program, like
its endowment, is bigger. The green of Spartan Stadium is, therefore, not
quite the green of big money, or not quite enough of it.

In the first Big Ten game I attended, Michigan State defeated Wisconsin.
It was an impressive victory over a sluggish group of Badgers. Up to this
point in the season, the Spartans had been collapsing against big teams in

the second half, but this time they took command, pushing the defending Conference champions all over the place. The Badgers did not exhibit
their Rose Bowl–winning form of 1993, and as the final seconds ticked off
the scoreboard, the State crowd chanted, with a characteristic mixture of
derisive accuracy and inferiority complex: "Overrated!" Thousands stayed
to hear the marching band give a postgame concert.

But I was continually drawn to the marginal antics of the rival mascots.
They wrestled, pantomimed, and yukked it up along the sidelines. Bucky
Badger is more of a basketball mascot with a lot of African American style,
always slippin 'n' slidin', dippin 'n' divin', movin 'n' groovin'. Sparty, or
rather the guy in the Sparty costume (so palpable is his costume), by contrast, is only slightly more mobile than his statue. He moves his puffed-up,
steroidal physique like a robot with Y chromosomes, lumbering about and
making ludicrously simpleminded gestures of enthusiasm. (The embodiment of brute stupidity, Sparty really has to be seen to be believed.) As
Sparty spanked Bucky and Bucky razzed the cheerleaders and both Bucky
and Sparty pointed at us in the stands time and again, I wondered what
relation these "fan-tasms" had to the bone-crushing game being played in
the center of all that green. Evidently, they have only a vestigial connection
with their original role as bringers of good luck.

I suspect that the vehemence of carnival spectatorship that all the
Buckys and Spartys represent alters our understanding of the game. Football has always been a violent game, but now, through the mute language
of chicken suits and Disneyan creatures, we are apparently doing new and
interesting violence to the old. They represent the fans more than they do
the team. They are our surrogates, looming up as ritual insults to our intel-
ligence. It is a wonder that most people find their antics merely benign.
I think Bucky and Sparty have become fixtures at football games because
they remind us, in a way that only citizens of the TV Age can fully appreciate, that the experience of playing football is ultimately incompatible with
the experience of watching it. While football in its most spectacular moments *looks* impossible (and is designed to produce such moments—the
Hail Mary pass, the fingertip catch, the broken tackle, the seam that opens
for the instant the halfback needs to slice through it, the hit that tosses a
figure of incomparable speed and strength through the air like a rag doll),
the game seduces spectators into believing that they are indeed part of the
action. So Bucky and Sparty and all their collegiate cousins, decked out

as they are for the Magic Kingdom, remind us that to watch football is to enter a fantasyland, that victory, defeat, and identification with a particular team properly belong to the realm of the *imaginary*—and that there is something a little silly about all of this. When Steve Young tells us that he is "going to Disneyland" after his team has just won the Super Bowl, he is participating in the cartoon logic of sports-as-mass-spectacle. Outrageous victory propels us into the realm of the imaginary. Only then are we fit for the company of Mickey and Goofy.

There is a fidgety quality to the football sideshow. For as much as the fans roar and cheer, they also worry, nail-bite, and coax the action in the direction of their hopes and wagers. In the stands, men are constantly explaining what happened or how they knew what would happen. You get the impression that people are very much afraid of losing by proxy, and Bucky and Sparty act out these emotions. It reminds me of George Plimpton's *Paper Lion*. The physically unprepossessing Plimpton trains as a quarterback with the Detroit Lions, setting himself the modest goal of running five plays against a "live" first-string NFL defense. Horribly muffing all but the last of his attempted plays, Plimpton learns the hard way what any armchair quarterback could have predicted: it is difficult to play in the National Football League. While trotting shamefacedly off the field, he is astonished to hear appreciative applause and laughter from the crowd. What Plimpton had attempted with epic seriousness, and consequently profound humiliation, was perceived by the fans as a brilliant bit of clowning. It had never occurred to them that he was serious. It is this disjunction between high humiliation on the field and low laughter in the stands that Bucky and Sparty silently register.

———

Such heroism and humiliation have always been at the heart of football. James Wright, a poet and true Midwesterner, explained the game's attraction this way in "Autumn Begins in Martin's Ferry, Ohio":

> In the Shreve High football stadium,
> I think of Polacks nursing long beers in Tiltonsville,
> And gray faces of Negroes in the blast furnace at Benwood,
> And the ruptured night watchman of Wheeling Steel,
> Dreaming of heroes.

All the proud fathers are ashamed to go home.
Their women cluck like starved pullets,
Dying for love.

Therefore,
Their sons grow suicidally beautiful
At the beginning of October,
And gallop terribly against each other's bodies.

In Wright's formulation, the young men who play football grow "suicidally beautiful" in direct proportion to their fathers' blue-collar immigrant defeat. In societal terms, the power of football to produce glory and beauty is purchased at the price of industrial quotidian and loveless marriage. There is a truth in Wright's equation ("therefore" makes it an equation): the rise of American football coincided with the rise of American industry and the influx of immigrants who sacrificed their bodies to the Machine Age, so as football field displaces factory, the body is sacrificed to the machinery of sport. It is an elegant conceit, but Wright wrote his poem about high school football in the early 1960s, and the game has evolved since then. Sportswriters constantly lament the professionalism that has corrupted the spirit of the game, the big money that has changed everything—and so they have, they do. It is not easy now to say that the glory of football stands in opposition to the drudgery of the factory or the workingman's oblivion of the bar—not even about high school football. If the stories I read in the papers are true, steroid use is rampant and boys exchange their potential suicidal beauty for suicidal muscle mass. The line—whether defense or offense, whether in high school, college, or pro football—has become the assembly line once more. Each man on the squad is hulkingly deformed to suit the demands of his specialized gridiron tasks. In the old days, players were known as Elroy "Crazylegs" Hirsch, "The Galloping Ghost," or Frank "Bruiser" Kinard, nicknames which conveyed an almost eccentric natural prowess. Today, we have "The Fridge," "The Rocket," "Neon Deion," and "Ironhead," suggesting that our own living legends are bionic, custom-built with technological bodywork and as unstoppable as their technology. The days of the triple threat and the two-way player are long gone; mechanization has taken command. Even such incomparable athletes as Joe Montana are wonders of prosthesis, and many lesser players with blown knees and frozen shoulders fall into the role of Wright's ruptured watchman in their twenties, all their bulk rendered staggeringly useless in the split second of a broken play, relived for the rest of their days in the gruesome precision of slow motion.

Football may be different today, or all that was latent in football may be bubbling to the surface now. Certainly, there is too much celebration in the end zone to think of it as suicidally beautiful anymore. It has lost the romantic aura of sacrificial beauty and acquired the commonsensical gloss of euthanasia. This is what I feel when I look on the unnatural green of Spartan Stadium and Spartan spirit. Natural suicidal beauty has become artificial suicidal beauty. Or perhaps, and I say this with perverse admiration, there is something both deforming and tolerant of deformity about football, something which bends the bodies and hearts of boys in puberty like an unrecognized secondary sex characteristic. I continue to wonder at the image of Jem, nearly thirteen when his arm was badly broken, in the opening of Harper Lee's *To Kill a Mockingbird*:

> When it healed, and Jem's fears of never being able to play football were assuaged, he was seldom self-conscious about his injury. His left arm was somewhat shorter than his right, when he stood or walked, the back of his hand was at right angles to his body, his thumb parallel to his thigh. He couldn't have cared less, so long as he could pass and punt.

For Jem and for many a real boy, the game promises to compensate, to redeem deformity and relieve painful self-consciousness. It is no wonder that boys and men chemically deform themselves to play football; they are responding to the deep logic of the game, which is the logic of warfare. And, I suppose, football relieves us all, as spectators, of self-consciousness about our own injuries.

There is a profound restlessness in the insatiable hunger for victory and the constant refusal to acknowledge humiliation and hurt. When I recall my own years playing "Pop Warner" football on the playgrounds of suburban Massachusetts in the early 1970s, I think of the coaches—men like my father who had spent their childhood in the Depression and war years, men who had witnessed the rise of professional sports on radio and television, men who had great respect for Vince Lombardi and his philosophy of winning. Although aware that we were only boys, they still could not re-strain their zeal for the glories of the game. They were nice men who acted tough, barking at us, making us run laps and do gut-wrenching leg lifts. They appraised us and tried to instill a competitive drive in us, preaching about the fourth quarter and the necessity of wanting it more than the other guy. They made no bones about how essential it was to endure pain and hardship for success, on the field and off. And there was another as-pect of Lombardi's philosophy that they drilled into our heads: execution, execution, execution. Every play is designed to go all the way, they would tell us, their eyes burning with Platonic Ideals. If every man does his job, even a simple dive play will result in a touchdown. Don't be a hot dog, don't be a show-off, just do your job to the best of your ability.

My father had been a quarterback in high school and college, and for him there was a deep joy in coaching. There was solace on the football field for the frustrations of marriage and career—not just the blue-collar miseries of Wright's poem, but the suburban white-collar ones of his own world. Having played for Benny Friedman—the great field general of the Michigan Wolverines in the 1920s—my father always emphasized intelli-gent, strategic play. When I was ten, he wanted me to be a quarterback too, so I played the position, but rather miserably. I performed like a poor dancing student, learning steps without any sense of the rhythm or overall motion of the dance. I was fine throwing the ball around with my friends, but in uniform I lost what little intuitive grasp of the game I possessed. I remember one broken play during practice when I held the ball out in a hand-off to a halfback who wasn't there, having run another play else-where. I just stood there until a linebacker from the defensive unit came through the line, took the hand-off, and ran for a touchdown. This was not what the coaches meant by competitive drive. I did better on defense, somewhat gleefully disrupting the plays of the opposition, but I never cared for all the paraphernalia, the pads and the helmets. I never cared for all the specialization that football requires, all the stop–action. With the exception of a fumble I once recovered in the end zone, in all the time I played organized football it never felt like *playing*. After a few seasons of this, I quit and took up other sports.

Perhaps my own experience has oversensitized me to football and pre-disposed me to judge the green of Spartan Stadium too harshly. But it seems to me that the color speaks to the restless underside of the game, at MSU and in our culture at large. Football has a tendency (as perhaps all games do) to become an end in itself. Why else would coaches and pundits always be at such pains to remind us that it is about life? Football *can be* about life, but it can also detach itself from the more meaningful aspects of experience. Football *may be* glorious for the athletes who play it at the highest levels, but for the spectator it can only be glorious when it is wedded to larger human aspirations—larger, at least, than the NFL and cable TV contracts and victory for victory's sake. "Winning isn't everything, it's the only thing," sayeth Lombardi, and many Americans nod in agreement with this pearl of pre-Vietnam wisdom. I suspect that most people hear it as a hardheaded retort to Grantland Rice's *Alumnus Football*:

> When the One Great Scorer comes to write your name
> He marks—not that you won or lost—but how you played the game.

But in fairness to Vince, he was talking about professional football, and as Ray Nitschke says about the pros, "The fans pay to see you win." Lombardi's dictum becomes problematic, however, when life (as well as college and high school football) endeavors to model itself on pro football. The game has always offered men and boys a choice between "everything" and "the only thing," that is, a degree of focus not often available in life, a chance to dispel everything else and concentrate on the only thing. What Spartan green reflects above all is this confusion of life and football; the way in which everything has become the only thing for many, marking it as a pure product of the twentieth-century American scene.

It must be conceded that television has had more to do with this confusion than any other single factor; in fact, if Mike Celizic's account of the November 1966 clash between first-ranked Notre Dame and second-ranked Michigan State in *The Biggest Game of Them All* is accurate, the debut of the contemporary collegiate-sports television machine took place in Spartan Stadium. In this grueling game—which was supposed to have decisively determined the best college team in the country, but instead ended in an enigmatic tie—the "innocence" of NCAA football (actually more "preprofessional" than "innocent") was sacrificed on the altar of the American Broadcasting Company. Still operating then as a witness, television used that experience to develop its potential to be a highly intrusive participant–observer. Now, of course, everyone plays for the camera, which binds players and fans in an ever-tighter circle of watcher and watched. We can see this relationship played out in the colorful commentary provided by a young boy for a game with his friends, in the confusion of athletes with role models, or in the corporate trend of hiring well-known coaches to give "motivational lectures" to sluggish salespeople. The line between life and sport blurs, rendering the very concept of victory hollow.

This too has a special resonance in East Lansing. Evidently, it has always been difficult to dredge a grand tradition out of the swamps and fields of central Michigan. Even Duffy Daugherty's mighty teams of the mid-1960s were pools of local talent and recruits from the segregated South, honed to excellence in the relative vacuum of East Lansing. Those wonderfully integrated teams were accepted not out of any great racial enlightenment, but out of a raw hunger for victory—and perhaps a need to fill the void. In his book, Celizic relates how the Spartans got their name. When Michigan State held a contest to come up with a nickname for the team in the 1920s, the winner was the "Michigan Staters," but some local journalists, unhappy with such a long moniker, took it upon themselves to call the team the "Spartans" (one of the runner-up names), if only for shorter headlines. I find myself regretting that "Michigan Staters" didn't catch on. The Michigan State Michigan Staters has a Zen-like redundancy that speaks an abiding truth about the campus, about the beautiful but mundane landscape that surrounds it, and especially about football.

People who bleed Spartan green might object to all this. When I look over the stadium and out to the green world surrounding it, the tension between the two strikes me as brutally honest. To say that MSU, in all its green blankness or blank greenness, is an institution dedicated above all to its own institutionhood is really just to utter a commonplace about corporate culture in America. Although it would be more shocking if college football were immune to this culture, I am still struck by what an undiluted expression of it football has become. But it would do a disservice to the aura of Spartan green to discuss the particulars of MSU's institutional blight. Green, the football team, and the strip of East Lansing are all synecdoches for the institution and its slogans; it is healthy, for the time being, to feel them in all their synecdochic power. New faculty are oriented to the campus by screening an MSU-produced video in which one is told that the school stands for "Excellence, Diversity, and Mission" (meaning the land-grant mission). When my friends, scattered around the country, call and ask me how it is here, I tell them about this official corporate slogan, and the reaction is almost always the same: silence followed by a long indrawn breath, followed by a longer sigh. You inhale it. You take it in and then you let it go. You hope it's air.

Or maybe you just ignore it, knowing that yet another puff of corporate smoke has drifted your way on a phrase of peculiarly American music, no cause for alarm. To participate in American sports culture is to court paradox, and Spartan green can take its place among a host of other paradoxical artifacts of this culture. It is certainly a product of the Midwest, at least of my Midwest, but equivalent sports-cultural artifacts can be found all over the country. I am reminded of the demands of Lombardi's philosophy and the "rest area" that bears his name at the end of the New Jersey Turnpike near the Meadowlands. It is a place of constant motion, a highway pit stop where in the 1980s, before it was remodeled, I used to see Lombardi's face, grinning gap-toothed at me eerily from a holograph, as I made my way to the men's room. Winning isn't the only thing, I would remind myself, it is also *nothing*, and—as in football—it is a rest area and no place of rest.

Pamela Haag

"The 50,000-Watt Sports Bar": Talk Radio and the Ethic of the Fan

*A*AAAAAAHHHHHHHH—*GOOD afternoon everybody how are you todayyyyy.* So begins another afternoon with Mad Dog Russo, the pied piper of sports talk radio, on New York's WFAN, a twenty-four-hour sports bivouac. After an escalating scream that threatens to go on forever, his monologue is delivered in a baffling voice reminiscent of Jerry Lewis or Elmer Fudd on helium, ranging wildly over the scales before settling into a high-pitched, driving screech as monologue graduates to diatribe. By the end, he is spitting words as if they've gotten jammed up at the end of a sentence and he can't fire them out fast enough. Unlike his relatively serious sidekick, Mike Francesa, whose laconic "arenerrs" and "drawrrs" betray his thick Long Island roots, The Dog seems to have come from some particular yet dialectically untraceable locale. He bewitches even the casual sports fan with his repertoire of malapropisms and strange turns of phrase. (He is not above calling the Depression the "Great Repression," for example.) "Hey, don't be *killing* John Doe about this," he likes to say, always concerned with justice as he "chats about the world

The *South Atlantic Quarterly* 95:2, Spring 1996.
Copyright © 1996 by Duke University Press.
CCC 0038-2876/96/$1.50.

of sports" with a cast of first-time callers and "long times," or regular listeners.

Mad Dog and Francesa are the flamboyant descendants of sports talk radio's founding father, Boston's Eddie Andelman, who began fielding telephone calls twenty-five years ago to fill dead spots on a sports show. "It's still a miracle to me that people listen and take this stuff seriously," Andelman marveled at the conclusion of recent contract negotiations during which he won a quarter-million-dollar salary for hosting his talk show. "I haven't ever been in a locker room, I never had free tickets, but I go to the game and have my opinions."[1] On the surface, having opinions is all it takes. The all-sports format of WFAN, inaugurated in 1987, has proved wildly successful, and although only a handful of twenty-four-hour sports talk stations aired a few years ago, now an estimated 100 compete nationwide to satisfy the thirst for sports doggerel.[2]

All sports. All the time. A format described by WFAN's cantankerous Howard Stern rival, Don Imus—a drug-rehabilitated morning-show host who counts Bob Dole and Bill Clinton among his regular guests—as "$18\frac{1}{2}$ hours of imbecilic prattle between contemptibly limited talk show hosts and twelve housebound agoraphobes with sports obsessions." Kentucky basketball coach Rick Pitino concurs: "These listeners, they're frustrated at home, can't get a date, don't do well at their jobs and are basically at the nadir of their lives."[3]

I became one of those twelve housebound agoraphobes who lived with the FAN running like white noise as I wrote my dissertation, a life stage which certainly qualifies as the nadir for many a young, untested scholar. I had begun listening to 660 many years earlier (then just a sports fan with a sane level of interest in scores and stories) because I could not believe what I was hearing when I first tuned in. Flipping the dial in the dead of night while driving on the turnpike, I heard a man call in to urge listeners, in the best self-help tradition, not to stray as he had and lose their families, their lives—"all because of the Mets." I laughed the whole way home. At some point thereafter, I crossed the invisible line between bemused ironic distance and true fandom. If nothing else, the FAN saved me from the maddening existential hum of my own thoughts, regardless of its effect on the literary grace of my academic projects. But on a deeper level, I began to feel that I was actually absorbing some strange form of sustenance or knowledge from those interminable shows, so greedy had I become for their Brooklyn twangs and dilatory nonarguments. I would subject friends trapped in my car to the show, under the guise of an objective, anthropological participant–observer interest ("get a load of this—it's wild stuff"), but actually because I couldn't stand to miss The Dog's monologue, especially when I knew that a juicy debate was brewing in New York's kinetic, exacting sports universe. The axioms of sports and the FAN delighted me because they seemed so indisputably *wise*. One of my favorite maxims while growing up as a Baltimore Orioles fan was legendary manager Earl Weaver's query to struggling pitchers: "Are you going to get any better, or is this it?" It seemed a question with broad applications, as did WFAN's familiar exhortations to teams ("always play [your] strongest game, not the opposition's") and to franchise players (who, to be truly divine, sometimes had to take a team and "carry it on their backs," and who should "always play to *win*, not to avoid *losing*"). As a result, I have come to believe that an ethical worldview cannot be cultivated in the 1990s without a few object lessons from sports. The FAN's tidy mythologies and rivalries have lulled me into a comfortable feeling that maybe life really is bounded by white lines and organized according to clear rules and penalties—and that at the end we will shake hands amiably, like good sports, with God. Life will prove to have been for fun, after all.

I have no business listening to the FAN, of course. It is targeted to a particular (male, White) ethnic "niche," as marketers call it, and it is steeped in both masculine camaraderie and the sort of visceral anti-intellectualism that led Mad Dog, for one, to reject Ken Burns's *Baseball* series because he didn't "want to hear what three professors at Harvard—Burns's friends—have to say about the sport. Hey, how about asking some barber in the Bronx about it?" I have wondered why, then, as a feminist academic (setting aside any self-ascriptions of false consciousness or perverse identification with the enemy), I listen to the show. How did WFAN come to appear the one safe and welcoming spot on the dial for me, a delightful refuge from the "hate radio" talk shows that emerged as the other viable programming format of the 1990s? Sports talk radio and hate radio are equally "masculine," to be sure, and equally hostile to academics and feminists. (Not to mention my own personality—I am incapable of responding to anything without mixing abstraction, intellectualism, and passion.) Even though it was spawned by the same deregulatory changes in the communications industry of the last ten years, however, there are compelling reasons to see the sports talk show as something other—and more redemptive—than the flip side of the angry White male's political harangues on the conservative airwaves. These sports shows—and the ethic of the fan—speak to an older, perhaps nearly extinct version of White masculinity and cultural provincialism.

———

At one end of the spectrum, the FAN caters to those victimized by the economy—unemployed and with no place to go during rush hours; at the other end, it seduces those who are "special"—important or successful enough to have cellular phones and houses safely distanced from their urban workplaces. In this regard WFAN is the airwave equivalent of the Department of Motor Vehicles—one of the last social melting pots where callers who abashedly confess to being physicians or lawyers when medical or legal expertise is solicited rub earlobes with those who are alienated from the economy altogether. Mostly, however, the FAN belongs to the anxious-in-between, those who spend obscene amounts of time commuting on the congested roadways from Connecticut to New Jersey, stalled at the Hudson crossings and staring grimly ahead, calling in from their car phones while snarled in traffic. (Talk-show hosts insist, "If you start breaking up, get off the line.") *Electronic Media*, a trade publication, explains radio's revival in the 1980s specifically as a function of this commuter plague, since most people listen in their cars.[4] "Those trapped in traffic jams are captive audiences for radio," observes the *LA Times*. "All you have to do is look at the freeways at quarter to five. Every traffic jam is an opportunity to a broadcaster. You're dealing with a medium that has very much a captive audience in the automobile. It's bordering on the oppressive."[5]

The radio marketing potential of commuter life could be fully exploited in the 1990s, following the FCC deregulatory trends of the 1980s. Ultimately, deregulation, which loosened mass-media ownership and content restrictions, both renewed interest in radio as an investment and inspired the eventual emergence of its two 1990s showcase formats: "hate radio" talk shows and all-sports programming. Taking his cue from Ronald Reagan's laissez-faire policies, FCC Chairman Mark Fowler vowed in 1982 to take "deregulation to the limits of existing law" and to convert communications into an entrepreneur's goldmine,[6] a necessary condition for the much discussed free-flowing information "revolution" so central to transnational corporate development today. Consistent with his marketplace position toward the communications industry, Fowler "was always saying, television is just a toaster with pictures, and it should be regulated like any other appliance," one FCC attorney recalls.[7] Radio "reforms," beginning in 1981, accordingly included abolishing requirements that station owners wait at least three years after buying a station before selling it and that stations air extensive news and public affairs programs as conditions for licensing; repealing the "fairness doctrine" that required stations covering controversial issues to provide "reasonable opportunities" for opposing views; abolishing public service and ascertainment requirements whereby stations demonstrated and explained their contribution to community programming, particularly through public logs, as a condition of license granting or renewal; raising the maximum number (from 24 to 60) of radio stations a broadcaster could own nationwide; and, finally, extending the duration of radio licenses from three years to seven. Radio, complained one former station owner, had become "strictly for business."[8]

Deregulation encouraged an intense quest for new and viable formats in this now relatively open environment which stimulated the growth of satellite programming and media conglomerates, for as station prices climbed conglomerates emerged as the only qualified buyers. The stations themselves saved money with syndicated programming. "The public isn't better served by this," argues Paul Goldman, owner of a Burlington, Vermont, station. "The listener gets a greater variety of programing, but the community loses as more and more information is beamed out of the sky."[9]

Infinity Broadcasting, the largest U.S. company devoted exclusively to owning and operating radio stations, owns WFAN. With audiences in each of the nation's top ten radio markets, Infinity boasts in its promotional material that the "geographic diversity" of its markets makes it less dependent on the "local economy or advertisers." Infinity has become more attentive to content since 1993, when the company acquired a 25 percent, controlling interest in Westwood One, the largest U.S. producer of sports, entertainment, and news programming, whose subsidiaries include Mutual Broadcasting, Talknet, NBC Radio, and The Source.

The ascendance of satellite programming, thanks to Infinity and other conglomerates, would seem to confirm a structural move toward what media commentator Herbert Schiller calls the modulated, homogenized "corporate voice": "Corporate speech has become an integral part of cultural production in general. The corporate voice constitutes the national symbolic environment. For this reason it becomes more and more difficult to maintain the difference between individual and corporate speech."[10] Ironically, however, Infinity's specific marketing strategies focus on cultivating popular, idiosyncratic on-air talent, acquiring stations with one-of-a-kind radio personalities, and attracting key demographic groups by means of specific program formats. Despite radio's trumpeted ubiquity, notably, its advertising appeal as a medium that is "everywhere," deregulation encouraged, if not mandated, its splintering into stations catering to targeted demographic groups.

Fowler praised the 1980s triumph of "niche marketing," or "narrowcasting" (buying stations and programming them for targeted audiences and advertisers), as the "magic" that businessmen could work "when left alone. My view is that because something like radio is a powerful medium that is all the more reason it should be free."[11] "Freedom" in this context, critics retorted, meant the replacement of "government regulation with marketplace regulation."[12] "If the airwaves were left to market forces," argued Andrew Schwartzmann of the Media Access Project, "freedom of speech would suffer because only material with sufficient commercial appeal would get on the air." Programs designed for marginal social groups (i.e., groups with little financial or consumer clout—the young, elderly, and poor), which had been protected under ascertainment policies that guaranteed programming variety within geographic communities, would vanish from the airwaves. Deregulation, with its specter of auctioned airwaves, constituted a "selling of our birthright," Schwartzmann warned. "Sure, we could probably get more for the Grand Canyon if we leased it out to Nike and let them put an Air Jordan logo on it."[13]

These criticisms notwithstanding, niche marketing has won the decade. "Niche media is what the 1990s will be about, finding new ways to reach people" unobtrusively.[14] The "magic" performed by Fowler's unregulated businessmen conjured up the two programming formats already mentioned: the now notorious "hate radio" of political talk shows, and the twenty-four-hour sports stations like WFAN. Both are aimed at the elusive "niche" that is universally recognized in the trade as the most desirable for selling advertising, the "Testosterone Set"—men between the ages of twenty-five and fifty-four—"boys at heart listeners," as the *Chicago Tribune* characterizes sports fanatics.[15] Sports radio, one expert notes, is "niche marketing at its most powerful . . . very few women, very few kids."[16] As another industry maven observes, "The stations are hoping to generate revenue by giving advertisers a way to make contact with a desirable but elusive audience, men ages 25 to 54." Any retailer would be happy to reach the 100,000 listeners typical of sports talk shows with a "cume"—those who listen for at least five minutes a week—of 300,000, *"with no waste."*[17] In other words, with few superfluous interlopers on "the boys' club of sports radio," advertisers can count on a well-defined niche to whom they can hawk men's clothing, ticket brokers, and cellular phones.[18]

Ceding the airwaves to the "free market" has, unsurprisingly, generated programming that mirrors the politics of those who champion laissez-faire policies generally. The "marketplace of ideas," as Newt Gingrich calls it, has dignified the rage expressed on incendiary radio shows as a virtual state of nature—the way that White male citizens would act if "left alone," unregulated in their social and economic relations. On the surface, the sports talk show is a venue for the embattled White male seeking recreational repose; thus it caters to this audience as surely as Rush Limbaugh articulates its discontents. Some sports talk stations define their listening audience explicitly, such as the one that advertises itself as "a station for men with hair on their backs," or the Atlanta station whose management bluntly states, "We make no pretensions [*sic*] about what we're doing here. The FAN is a guy's radio station. We're aiming at the men's bracket which is the hardest to reach."[19] If these comments affirm *Playboy*'s recent assessment of sports radio as the only arena left to White men wounded by the indignities of feminism, affirmative action, and other groups' quests for social equality, the shows themselves inevitably create more complex faultlines.[20]

===

I am one of the listeners who creates "waste" for sports radio advertisers. I fall outside of the targeted audience to whom Rogaine ("MEN! Are you losing your . . . *HAIR*?"), cellular phones, and romantic reconciliations at the Kew Motor Lodge are pitched. But the ethic of the fan disrupts the practice of "narrowcasting" and effectively undermines the "market," which persists as an audience. However ardently WFAN marketers and advertisers pursue the Testosterone Set, for example, Mad Dog, who exhibits a certain goofiness toward the "ladies," continues to invite more women into his listening audience and to applaud those who call in because he is committed to the democratic appeal of sports. He reminds me of that genre of men who seem unrefined or remote until the subject of sports comes up, at which point they rise to an unprecedented rhetorical grace and passion, recounting in exquisite detail pivotal moments in their franchise's history. I count my own family among the many whose intimate relationships were largely consolidated or expressed through a shared passion for sports.

The Dog appears to be a trespasser in the world of gender relations. Describing his wedding plans to Francesa, he reported, "I told those caterers that there'd be a lot of sports fans at the reception, and that they should make sure to have TVs in the basement so we can watch the Derby." But on the air he displays an instinctive, if surprising, decorum toward female callers that no marketing strategy or etiquette manual could equip him to practice. This is not to suggest that the sports show format isn't implicitly structured by exclusions and the heterosexual matrix. Francesca and The Dog, in fact, attest to Eve Sedgwick's brilliant observation that homosexuality is the "open secret" in American culture, the thing that must be invoked and then "closeted" to protect homosocial relations such as theirs—Mike and Mad Dog bicker like a married couple—from the potential stigma of gay desire.[21]

A similar argument might be made about the generic treatment of racial issues—historically central to American sports—on these talk shows, where the racism is displayed not in seething hostility or political resentment but in a quixotic, sometimes hysterical determination to act as if race does not matter. The universal sports talk refrain is "I don't care if you're purple, orange, green, or yellow. It's an issue of fairness, and I would have the same complaint of a White athlete." There is a deeply held belief that reverse racism is widely practiced. When a Black coach referred to a player as "a dumb White quarterback," the FAN audience could not have been more outraged. The mere identification of a racial characteristic, even "Whiteness," seemed to violate the code of race-blind fandom. The ensuing discussions did not acknowledge that White Americans, having structural privileges, are not implicated in or affected by racial insults in the same ways as Black Americans. Rather, antiracism is apparently all about niceness: if a person is good and means well, then he is by definition not a racist. It is a worldview deeply rooted in the efficacy of individual intentions and goodwill rather than critiques of injustice or power.

Nevertheless, while surveying airwaves overrun by the incivilities of the chronically indignant populist Right may lead to the conclusion that sports talk suffers from the same structured exclusions as all other discourses (an acute, if fashionable, insight of poststructuralist theory), that does not get us very far toward imagining a new way of conducting social relations on a more civil and decent basis. Substantively, the ethic of fandom creates a world in which one's participation or membership is conditioned by longtime loyalties. (Fans always preface their comments with the legitimizing phrase "I've been a fan forever.") Here, within the boundaries of the Disneyland universe of sports, people tacitly agree to treat others respectfully even while passionately disagreeing about everything else. Sports talk radio is actually the opposite of hate radio because topics that become too controversial or contentious no longer qualify as "sports"; hosts vigilantly patrol the boundaries of sports-acceptability on the show and halt any conversation that introduces irresolvable political hatred. This means that the inclusive ethic of fandom is effectively elaborated through a roster of topics that maintains a safe distance from the explicitly political, but the ethic at least survives as a blueprint for what theorists had imagined as an ideal politics and public discourse of civil society. This sphere of fandom is one in which people can speak both passionately and respectfully. They can care deeply about issues, but no one will die for expressing opinions on them—unlike those involved in, say, the abortion debate.

It is undoubtedly pathetic to feel compelled to speak so seriously and redemptively about something like sports radio. But some of the most reassuringly decent moments in history pass unrecorded in the ephemera of daily life, and not much on the airwaves other than sports talk offers a paradigm of how we might imagine a public discourse among diverse strangers that is at once impassioned and safe, conforming to some Deweyan dream of the "public." In this respect, talk radio and *sports* talk radio, although marketed for the same discontented White men, seem qualitatively different, one hinging on an exaggerated distinction between a White male constituency and its vilified foes—in short, on the reinforcement of the audience *as* the exclusive market niche—and the other hinging on a sincere, if awkward, impulse to reach out to "ladies," through sports, on terms of kindness.

———

Baltimore had its own Mad Dog in Charley Eckman, a "certified Baltimore character," who died recently. "Call a cab," he used to rasp when some sports decision upset him; "better make it two cabs," if something even more scandalous had happened. As a former basketball coach, he had been fond of such sayings as "there's two plays— *South Pacific* and 'Put the Ball in the Basket.' " His obituary noted that "when a listener called his radio show inquiring if a horse had won the third race at Pimlico, his reply showed no mercy. 'Ain't no way, sweetheart. Whatzamatter, honey, your old man have a fin on King Flame?' " [22] This version of White masculinity is as anachronistic as Eckman's vocabulary. It is prefeminist, to be sure, yet rooted in a good-humored playfulness toward women that could, at the very least, be transformative because it was based on a *liking* for people and a fondness for a listening audience who became a community through sports. Much as I may roll my eyes at the "honeys" and "sweethearts," they cannot be compared to the vitriolic terms of today's conservative idiom and the new properties of White citizenship it has spawned. As one of his colleagues recalled about Eckman, "There was never a person he didn't like. He lived for the city of Baltimore and the state." [23]

The idea of living for a city—of identifying oneself by place—perhaps offsets some of the rage we hear on political talk shows. The conservative imagination idealizes local, almost tribal governance, yet envisions such locales as economically, racially, and ideologically homogeneous, semiprivatized communities free of burdensome obligations toward weak or insufficiently rugged individuals. While conservatives are committed to the *idea* of the local, they anathematize any crystallization of it that might "force" well-off taxpayers to take responsibility for those less economically secure. By contrast, fandom, which has often inflamed or enacted racial tensions (one thinks of Jackie Robinson, Muhammad Ali, and the 1968 Olympics, for example), has also defused those tensions by fostering loyalty to place and a sense of community based entirely on pairings of teams and cities.

My father, an old-time War on Poverty liberal, defends the city of Baltimore with unrivaled intensity. At a reception recently, a visiting musician asked him where he was from. "Well, I'm *from* Indiana. But of course I don't claim that identity anymore," he responded, as if denying that he was a Serb. When asked why not, he replied with all the patience he could muster, "Because they stole our football team." Having grown up with it, I never used to find anything unusual in my father's geography of the vilified and the sanctified. It didn't strike me as odd to avoid shopping in certain states because they "stole" Maryland's business through low corporate taxes, to boycott Pittsburgh and Charlotte, North Carolina, because they had beaten out Baltimore in major sporting bids, to refuse to shop or live in the county (our house was only half a mile from the county line) because it drained off the city's rightful tax base. I thought everyone had a moral position on communities, cities, and states during the urban-renewal heyday in which I grew up.

Part of this intense affinity for Baltimore comes from the city's idiosyncratic status as both southern and northern. And when Baltimoreans ask where you went to school, they mean high school, not college. Once I moved out of Baltimore, my new friends and acquaintances tended to be wealthier, better educated, and more personally ambitious than the people I had known there. They had a "rootless cosmopolitanism" about them, as a friend of mine once characterized it. They usually hailed from Westchester or northern New Jersey, but it would often be months before I discovered where they had grown up. It just never seemed that interesting or relevant because those places hadn't imprinted themselves on their minds.

It is no accident that sports talk, which mines the lore of regions and exploits their provincial twangs and idiosyncrasies, endures as a relatively polite discourse for a largely White male constituency. Loyalty to place, to communities founded by geographic serendipity rather than by design (with racial exclusions ultimately achieved through property ownership) or by religious/ideological homogeneity, perhaps modifies racist and sexist sentiments. At the very least, our shared investment in the operatic fortunes of Baltimore teams has saved my own family from otherwise hopelessly contentious, internecine political and personal differences. Some of my fondest memories involve being thankful that another stormy debate had been deflected when my brother, a passionate master of sports mythology, trivia, and lore, began to tell a story about the Baltimore Colts (or "Coats," in Baltimore dialect). He'd reminisce on games played before Colts owner Robert Irsay furtively relocated the team to Indianapolis in 1984, with stunningly undisguised cowardice, in the middle of the night. This is what really feels like "coming home" to me—the moment I hear the compulsively retold tale again, relieved of the pressures of political and social vigilance, allowed the slothful pleasure of nostalgia.

And relieved of the pressure of feeling so annoyed and exasperated all the time: when you discuss sports, you are especially reminded of why you *like* people, occasions sorely lacking in the joyless, embattled discussions of 1990s politics. It's hard for me to imagine that the callers I chuckle with on WFAN might do evil and unkind things in other arenas of their lives because fandom endows them with such passion and virtue. Everyone who listens closely to sports talk and legend knows that what's being discussed isn't necessarily sports. Through displacement, sports talk speaks to a particular moment in the fan's life and to a special feeling of regional affinity that is associated with it. As my brother comments, "In every town with any kind of team, there's some fool like me with as many stories about his franchise as I have about the Colts."

Sports talk radio exploits the same kind of nostalgia for regionalism and, to some extent, recreates it. In any major radio market, the typology of the sports-talk-show host will dictate a middle-aged man (the briefly famous "sports babe" of ESPN Radio is a notable exception) with an extreme or unusual voice whose speech is typically marked by dialect, wobbly syntax, and poor grammar. His rhetorical style will tend toward malapropism, the expression of passionate opinions about seemingly trivial events, and an ability to finesse intimacy with anonymous callers. The typology notwithstanding, these radio personalities are idiosyncratic and decidedly noncorporate voices; steeped in regional specificity, many of them, ironically, want to "be everywhere," an ambition that can only be achieved through syndication.[24]

San Francisco sports-talk-show host Scott Ferrall has garnered what the *Chronicle* describes as a "cultlike status" among Generation X listeners, who "either love him" or "despise" him: "You need a seat belt when you listen to Ferrall. He talks as fast as an auctioneer, his voice is gravelly and instinctive. He favors truncated words. He'll say anything. . . . He is to sports talk radio what Camille Paglia is to academic discourse."[25] Ferrall produces "talk show graffiti," the *Chronicle* concludes, aptly capturing the outlaw quality of his voice and delivery, so distinctive in an age of more modulated, even slick, communication styles. Each city, of course, has its own Mad Dog, Eckman, or Ferrall. Chicago has Mike North, who is paired with African American, Harvard-educated, ex–football player Dan Jiggetts. "North comes under attack for his untrained voice and lack of professionalism," notes the *Chicago Tribune.*

> To North, "Da Bears" is the natural way to pronounce the name of his favorite football team. "Some guys talk different when they go on the radio," North says, "You talk to me on the air, I'm the same." In some

ways North's West Side accent (even though he's from the North Side) is the *station's biggest asset.*[26]

In New Orleans, it is Buddy DeLiberto ("Buddy D") who offers the "free flow of ideas, uninhibited expression, the outpouring of dysfunction unique to talk radio."[27] Pete Rose fields calls from a bar in Florida, but he aspires, like Ferrall, to become the "Rush Limbaugh of sports." With characteristic confusion, he explains, "I'm just learning how to do this now where I can use my personality, you know, my antidotes and stories."[28] Meanwhile in Chicago, Coppock, who describes himself as a "shameless self-promoter," dons a raccoon coat and loud ties, and "cultivates a voice with the range of a fog horn." On his radio show, he "delights in jargon and pretense . . . calling everybody pal and buddy."[29]

Callers, the pals and buddies of the radio-electrified night, are actually the "product" that a station sells to its advertisers, but in the world of sports talk they are considered "the stars of the show."[30] Each city has its cast of celebrity callers: St. Louis has "Fred from Fliassen," "Diamond Lil," "Deep Throat," "Jackie O," "Ted the Cop," "Bob the Economist," and "Black Jesus," while New Orleans is home to "The Tiptoe Burglar," "Dr. Kevorkian," and "Bubba on the Magic Carpet." Chicago boasts "Sister Mary Chain of Lakes, the Handicapping Nun," Atlanta "The Black Quarterback from the Valley of the Dry Bones" and "The Big Dog from Windsor." Under such colorful aliases, certain callers in every city acquire a celebrity status in their own right and blur the distinction between talk-show host and audience.[31] Hosts such as Mad Dog similarly blur the boundaries between advertising and entertainment. Given his idiosyncratic pronunciation and tendency to stop in the middle of a pitch for the Men's Hair Club or the Vermont Teddy Bear Company and confess to his sidekick, "I don't know if I can pronounce this word, Mikey," it is sometimes as entertaining to hear The Dog hawking wares as it is to listen to his monologue; his idiosyncrasies can raise even the most banal messages to the heights of low comedy. When Chicago sports-show host Dan Azzaro produces and sells a tape of his specialty — parodies of commercials — products-marketing becomes a product in its own right.[32]

The fact that hosts and callers represent the same types in every city, yet also manage to seem unique and idiosyncratic, allies sports talk shows with the genre of TV programming exemplified by such series as the stylish (and regrettably canceled) *My So-Called Life* and MTV's *Real World*, which records and then narrativizes the day-to-day activities of several Generation Xers living together in a San Francisco apartment. *My So-Called Life* for middle-aged White men, WFAN presents the banal soundtracks of other people's lives as entertainment. Inexplicably drawn in by monologues sprinkled generously with "it's likes," "ums," "you knows," and "I'm all/she's all"—a stream of unedited stuttering and verbal incoherence that culminates in some vague, cliché-filled confrontation between stock characters—we listen to people struggling for an authentic way to express themselves and their desires: *we listen*, precisely. Both Generation Xers and the coveted Testosterone Set that keeps sports radio rolling seem to thirst for some unmediated communication or human interaction, needing to connect with, or at least to eavesdrop on, everyday life—ironically, by consuming it as entertainment.[33] Neither a television show like *My So-Called Life* nor talk radio more generally aims for stylish production, but rather for the halting, unrehearsed authenticity of the impassioned banal. Mike Francesca and The Dog augment this effect by not discussing their show more than ten minutes beforehand and by openly confessing their discontents with each other and the job—the onerous road trips, salary disputes, and so on. Qualitatively, their show strays as far as possible from the "corporate voice" that undergirds it, the homogeneous and ubiquitous sound of satellite broadcasts that seem to emanate from nowhere in particular, but seem to be received everywhere. The main criticism of talk radio by the sports world—that it circulates bull and represents the mental dregs of sports when it should be knowledgeable and informative—thus misses the point. Sports talk revels in useless information and in so doing flouts the Information Age axiom that communication, and the access to facts it represents, determines economic viability and identity. A meandering, dull sort of front-porch talk—redundant and aimless but steeped in passion and knowledge, if not information—in an age when communication is expected to *do* something, sports talk demonstrates an older function of communication, that of concretizing social rather than economic communities. As columnist Mike Royko says in parodying sports talk radio:

> You will hear the host, Bill Babble, and the city's most dedicated sports fans saying things like, "Yo, jo, how you going, yo? I believe you be-

cause you tell it like it is. . . . Hey, the way it is, is the way it is . . . because if you don't tell it the way it is, you're telling it the way it isn't and the way it isn't will never be the way it is."[34]

The very conditions that have made sports talk radio such a dazzling format for the 1990s—deregulation, national syndication, and an easily exploited captive audience of commuters—are ironically belied by its recourse to, and revitalization of, local or regional idiosyncrasy. Sports talk radio, in fact, confirms some of George Lipsitz's observations on television's introduction of new popular forms. Establishing itself in the suburban scene of the 1950s, many of television's early shows nevertheless recalled a 1930s urban lifestyle and community, thereby veiling the extent to which the new medium and postwar class formations had obliterated this community.[35] Sports talk radio, despite being disseminated and popularized by the stations of such conglomerates as Infinity, seems to thrive precisely insofar as it remains adamantly quirky and regional. Perhaps in reaction to the "corporate voice," listeners seem to crave dysfunctional speech—verbal idiosyncrasies that, in an age of modulated communication, have become quaint and something to be treasured. When I listen to sports talk radio, I feel some renewed optimism. It comes not from any guiltily reinvigorated faith in rightfully challenged liberal pretenses about "agreeing to disagree" or in the possibility of everybody's being treated the same, whether "purple, yellow, orange, or green." Instead, it comes from the evidence on sports talk shows that people *do* want to be thrown together in unexpected, impassioned, even random social relations and communities. They want to mix with people they have nothing (but sports) in common with. They want to be *from* somewhere again, to be part of a heterogeneous tribe rather than a narrowly defined political cabal.

As a genre, sports talk radio promulgates a provincialism that is at odds with the economic conditions under which the stations flourish and the audience lives. Many listeners tune in during the approximately three hours a day they spend commuting from one locale to another, belying the regional coherence evoked by the talk-show hosts. Indeed, nothing characterizes Generation X more than the no-stick surface of its lifestyle, a transience that would seem to preclude any attachment to places. Most of the stations are owned by one of only a few national corporations. The FAN's arch-rival, WIP in Philadelphia ("Men! Don't get 'wipped' into part-time sports coverage!"), is actually owned by Infinity as well, making this a false, Pepsi–Coke rivalry. The local or quotidian has, in short, become something of a genre in its own right, albeit a deceptively packaged and marketed one. The genre's commodification resembles that of "history," which can now be variously marketed in a theme park or a movie such as *Forrest Gump* that invokes history only to allow its protagonist to run through it unchanged and unscathed, utterly lacking any sense of his own historicity. The quest for what communications mavens think of, paradoxically, as "national local" broadcasting captures sports talk radio's peculiar status as well. As the *Washington Business Journal* reported in 1990,

> Radio officials believe isolated radio stations could become power-houses by having access to satellite transmission. For instance, a religious station in Louisiana limited by its signal could, through satellite, rain its programing down on listeners with specially tuned radios nationwide. The purpose of a satellite broadcasting service is very beneficial for the *local broadcaster* because he can *broadcast nationally*.[36]

I wonder what construction of "local" would encompass shows "broadcast nationally." "Local" in this sense would evidently define the generic properties of a broadcaster or program, perhaps with reference to origins in a particular culture and place, rather than a station's signal range or territory per se.

The genre of sports talk radio, in its most successful modes, is anachronistically committed to this sense of the local as a discourse and to fandom as a means, however awkwardly realized, of inclusion. If we wish to find any signs of grace and dignity in interactions between strangers these days, we cannot afford to ignore them in such popular venues as fandom and sports talk radio. They can teach us how to speak both civilly and passionately to one another, how to make a community of and for a lot of people who lead isolated, often lonely lives in America. Sports talk is not rocket science, but a discourse that orbits around what many feel is a culturally trivial activity. Nevertheless, as Richard Rorty has observed, despite the sophistication of our political and theoretical analyses, we do not have much more than the kindness and decency of others to rely on politically.[37] These days, we must take such an ethic where we find it. As WFAN listeners like to affirm at the end of a testy call, "Well, *Dawg*, you're crazy wrong about the Knicks as usual, but I'll be listening tomorrow anyway."

Notes

Thanks to Jim Fisher, a true sport, and to all the other people I've bored with my WFAN obsession.

1 Susan Bickelhaup, "Andelman Is Free to Join the WEEI," *Boston Globe*, 4 July 1991, 6: 1.
2 See WFAN promotional material; and Lisa Leigh Parney, "Sports Talk Scores with Radio Listeners," *Christian Science Monitor*, 2 September 1994, 12.
3 As quoted in Rick Reilly, "Look out for the Bull! The Prattle Emanating from Sports Talk Shows Is Polluting the Air Waves," *Sports Illustrated*, 14 March 1994, 76.
4 See Eileen Norris, "The 1980s: A Decade in Review," *Electronic Media*, 1 January 1990.
5 "Radio in the 1980s," *Los Angeles Times*, 27 December 1989.
6 As quoted in Martha Middleton, "A Clear Signal from the FCC: Deregulation Is Key," *National Law Journal*, 21 January 1985, 1.
7 Ibid.
8 "Radio in the 1980s." See also Jill Rush, "Local Broadcasters Upset over New Fairness Doctrine Bill," *Indianapolis Business Journal*, 2 November 1987, 14; David Kelly, "FCC Responds to Hill's Static," *Hollywood Reporter*, 18 March 1993; Tanya Bickley, "Don't Touch that Radio Dial," *Christian Science Monitor*, 7 March 1980, 23; Middleton, "Clear Signal from the FCC," 1; Jay Sharbutt, "FCC's Patrick Boosts Deregulation's Effects," *Los Angeles Times*, 23 September 1988, 24; and Norris, "The 1980s," 28.
9 As quoted in Timothy McQuiston, "Radio: Vermont Stations Proliferate under FCC Ruling," *Vermont Business Magazine* (April 1990): 11.
10 Herbert Schiller, *Culture, Inc.* (New York, 1989), 40.
11 Middleton, "Clear Signal from the FCC," 2–3.
12 Bickley, "Don't Touch that Radio Dial," 23–24.
13 As quoted in Mark Lewyn, "Airwaves Wars," *Business Week*, 23 July 1990, 48.
14 Dan Kening, "Radio Syndicator Stays ahead of Game," *Chicago Tribune*, 15 September 1991.
15 Paul Galloway, "Coppock on Coppock," *Chicago Tribune*, 18 July 1993, 5; Frank Ahrens, "For All-Sports Radio, Fans Are All Ears," *Washington Post*, 11 February 1993, B: 1.
16 Kening, "Radio Syndicator."
17 "Sports Nightly Radio," *Chicago Tribune*, 16 November 1993, 5: 2. See also Parney, "Sports Talk Scores," 12; Bill Stoneman, "Radio Stations Change Formats to Find Right Niche," *Capital District Business Review*, 21 November 1988, 1; and Raymond Snoddy, "Tuning in to Radio Diversity," *Financial Times*, 23 January 1988, 6.
18 "Sports Nightly Radio," 5: 2. See also McQuiston, "Radio"; David Nickell, "AM/FM Warfare," *South Florida Business Journal*, 14 March 1988, 6; and Erik Larsen, *The Naked Consumer* (New York, 1992), 79.
19 Prentis Rogers, "Management Denies Fan Talk on the Way Out," *Atlanta Constitution*, 16 November 1993, D: 2; see also Ahrens, "For All-Sports Radio."
20 Kevin Cook, "Media," *Playboy* (April 1993): 20.
21 Eve Kosofsky Sedgwick, *The Epistemology of the Closet* (Berkeley, 1990).
22 Fred Rasmussen, "Sports Personality Charley Eckman Dies; He was 'Certified Baltimore Character,'" *Baltimore Sun*, 4 July 1995, 1.

23 Ibid.

24 Glenn Sheeley, "Talking Pete Rose Radio," *Atlanta Constitution*, 23 March 1993, E: 2.

25 Jonathan Curiel, "Hey Ferrall! You Freak! Pour Me a Tall One!" *San Francisco Chronicle*, 19 February 1995, 1.

26 Robert Marcus, "WSCR: Little Station Gains Big Reputation," *Chicago Tribune*, 28 January 1993, 4: 1.

27 Mark Lorando, "Buddy D's the Talk of the Town," *New Orleans Times–Picayune*, 30 March 1994, E:1:3; see also Marty Mule, "Buddy D. Delighted to Be Talk of the Town," *New Orleans Times–Picayune*, 22 January 1995, C:17:2.

28 Sheeley, "Talking Pete Rose Radio," 1: 2.

29 Galloway, "Coppock on Coppock," 1: 2.

30 Joe Strauss, "Caller Approaches Celebrity Status," *Atlanta Constitution*, 30 June 1993, E: 7.

31 See Jimmy Smith, "Radio Days," *New Orleans Times–Picayune*, 18 October 1994, E: 1; William Rhoden, "A Celebrity Caller Is King for a Day," *New York Times*, 26 December 1994, A: 49; and John McGuire, "Dialing for Hollers: Regulars Hit Phones and Bring Quirkiness to Radio Talk Shows," *St. Louis Post–Dispatch*, 3 January 1993, F: 1.

32 See Dan Kening, "Dan Azzaro's Fan Talk Sees the Humor in Sports," *Chicago Tribune*, 17 March 1992, 4.

33 Lawrence Grossberg astutely comments on the substance of "everyday life" and its fragility, arguing that only those with sufficient economic and social security can actually have an everyday life; see *We Gotta Get out of This Place* (New York, 1992).

34 Mike Royko, "Cubs Babble Picks up Right Where It Left Off," *Chicago Tribune*, 4 April 1995, 1: 3.

35 See George Lipsitz, *Time Passages: Collective Memory in American Popular Culture* (Minneapolis, 1991).

36 Doug Abrahms, "District Group Seeks Permit for Satellite-Based Radio Net," *Washington Business Journal*, 28 May 1990, 1.

37 Richard Rorty, "Wild Orchids and Trotsky," in *Wild Orchids and Trotsky: Notes from the University*, ed. Mark Edmundson (New York, 1993), 50.

Michael Oriard

Home Teams

As I began this draft, the 1995 NBA playoffs were in the second round, and my teenaged son Colin's favorite team, the Indianapolis Pacers, was still alive. Next to the Pacers, Colin liked the Los Angeles Lakers and the Denver Nuggets best. Among the college teams that year, he rooted for Wake Forest and Maryland. During football season, he liked New England, San Francisco, and Kansas City in the NFL, while his favorite college teams were Notre Dame and Nebraska. And once baseball got into full swing, he followed the White Sox, Red Sox, and Rockies most avidly. In recent years he has at various times loved the Oakland Athletics, Atlanta Braves, Charlotte Hornets, Memphis State Tigers, and Cincinnati Bearcats—often for a particular player (José Canseco, Larry Johnson, Anfernee Hardaway, or Nick Van Exel)—but in the case of the Braves because WTBS brought them into our home night after night throughout the summer.

We live in Corvallis, Oregon, 80 miles south of Portland and the Trailblazers, 1,000 miles from Los Angeles, 2,500 from Indianapolis, and 3,000 from College Park, Maryland. Corvallis is

The *South Atlantic Quarterly* 95:2, Spring 1996.
Copyright © 1996 by Duke University Press.
CCC 0038-2876/96/$1.50.

home to Oregon State University, whose football and basketball teams have failed to win my son's loyalty because they have failed to win PAC-10 titles. Colin followed the Trailblazers during the seasons when they reached the NBA finals, but he's lost interest as they've lost close to half their games in recent years. Were he permitted, Colin would live about six feet away from our television set, where all his teams reside, where every team is the home team. At my son's age I lived in Spokane, Washington, in the early 1960s. "My" college basketball team was the Gonzaga University Bulldogs. A GU guard named Frank Burgess had won a national scoring championship when I was in the sixth grade at Sacred Heart; I had a Polaroid photo of myself taken with Burgess at the school's fundraising carnival that year. Gonzaga did not have a football team, but Washington State College in Pullman, about ninety miles south of Spokane, did; and the Cougars were my team. I paid little attention to pro basketball, but I was a Cardinals fan in baseball and a Rams fan in football. With no teams west of the Mississippi, I had selected St. Louis when I first became conscious of baseball in the mid-1950s because of Stan Musial. (My older brother picked the Red Sox and Ted Williams.) In the early 1960s, I added the Los Angeles Dodgers to my roster not because they had moved to the West Coast, but because most of their star players passed through their Triple-A farm club in Spokane. I chose the LA Rams from a pool of two NFL teams— the other was San Francisco—because those were the ones that appeared on Sunday television in Spokane. I picked LA over the 49ers partly for the swirling ram horn on the helmets.

My son and I are to some degree representative of our generations. My childhood sporting world was more local, his is more national; mine was largely defined by geography, his by television. Mine was characterized by scarcity, and by comedy or tragedy; his by abundance, and by farce or melodrama. My TV *Game of the Week* has become his dozen games of the day on ESPN's *Sports Center*. My hopes rose and fell with the fortunes of my local teams from season to season; he always has a winner to back, changing "loyalties" as necessary from one year to the next. I had a couple of "home teams"; every team, and no team, is his.

I am targeting the impact of television on fans' relation to sports here not to add another verse to the Luddite anti-TV chorus, but to pinpoint one aspect of U.S. spectator sports that remained essential from their rise in the middle of the nineteenth century to the end of the pretelevision age in the middle of the twentieth: their local-rootedness. Over the centuries before organized spectator sports emerged in the West—from the original Olympic games through the folk games of medieval Europe and beyond—sports had been defined even more unequivocally by place (as well as by class). The rise of spectator sports in the nineteenth century did not initially alter the traditional nature of sports, but it unloosed the forces that would eventually do so. If we set aside the economic and institutional transformation of sports to focus on the fans' experiences of the games, what seems clear is that as popular spectator sports have become democratized (however incompletely) and mediated (first by the press, then by radio and film, and finally by television), they have been less closely identified with particular groups and places. The press, beginning in the late nineteenth century and then enhanced by radio in the second quarter of the twentieth, gradually established a national sporting culture within which, however, teams generally retained their local identities. To a radically greater degree, television since the 1960s has freed, or unmoored, teams from this local-rootedness.

The change has not been simply one of loss. Nostalgic golden-agers too easily forget, for example, that segregation—Jim Crow baseball and football—was one consequence of tribal identification with sports. Television and the integration of sports advanced together and are more than coincidentally related. I would hesitantly suggest that television has by this time nearly deracinated the Black athletes who dominate football and basketball for young viewers such as my son (as it has similarly deracinated Black entertainers). Their walk, their talk, their gestures, and their dress are now emulated by White kids like Colin, who remain oblivious to the irony of this emulation in a still racially troubled America. White kids as well as Black want to "be like Mike"; White kids as well as Black low-ride and wear their baseball caps backward. Colin is acutely aware that his favorite athletes and musicians are Black, but he apprehends their Blackness chiefly as language and gesture, as dress and style. (Whether televised sports ultimately teach lessons in race relations that will prove beneficial to society as a whole, I do not know, but Black athletes have certainly benefited from sports' usurpation by the national media. It is also obvious, however, that elements of tribalism, including racism, persist among sports fans despite television, just as more virulent kinds of tribalism persist in our late-twentieth-century world despite the various forces of globalizing modernity.)

I cite the example of Jim Crow sports not to initiate a discussion of race, but to indicate that the loss of local-rootedness is not simply an erosion of sporting values. I am less interested here in judging than in exploring this local-rootedness, specifically in football, during the period from American sports' so-called golden age of the 1920s up to the dawn of the TV era.

≡≡≡

Red Grange's 1925 professional debut with the Chicago Bears provides a useful case study in the power of local-rootedness for the period as a whole. While Grange was by no means football's first star, he was arguably its first celebrity. His coronation by the press took place in his junior year of college, on 19 October 1924, the day after Illinois thumped Michigan (39–14), with Grange scoring five touchdowns, passing for a sixth, and gaining 402 yards rushing. Grantland Rice immortalized Notre Dame's "Four Horsemen" on the same day, but Grange's fame exceeded theirs in the intercollegiate world, perhaps because it was concentrated in a single player rather than spread over a quartet. At a time when sports-page headlines about football games rarely named players but only teams, Grange got marquee billing week after week during his last two years at Illinois. Over the course of his senior season, newspaper reports of Grange's exploits in games were even supplemented by a serialized biography, syndicated throughout the country, all of which amounted to unprecedented recognition of an individual player in an amateur team sport. The story of an unpromising lad who built himself up into a spectacular intercollegiate ballcarrier, most famously by hefting blocks of ice for eight summers in Wheaton, Illinois, became instant history and legend.

Given Grange's celebrity, the question of his postgraduate plans became increasingly urgent over the closing weeks of the 1925 football season, as rumors periodically leaked out of Champaign that the Redhead/Galloping Ghost/Wheaton Ice Man might turn pro. In 1925, professional football was less than unimportant in the United States; it was felt by the majority of fans to corrupt the sport's essential spirit. "Professionalism" had periodically blighted the intercollegiate game since its beginnings in the last quarter of the nineteenth century. The very term stigmatized the recruiting of players, the paying of coaches, and the playing of baseball for pay at summer resorts—any activity that brought money openly into contact with college football or punctured the illusion that players were anything but regular students engaged in an extracurricular activity. Although professional baseball had already earned a cherished place in American life by the 1920s, professional football continued to be perceived as the dark underside of the college game.

When Red Grange announced at the end of the 1925 college season that he was turning professional—without completing his senior year at Illinois—his decision consequently provoked a deluge of articles and commentaries in the sporting press that might seem incomprehensible now in our NFL-saturated times. While the Harvard and Yale campus dailies, Grange's own coach at Illinois, and the intercollegiate world in general accused Red of betraying his alma mater and profaning sacred amateurism, the extracollegiate world reacted more pragmatically, asking how anyone could pass up the riches that Grange immediately earned. Although journalists spoke with no consensus, they generally took Grange's side. An editorial in the *New York Times*, for example, insisted that Grange had the "one talent which it is death to hide" and "enormously profitable to exploit," so "there [was] no reason in morals or esthetics why the rewards should be withheld from the most famous name in the American ice industry since Eliza crossed the Ohio in front of the bloodhounds."[1]

The *Times* spoke with metropolitan worldliness from an NFL city; in the provinces local sports editors variously took up each side of the issue.[2] The most consistent, and compelling, defenses of Grange's action took one of two forms: an argument that college football would survive unharmed, or a display of awe at the amount of money Grange immediately began to earn. From New York to Omaha to Seattle, headlines proclaimed: "Red Grange Gets $82,000 in Eleven Days; $16,000 a Game Is His Average as a Pro"; and "Grange's Profits since Leaving University of Illinois Total Nearly $500,000." (These figures were consistently inflated.) One cartoon depicted the Redhead running alongside Father Time (reminder of fleeting fame), with a bag of gold under his arm representing "The Million He's Out to Make."[3] A feature article in the *American Weekly*, the Hearst chain's nationally syndicated Sunday supplement, described the "Beggers [*sic*], Fakers, Get-Rich-Quick Schemers, Charity Workers, Designing Women and the Income Tax Foxes" who were "Tormenting the Famous Football Star." Not just Grange's share of the gate for the football games, but also his endorsements and movie contract (originally reported at $300,000) received a full accounting (Figure 1):

> $1,000 for admitting that a cigarette smelled all right, though he does not smoke; $10,000 for wearing a sweater and agreeing that it was

Figure 1. "Trying to Get Some of 'Red' Grange's Easy Money," *The American Weekly* (Hearst Syndicate Sunday supplement), *Seattle Post–Intelligencer*, 3 January 1926. Reproduced courtesy of the *Seattle Post–Intelligencer*.

warm; $5,000 for putting his swift feet in a pair of somebody's shoes; $2,000 for enjoying a ride in a certain automobile; $10,000 for permitting his name to be attached to a red-headed football doll; $10,000 more for his expert judgement that a certain firm's football felt as snug in his arm as any he had ever carried over a goal line, etc., etc.[4]

The writer was not critical of these extravagant giveaways but sympathetic to their beneficiary, who had become a target for the truly undeserving: tax collectors and pitchmen for various charities; "vamps of all kinds, with love on their lips and dollar signs in their eyes"; even a supposed "welfare organization that worked to uplift the East Side poor of New York," but whose "uplift" turned out to consist "of Communist propaganda, which he does not care for. 'Red' Grange is not 'red' and does not think a football team could be run on Soviet lines."[5] To those unmoved by pleas for the purity of amateur sports, Red Grange could stand as a hero for the emerging age of consumption.

College authorities genuinely—if mistakenly or even hypocritically—felt threatened by Grange's defection to the National Football League. Bans on all forms of professionalism enacted in December 1925 by the Southern Conference and the Missouri Valley Conference were reported in newspapers alongside coverage of Grange's tour and provoked responses from local sports editors. Other aspects of the controversy were driven by barely disguised class prejudice. The NFL in 1925 had an unsavory reputation for spiritless brutality, corruption by association with gambling, and "professionalism" itself. The class bias that underwrote this disdain was belied by the reality of professional football. Historian Steven Riess has determined that during the 1920s only 20 percent of the players in the NFL had not attended college. (By 1933, the figure had shrunk to two percent.)[6] In general, histories of professional football suggest that the majority of those non-college men played in the earliest years of the NFL (before Grange turned pro) when most teams were located in small industrial towns and manned by blue-collar workers. Players received $75 to $100 per game, playing football on weekends to supplement their income from regular employment.[7] Nevertheless, pro football was by no means a "working-class" sport. Even if that entire 20 percent had played before 1925, well over half of the professionals that year were college men. At a time when about 10 percent of all eighteen-year-olds went to college, pro football players were markedly better educated than the population as a whole. Riess cites the example of the Providence Steamrollers, nine of whose twenty-two players in 1924 attended local Brown University.[8] By 1925, all but one player on the Pottsville Maroons—a team formed in a largely Catholic, recent-immigrant, working-class region—were college graduates.[9] The class bias against pro football that crept into the Red Grange controversy remained impervious to such counterevidence. As one savvy reporter at the time commented in the *Dallas Morning News,* no one complained about the money earned by Jack Dempsey or Babe Ruth, but that was because Dempsey was "an alumnus of the brake beam and fellow of the handout," while Ruth was "the most famous alumnus of a Baltimore orphanage and a magna cum [laude] graduate of the National Sand Lots." For such as these, pay-for-play violated no sacred principle. When Grange turned pro, on the other hand, it was— in the writer's lively analogy—"as if Mary, the minister's pretty daughter, who sang in the little church choir, had snapped her hymn book shut and stepped out of her gingham and signed on with some tawdry burlesque troop to chirp shoddy ditties and kick toward the rafters a shamelessly unclothed limb."[10]

≡≡≡

Class prejudice could not, of course, be openly expressed in the sports pages, given sports' claims to open competition and fair play. Once the initial furor abated, the fact remained that Red Grange, until recently the most famous amateur football player in the land, was now a professional, and he changed the professional game permanently. Every popular history of the NFL has singled out Grange's professional debut with the Chicago Bears on Thanksgiving Day 1925, and the barnstorming tour that followed, as the turning point in the game's early history, but its significance has been variously interpreted as

—yet another crisis over "professionalism" and the "overemphasis" of football in college;
—the event that saved the struggling pro league from oblivion;
—the incident that resulted in the NFL's agreeing not to sign any college player until his class had graduated (a cornerstone of the college draft system until successfully challenged in the 1980s);
—the first triumph of the arts of promotion and marketing that the NFL would eventually perfect.

For my purposes, what Grange's inaugural tour of NFL cities with the Bears, followed by his swing through the South and West for exhibition games with local all-star teams, most interestingly reveals is not how the NFL first gained a popular following, but why it was not yet able to do so. Before the age of television, football's essential local-rootedness kept the professional game from attracting any broad following outside the cities where franchises were located. Grange's tour was an unprecedented media event for the sport of football, but the medium was the press, not television, and the press primarily serves local cultures.

First, the facts. Grange turned pro immediately after his final college game on 21 November 1925 and debuted with George Halas's Chicago Bears at Wrigley Field five days later, playing the crosstown Cardinals before a sellout crowd of 36,000.[11] Following an itinerary orchestrated by Grange's agent — Charlie "Cash-and-Carry" Pyle, the Champaign theater owner who, along with Tex Rickard, founded modern sports promotions — the Bears then played nine more games, in eight cities, over the next sixteen days against

> —the Columbus Tigers on the following Sunday, 29 November, again at Wrigley Field, this time before 28,000 spectators;
> —the Donnelly Stars in St. Louis the following Wednesday, before a crowd of 8,000;
> —the Frankford Yellow Jackets in Philadelphia on Saturday, with 40,000 in the stands;
> —the New York Giants in the Polo Grounds the next day, to catch a Sunday crowd of 65,000;
> —three different teams in three days (after one day off): a team of locals in Washington, DC, the Providence Steamrollers in Boston, and some local all-stars in Pittsburgh;
> —the Detroit Panthers in Detroit (after another day off), before only 6,000 (angry) fans as Grange sat out with an injury;
> —the Giants, in a Chicago rematch on 13 December before a Wrigley Field crowd that had shrunk to 15,000, as Grange sat on the bench for the second straight game, nursing a damaged arm.

Retellings of this story tend to emphasize the herculean stamina of an eighteen-man squad playing ten games in seventeen days, harking back to a time when men were men, not the pantywaists who barely manage to stay upright for a single game each week, playing only on offense or defense, perhaps only on passing or short-yardage downs. The modern reader might more properly marvel that professional football was gentle enough in 1925 to conceive of its being played on a baseball schedule. I am interested, however, not in comparative masculinities but in public relations, particularly the public to whom Grange and his fellow professionals were relating in the fall and winter of 1925–26.

After their rematch with the Giants on 13 December, the Bears took an eight-day breather before embarking on a 7,000-mile trip through the South and West, a schedule-as-you-go barnstorming tour of nine cities. Land-boom Florida was the first stop, where a 25,000-seat stadium had been erected in Coral Gables by promoters who expected to make a killing at $5.50 to $18.00 a seat. (Tickets for NFL games normally cost fifty cents or a dollar.) Fewer than 10,000 fans showed up to see Grange and the Bears beat an all-star team on Christmas Day. Contests in Tampa on New Year's Day (against 41-year-old Jim Thorpe and his hastily assembled Tampa Cardinals) and in Jacksonville the following day (against the recently formed Jacksonville All-Stars led by ex-Stanford star Ernie Nevers, making his own professional debut) completed the Bears' swing through Florida. New Orleans was next up, on 10 January, for a match with an all-Southern team led by Tulane's Lester Lautenschlager. Apparently, the Bears found no takers in Texas. (Possible games in Houston, San Antonio, and Dallas, as well as in Atlanta and Birmingham, had been announced in the press on 19 December but did not materialize.[12]) The team then landed in Los Angeles and worked the Pacific Coast for the next two weeks. A crowd of 70,000 filled the LA Coliseum on 16 January as Grange and company took on the locally assembled Los Angeles Tigers led by George Wilson, an all-American halfback from the University of Washington team that had recently lost to Alabama in the Rose Bowl. The next day, in San Diego, the Bears took on the All-Californians, largely the same team and again led by George Wilson, but renamed for the sake of the locals.[13] A week later, Wilson and a new supporting cast took another shot at Grange and the Bears in San Francisco before 20,000 spectators in Kezar Stadium, and for the first time the Bears lost. Wilson then accompanied Grange north to Portland and Seattle to lead the opposition for the last two exhibition games: in Portland on 30 January, against a team calling itself the Waterfront

Longshoremen; and in Seattle the following day, against the Washington All-Stars, a team organized for that occasion.

By Grange's count, the nine-city tour attracted 150,000 fans, while in eighteen games over a 66-day period he had played before more than 400,000 spectators and earned $125,000 in salary and another $85,000 in endorsements. (For perspective, consider that in 1925 a new car cost about $400, and the average pro football salary was around $100 a game.[14]) "The important thing to note about the tour," according to Grange's collaborator on his 1953 gee-whiz autobiography, "was that professional football got the exposure it desperately needed, fans were impressed with the quality of play, and the NFL finally came of age."[15] Grange's own assessment was similar: "We made enough pro-football converts all over the land to give the sport the shot in the arm it so badly needed and, from the 1925 season on, professional football began to grow steadily in popularity."[16]

Not exactly. My alternative sources for Grange's tour are the newspapers in the cities where he played, and they tell a slightly different story. For one thing, Grange's numbers are at least a bit inflated: the barnstorming tour through the South and West attracted closer to 135,000 than 150,000 spectators, but more telling is the fact that over half of them attended a single game (in Los Angeles), while only one other drew more than 10,000.[17] For the entire eighteen games, the newspapers' total is closer to 300,000 than 400,000, or an average attendance of about 17,000, but if the games in the Polo Grounds and the LA Coliseum are excluded, the average is closer to 10,000.[18] To put these numbers in perspective, crowds at the Bears' home games in 1925 also averaged 10,000; league-wide the average was half that number.[19]

Although these revised figures seem to deflate Grange's impact, a comparison of attendance at the stops on the Bears' tour reveals that a healthy Grange did in fact draw significantly larger crowds than usual, while an injured Grange kept many fans away. The Bears' first two games at Wrigley Field drew 36,000 and 28,000, respectively, while their Grange-less final game at Wrigley attracted only 15,000. The Grange-led Bears games in other NFL cities — Columbus, Philadelphia, Providence, Detroit, and New York — drew 28,000, 35,000, 25,000, 5,000, and 65,000, respectively (according to the *New York Daily News*, not Grange). He sat out the Detroit game, hence the paltry 5,000 spectators (no more than a typical game drew that season). Attendance at the games in which Grange played was thus several times higher than the league average. The 65,000 fans who filled the Polo Grounds more than doubled the Giants' previous record crowd of 30,000 (on 22 November) and even more dramatically outstripped the 18,000, 20,000, and 27,000 spectators for other games that season. (An 8 November game played in heavy rain drew all of 4,000.)[20] The Giants were new to the NFL in 1925. The *New York Times* report of their first game, in New Brighton, Connecticut, introduced them to a readership that may not even have known they existed: "The New York Giants, a professional football eleven, inaugurated their season here this afternoon."[21] From this quiet beginning well before Red Grange's advent, then, the Giants attracted an impressively large following in a short time, but Grange's arrival with the Bears caused an explosion of new interest. Similarly in Chicago, the Bears and the Cardinals received very modest coverage by the *Tribune* in 1925 (with the Cards usually taking top billing) until Grange's joining the Bears provoked headlines, major stories, and commentary day after day. The broadcast of Grange's Thanksgiving Day debut by WGN was the first, and only, radio broadcast of a pro football game that season. (College football fans, in contrast, had a choice of four local games on Chicago stations each Saturday.) In the other cities where pro football was already known, Red Grange's power to draw new fans to the ballpark is likewise irrefutable.

On his tour through the South and West, Grange brought professional football to places that had never seen it. Given the coverage by local papers, we can readily assume that it was chiefly Grange who drew fans to these games. Even the meager five or six thousand who turned out in New Orleans, Portland, and Seattle would likely not have come at all for the Grange-less Bears. Wherever the Bears played, the draw was Red Grange, not professional football. Commenting on the enormous crowd at the Polo Grounds for the Bears–Giants game, an impressed *New York Times* editorialist suggested that professional football was especially appealing to local fans "who do not go to college football exhibitions, mainly because tickets are scarce and the cost prohibitive."[22] Intercollegiate football had a huge audience, which pro football still lacked in 1925. In contrast to the average crowds of 17,000 that Grange drew when he played with the Bears (an average of 10,000, remember, if the New York and Los Angeles games are excluded), his last college game, against Ohio State in Columbus, drew 85,000; for all seven Illinois games that year, attendance totaled 371,000 — an average of 53,000 spectators per game.[23] Grange brought some, but not all, of that fandom with him to the Bears; even without him, however, the University of Illinois football team would have drawn huge crowds in 1925.

Beyond such accounting, what contemporary newspapers uniformly reveal is that before Grange turned pro, following his storied college career, professional football commanded virtually no interest outside the cities where it was played and that his highly publicized first foray into the professional ranks generated considerable local interest in the pro game for the first time ever. This interest did not survive the end of his 1925–26 tour, however. Local papers (and presumably their readers) were profoundly interested in the Grange phenomenon—but in only that. Grange's professional debut did not mark an initial imprinting of pro football on the general public consciousness that would then be gradually and continuously deepened throughout the following decades; rather, it foretold how the pro game would eventually win the hearts of American football fans, but not for another three decades.

The NFL had an image problem in 1925 that limited its popularity, but a more important factor was football's local-rootedness: the NFL could not connect with fans outside the relatively few cities where franchises were located. Red Grange's pro debut provided this connection, but only temporarily because it was indirect. While football fans in such cities as Tampa, New Orleans, Los Angeles, and Seattle could not claim Grange as one of their own, they could feel kinship with him as the model against whom they measured their local heroes. Everywhere that Grange played on his barnstorming tour, college football was played (or played nearby) by a team of local boys who represented a community or region as well as a school. Red Grange represented the pinnacle of college football in 1925, but this pinnacle was on terrain that included college teams all over the country. The 1925 map of the National Football League, on the other hand, was limited to New York, Chicago, Detroit, and a handful of other Eastern cities, together with small towns such as Pottsville, Rock Island, Hammond, and Dayton. The six touchdowns Grange scored rushing and passing against Michigan in 1924—95 yards on the opening kickoff, followed by runs of 67, 56, and 45 yards—had been trumpeted on every sports page in the country, though differently in each city or region. In Atlanta, the *Constitution* featured Grange's heroics (alongside those of Notre Dame's Four Horsemen against Army) on the second page of the sports section, while the Georgia Tech–Penn State and Georgia–Furman games commanded page one. In Omaha, Grange and the Four Horsemen took most of page three of the *World–Herald*, with page one reserved for the Nebraska–Colgate and Creighton–Morningside games, as well as a local high school contest. In Dallas, Grange grabbed page one of the *Morning News*, but not top billing, which went to Texas Christian University's game against Simmons College. For two years before Grange turned pro, he had set the standard for collegiate running backs everywhere, the standard against whom Easterners measured Andy Oberlander, Californians measured Ernie Nevers, and Northwesterners measured George Wilson. By the time he turned pro, then, Grange belonged, if only indirectly, to the entire country. He was not just a football celebrity but an embodiment of college football itself, the game that was played in every state in the union. When he turned pro, fans came out less to see professional football than to see Grange, but at the end of the tour their connection to pro football via Grange was too weak to sustain their interest in either the National Football League or the American Football League that Grange started in competition.

The impact of the Grange phenomenon on professional football attendance beyond his debut season was negligible, although Grange himself continued to be an attraction on the field. In 1926, Grange's New York Yankees, in his rival American Football League, drew crowds of about 19,000, while the NFL's Giants averaged about 12,000 spectators per game. (Together, those averages slightly exceeded the largest crowd drawn by the Giants during their 1925—pre-Grange—season.) When both teams were playing at home on a given Sunday, the Yankees outdrew the Giants by nearly two to one. Thus Grange can be credited with expanding the audience for professional football in New York. But Grange's aura could not enfold the other eight teams in the upstart league, all but one of which went bankrupt before the end of the season. That team, the league's champion Philadelphia Quakers, played the New York Giants in a postseason contest before all of 5,000 fans in the Polo Grounds. With the demise of the AFL after a single season, Grange's Yankees joined the NFL in 1927, but the team folded a year later, with Grange returning to the Bears.[24] As for the city where Grange first played pro football and where his exploits at the University of Illinois had always been big news, the *Chicago Tribune* expanded its coverage of professional football in 1926, seemingly as a direct consequence of Grange's having focused new attention on the pros, and WGN began broadcasting a pro game on Sundays. But the Bears and the

Cardinals, together with the AFL Bulls now, regularly attracted no more than 15,000 fans among them—except for the one Sunday when Grange came to town and outdrew the combined attendance for professional games on every other Sunday. Grange's Yankees played the Chicago Bulls before 16,000 fans on 17 October as the Bears played the Cardinals before 12,000. The following Sunday, in contrast, the Bulls drew only 3,000 fans for their game against Cleveland, while the Bears took on Ernie Nevers and the Duluth Eskimos before another crowd of 12,000. With the exception of their game against Grange's Yankees, the Bulls never drew more than 7,000 spectators, and attendance even dropped to 1,500 at one game.[25]

In short, within the world of professional football Red Grange created a momentary sensation but could not sustain this heightened interest in the pro game. What he did for professional football by leading other college stars into its ranks, however, proved more lasting. In addition, having to compete with Grange's AFL for fan support apparently helped to convince NFL Commissioner Joe Carr that his league's future stability lay in metropolitan franchises[26]—thus, its reduction from twenty-two teams in 1926, many of them in small industrial cities, to twelve in 1927 and to ten in 1933, when the two-division structure of the modern NFL was finally established. Grange did much for the NFL in the long term, then, but he was not able to make the professional game itself immediately more attractive to football fans.

Outside the circuit of NFL franchises, fans in those southern and western cities where Grange barnstormed over the winter of 1925–26 afterward returned to the football that represented them, the college game in their own cities or regions. Local coverage of Grange's barnstorming tour followed a consistent pattern: resistance to its commercial aspects until a local contest was scheduled, mounting interest as this game approached, declining interest in its aftermath, and no interest at all in professional football during the next season. While Grange had been the brightest comet in the 1925 intercollegiate football cosmos, and his professional debut its tail, by 1926 he had become yesterday's college star; today had its own. Even at the height of the general obsession, both sporting and economic, with the Galloping Ghost, press coverage of Grange's tour stops invariably played up the local angle. The *Florida Times–Union*, for example, paid particular attention to the southern ex-collegians on the Jacksonville All-Stars and was more interested in whether the local team, organized around Ernie Nevers, would make its own tour. "Name of City to Be Carried over Nation in Great Tour," declared a hopeful subheadline on 29 December, about two weeks before an injury to Nevers in the All-Stars' second game, against the New York Giants, forced the team to disband.[27] Most accounts of the 2 January game in Jacksonville credited Nevers with outplaying Grange, but West Coast papers were particularly conspicuous in praising the ex-Stanford star, while also playing up Nevers's abortive exhibition tour.[28] In Atlanta, the *Constitution* singled out another of the All-Stars — Red Barron, formerly of Georgia Tech — for having outplayed both Grange and Nevers, then lost interest in Grange entirely once the southern swing of his tour had ended.[29] In New Orleans, Tulane's "Brother" Brown shared star billing with Grange in the *Times–Picayune* report on the game.[30]

Once the Bears hit the West Coast, local writers consistently found the playing of Washington's George Wilson superior to Grange's, particularly in Seattle.[31] In San Francisco, the performance of the University of Nevada's Jimmy Bradshaw was declared better than that of both all-Americans, while in Portland the pregame hype for the Longshoremen included rating ex-Gonzaga star and current NFL pro Houston Stockton superior to Grange.[32] The *Portland Oregonian* expressed little interest in Grange until he arrived in California, and no serious interest until 20 January when a game in Portland was finally arranged. By game day, indifference had been altogether transformed into wonder: a pregame report marveled that "out here in the far northwest" Portlanders would no longer be limited to reading about a "red-headed will o' the wisp named Grange," but would have the opportunity to see in action the greatest football hero in "these halcyon days of apotheosized sport."[33] In Omaha, far from any stop by the Red Grange express, coverage of the entire tour was conspicuously meager and largely negative, emphasizing the dullness of pro games, the boos of the crowds, Grange's own failures, his near arrest for speeding in Tampa, and nothing at all after the contest in Los Angeles.[34]

———

The coverage of the Grange tour, and its aftermath, by the *Los Angeles Times* can serve as a particularly rich but representative case for press attitudes in those communities briefly graced by the Redhead's presence. Grange fever ran hottest in Los Angeles among the stops on his tour, and its aftereffects lingered longer, but within a year the city and its citizens had recovered. When Damon Runyon arrived in Los Angeles to cover the game, he expressed astonishment at the preparations. "They have spread a welcome mat for [Grange] at the gates of the city," Runyon reported to his millions of readers, "and have arranged to food him and speech him within an inch of his well-known life."[35] Coverage by the *Los Angeles Times* of Grange's exploits as a pro had been restrained until 1 January, when the local game was announced, at which point the boundary between reporting and promoting blurred to indistinction. "Exclusive Dispatches"—likely fed to the *Times* by Grange's agent, Charlie Pyle—carried breathless accounts of the games between the Redhead and the "Blonde Behemoth," Ernie Nevers, with his Jacksonville All-Stars and the All-Southerners in New Orleans. The *Times*'s own writers also kept Angelenos informed on an almost daily basis as local promoter "Puss" Halbriter signed players for the LA Tigers to provide the opposition. With the Bears' arrival in Los Angeles on 14 January, *Times* staff writer Braven Dyer took over the Grange beat, and his prose strained even harder than that of the "Exclusive Dispatches":

> "Red" Grange, the famous Wheaton ice man, makes his first call at Los Angeles today. He will not deliver the goods until Saturday, however, stopping here in advance merely to become familiar with the route. Ice men have long been mentioned in song and verse, but the Wheaton gentleman is the most noted of them all, principally because the avenues of publicity are more numerous today than they were when the first carrier of frozen water deposited his load in Mother Eve's ice box.[36]

The *Times*, in fact, had a stake in the game as one of five newspapers sponsoring the contest (with their share of the profits going to charity), but its publisher, Harry Chandler, generally seized any opportunity to boost growth in Los Angeles.[37] Dyer's reports—with pagewide headlines, multiple photos, and sidebars—took up over half of the first page of the sports section each day, culminating in a spectacular spread of nearly two pages covering every angle of the game itself—won by the Bears, 17–7 (Figure 2). As usual, Grange was pushed off center stage by the local hero—in this case, George Wilson. "Knocked cold as a tombstone the first half," Dyer's report on the game began, "George Wilson, Washington's all-American half-back, returned to the struggle near the end of the third quarter of yesterday's game at the Coliseum and just as he had dominated the con-

Figure 2. Front page of the sports section, *Los Angeles Times*, 17 January 1926. Coverage such as this, although not always so lavish in layout, accompanied Grange throughout his tour in January and February of 1926. Reproduced courtesy of the *Los Angeles Times*.

test in the early part of the afternoon so did he put the big punch in the battle with his marvelous work as the shades of night were falling fast." [38]

To this point, Grange's Los Angeles visit, as reported in the *Times*, was an orgy of football and fame, but the day after the game brought a more sober reckoning. Dyer's piece was on Red's share of the gate, an estimated $135,000, of which he would get $40,000 for himself (less Pyle's cut), while $10,000 would be divided among his teammates. Wilson would pocket $5,000, and the other twenty-eight Tigers $200 each. Twenty-five thousand was to be distributed to the sponsoring newspapers' five charities, leaving $50,000 or so, out of which "Puss" Halbriter would pay Coliseum rent and other game expenses before presumably pocketing a fair chunk himself. [39] These postgame estimates proved to be reasonably accurate when the official accounting was reported ten days later. A total gate of $144,556.66, less $11,580.60 for Coliseum rent, $12,944.56 for taxes, $15,000 in profit for Halbriter, and $47,711.84 for Pyle, Grange, and the Bears (the share for Wilson and the Tigers was not mentioned), left $39,433.63 to be divided among the five charities. [40] In the buildup to the contest, fans had been invited to regard Grange as an athletic hero; in the aftermath, they pondered on Grange as a businessman.

After the spectacular success of the first game, there was some consideration of a second, but Dyer announced on 19 January that Halbriter was content to "rest on his laurels." Dyer followed the Bears to San Francisco, sending back reports that now had a more ironical bite: "Harold 'Red' Grange, Wheaton's fortune-seeking ice man, continues his pursuit of the almighty dollar tomorrow afternoon when he meets the San Francisco Tigers." Dyer seemed pleased to report from the Bay City that George Wilson, "the man who out-Granged Grange, but got beat in Los Angeles," came out on top this time. [41] He also reported on a rift between Pyle and the Bears, and its consequences for the team: although the rest of the Bears liked Grange, they took out their dislike of Pyle on him by giving Grange few opportunities to play the hero. In this same spirit of postgame deflation, the *Times* even punctured a bit of the euphoria over the LA Coliseum game by reporting that official counts of the attendance put the number not at a record 70,000 but at 61,923—8,000 fewer fans than had seen the USC–Stanford game that fall. [42] Pro football had come in second to college football in Los Angeles after all. But pro football was not ignored altogether in these post-LA accounts: the *Times* prominently covered the

Bears' two remaining games in Portland and Seattle, but with only "Exclusive Dispatches" rather than reports from its own staff writer.

With its blend of promotional hype, ironic deflation, and straight reporting, the *Los Angeles Times* constructed a variety of "Red Granges" for a variety of tastes, while keeping Grange and professional football in the awareness of football fans of all kinds through the month of January 1926. Unlike other cities on the Grange tour, Los Angeles (and San Francisco) remained interested in professional football even after the Bears' tour ended because the Coliseum spectacular had prompted local promoters to establish the pro game more permanently in Los Angeles. Within days of Grange's final game on his West Coast swing—the timing obviously not coincidental—Wilson was negotiating for his own club of West Coast ex-collegians; and local investors, backed by the Pacific Coast Baseball League, announced the creation of a new pro loop in California. Later in the year, a local group obtained an NFL franchise for the Los Angeles Buccaneers, another team formed to capitalize on the interest in football that Grange had generated. After having paid virtually no attention to pro football before Grange hit California, LA fans now had several ways to affiliate themselves with it: the American Football League, which boasted Grange himself plus George Wilson and his Wildcats; the NFL, which had the Buccaneers and Stanford's Ernie Nevers, who had joined the Duluth Eskimos; and the new Pacific Coast League, which included teams in Hollywood and Los Angeles as well as in San Francisco and Oakland. A typical Monday morning *LA Times* sports page in the fall of 1926 carried half-column reports on two Coast League games, Los Angeles–Oakland and Hollywood–San Francisco; an AFL game in which Wilson's Wildcats had defeated Grange's Yankees; and an NFL game in which the Los Angeles Buccaneers (led by Cal's Brick Muller) had trounced Brooklyn.[43] The newspaper's total coverage, though greatly expanded over its occasional few lines on the NFL in 1925, never approached that given to USC and its intercollegiate conference rivals, and it diminished over the course of the season.

By 1927, that coverage had been cut back to its meager pre–Grange tour level. The Pacific Coast League had failed by then, along with Grange's American Football League. Los Angeles's own 1926 AFL and NFL clubs had belonged to Angelenos only nominally: Wilson's Wildcats, though primarily a team of Californians, operated out of Rock Island, Illinois, while the so-called Los Angeles Buccaneers were based in Chicago; after playing all their games on the road, both teams folded at the end of their first season. Train travel to the West Coast was prohibitively expensive for professional clubs whose finances were shaky from the outset and whose crowd appeal was slight in 1926. (When Notre Dame traveled to Los Angeles to play USC, on the other hand, the capacity crowds of 75,000 more than covered the team's expenses.) In 1927, Nevers was still playing for the Eskimos and Wilson had found a home with the NFL's Providence Steamrollers, but their links to Los Angeles had been stretched too thin to sustain local interest. Pro football news nearly disappeared from the *Los Angeles Times* after one season and did not reappear until 1934, with the next LA pro franchise. Los Angeles continued sporadically to provide a home for marginal pro teams, both big league and minor, until 1944, when the Rams settled there permanently and Angelenos at last had a top-level team of their own. With the Rams in town, the popularity of professional football in Los Angeles rivaled that of its collegiate powerhouses, USC and UCLA, by the 1950s. Then, as before, football's appeal depended on local-rootedness; without a "home team," there could be little interest in the game. And in LA as elsewhere, football's local-rootedness continued to define its essential role in American life until television began its transformation.

═══
═══

The lesson of the Red Grange case—that pretelevision fans needed a local connection to football—is confirmed by contemporary newspaper coverage of college and pro games around the country. The lack of interest in professional football before the 1950s outside the cities where pro teams were located is perhaps the most obvious confirmation of the sport's local-rootedness. In cities such as Atlanta, Omaha, and Dallas, coverage of NFL games through the 1950s was limited to brief wire-service reports on Mondays and updates on a local favorite's post-college career. In Omaha, for example, the *World–Herald* belatedly took note (in 1933 and 1934) of the Bears' Link Lyman, a former University of Nebraska tackle who had been playing in the NFL since 1922. In the 1950s, the *World–Herald* followed the career of a truly local boy, running back Joe Arenas from Omaha University, more closely throughout his seven years with the San Francisco 49ers. But in Omaha, as in other non–NFL franchise cities, such coverage depended on wire-service accounts that singled out the local hero; no staff writer was put on the NFL beat prior to the age of television. The *World–Herald*'s NFL

coverage gradually expanded in the 1950s, notably—and most significantly
—in 1959, following the televised overtime championship game between
the Baltimore Colts and the New York Giants on 28 December 1958, which
numerous commentators cite as the beginning of football's TV era. Only a
tenuous and intermittent connection to certain teams through local players
was possible before television made every team a potential "home team."

The Omaha pattern was repeated in such cities as Atlanta and Dallas. In
Atlanta—and, I suspect, throughout the South, football-rabid but removed
from NFL cities—coverage of professional football was most conspicuously
negligible throughout the 1940s, despite the fact that the University of
Georgia's Frank Sinkwich and Charles Trippi moved on to the NFL. In the
1950s, when the Washington Redskins emerged as the Southeast's regional
team and their games began to be broadcast weekly on local television, the
Constitution and the *Journal* took more notice, assigning staff writers to
cover the team in 1958. In Dallas, the short-lived American Football League
(with teams also in Louisville, Memphis, St. Louis, Tulsa, and Charlotte)
had generated more coverage for the NFL, too, in 1934, although accounts
of games in both leagues still took up less space in the Monday edition
of the *Morning News* than its daily coverage of college football. Following
the demise of the AFL after one season, the Dallas paper's coverage of the
NFL dwindled again in 1935 and 1936. The pro career of TCU's Sammy
Baugh, beginning in 1937, provoked the first sustained local interest, and
in the late 1940s and 1950s the Detroit Lions became Dallas's quasi-home
team because of ex-college stars Bobby Layne (University of Texas) and,
particularly, Doak Walker (SMU). But even with Layne and Walker as the
focus of attention, coverage of NFL football in the *Dallas Morning News*
through 1958 was largely limited to Monday's single page on the previous
day's games. More pregame coverage appeared in 1959 (following the televised 1958 championship game); then suddenly, in 1960, with the arrival
of the Cowboys and the Texans as local teams in rival leagues, professional
football finally garnered the extended coverage long given to SMU and its
Southwest Conference opponents.

This unequal coverage of intercollegiate and professional football in the
daily press illustrates the importance of a local connection, the essentially
local nature of football prior to the age of television: where professional
football had never taken root before, TV was able to create a local audience. Football games had been broadcast over radio since 1921 (beginning

with the Pitt–West Virginia game over Pittsburgh's KDKA), and over the radio networks since 1926, when NBC's Blue Network was created. Regular radio broadcasts of local college games began in New York in 1922, Chicago in 1923, Portland, Oregon, in 1925, Dallas and Omaha in 1926, and Atlanta in 1928. While the New York and Chicago stations also broadcast the games of their local pro teams as early as 1926, it was not until 1937 that even the NFL championship game was broadcast over a network, and it was another decade before games were regularly picked up outside NFL cities. For most of the country, radio had a negligible impact on pro football's audience, as regular weekly games were carried locally only a year or two before football began to be televised.[44]

A significant delay in broadcasting professional games over both the radio and the television networks was another sign of the relative lack of interest in pro football outside the cities where it was played. But the NFL welcomed TV, showing none of the reluctance displayed by the NCAA, and thus began to enlarge its fan base, which would overtake college football's by the end of the 1960s. The NCAA fought the televising of football games in the 1950s to protect attendance, while the NFL embraced it with only the proviso that games would be blacked out locally when teams played at home.[45] Professional football not only had to overcome an unsavory reputation, it required a local presence that only television could create outside NFL cities. Radio did not have television's power to create fans where none had existed before, but was dependent on listeners' prior interest and their familiarity with teams and players. Through its more powerful illusion of immediacy and its ability to make visible what had never before been seen, television could create interest, not just increase it.

Every game on television is literally a "home" game. As a kid in Spokane, I could adopt the Los Angeles Rams as my team without ever having attended one of their games or seen any professional player in person. So could my father, who felt more of a connection to the adults in the NFL than to the kids at nearby Washington State College. The sudden-death championship game between the Giants and the Colts in 1958—watched by my father and me, along with the millions of others around the country—is rightly considered a turning point in the history of professional football. Without television, it would have been just another pro game played by strangers somewhere else.

The period from the 1920s through the 1950s was the golden age of college football, then, and the intercollegiate game played a unique role in fostering local identity and pride. If there is a Football Law of Local Interest, one corollary would seem to be that the most important games are the ones played by the community's high school team. In towns far removed from any major university, this is almost certainly the case. But what college football offered over the first half of the twentieth century that high school football could not was a local connection within comparative regional and national contexts. Large state universities offered all citizens not only a team of their own, but also a scale on which to measure that team against regional and national standards—a grid as well as a gridiron.

American football during the first half of the twentieth century looked different in different parts of the country, its geography mapped like that *New Yorker* cartoon in which home is the center of the universe, with distant regions increasingly foreshortened until they disappear over the horizon. Local boosterism aside, football power was centered in the East from its beginnings in the 1870s until it shifted westward, to Big Ten country, by the 1920s, then southward during the 1940s. But provincial newspapers always made local games the center of the football universe, both in the amount of coverage they were given and in their page-one status within the sports section. In Atlanta, southeastern football was the principal game in town, followed in decreasing order of importance by games played in the East, the Midwest, the Southwest, and the West. In Omaha, the corn belt teams, then those of the upper Midwest, reigned supreme, followed by eastern, southwestern, western, and southern football. And in Dallas, southwestern football took precedence over eastern, southern, midwestern, and western games, in that order. By the 1950s, coverage of football played elsewhere became more extensive and uniform, as papers in every U.S. city depended on the same few wire services, which chiefly covered games played among the current top twenty teams. But the local teams were always primary, the rest of the country secondary. Football's local-rootedness played out powerfully through the widening circles of state, region, and nation, as conferences fed intraregional rivalries, "intersectional games" (including bowl games) pitted region against region, and polls ranked the national elite.

Notre Dame played a unique role in developing intersectional conscious-ness. Murray Sperber has documented the fact that the fathers at Notre Dame did not initially intend to develop a *national* football team, but did so out of a desperate need to build a schedule in the face of boycotts by the nearby Big Ten schools. Once the team's national identity had become established under Knute Rockne in the mid-1920s, particularly among working-class and recent-immigrant Americans, Notre Dame administrators played brilliantly to their advantages by building a university through a football team. What this meant, not for Notre Dame but for the distant teams on its schedule, was that the Fighting Irish (or the "Ramblers," as they were more commonly known for their regular travel to distant places) became a unique touchstone by which the provinces could measure their progress on a national football scale. Notre Dame's excursions to Atlanta to play Georgia Tech, to Dallas to play SMU, to Los Angeles to play USC, and to Lincoln, New Orleans, Seattle, and so on, were both major social events and occasions for local self-analysis.

College football from the 1920s through the 1950s, more than any other major sport (perhaps more than any other major activity), provided and sustained a dialectic between region and nation, province and capital. Major league baseball had some of this quality, too, but the fact that teams were based in major metropolitan areas—until the late 1950s, exclusively east of the Mississippi, with Baltimore and St. Louis the furthest south—made baseball different. While the local baseball team was in a minor league and played within the region, the local football team was intercol-legiate and competed nationally. Most major college football teams were located in small towns. They represented local pride within a national context, playing intersectional games to achieve a national ranking. The accident that only the South had the weather for bowl games contributed importantly to the second, southward shift of football's geographical cen-ter. Beyond the factor of relative excellence, specific local identities also became attached to college football teams' styles of play ("power football" in the Big Ten, "wide-open passing" in the Southwest, and so on), which were woven by local sportswriters into narratives that expressed regional and community self-portraits embodied by the local football team.

Football had a national dimension during this period as well, repre-sented in the narratives of large-circulation magazines such as the *Saturday Evening Post* and *Collier's*, pulp magazines, and network radio broadcasts, films, and newsreels. Television—and, more particularly, the recent ubiquity of sports on television—has shifted football's balance between the local and the national. This is not to deny that Nebraskans and Oklahomans and Penn Staters have retained the home-team consciousness that is at the heart of football's local-rootedness. But as I watch my own kids switch favorites from season to season, sampling the smorgasbord available on ESPN and the networks—at a time, of course, when football languishes in Corvallis—I realize that their relation to the game is significantly different from my own as a kid. From a historical perspective, local-rootedness is in the nature of football (and of sports generally), and television alters the relation of football (and of sports generally) to its fans. As a cultural text, football is both real (the game played on the field) and representational (the game interpreted in the media), both immediate (the game played or watched in person) and mediated (the game read about in the press, heard over the radio, viewed on film or television). What football means and has meant in American life cannot be considered apart from the media through which we have had our primary access to it. And, as part of the immensely larger processes of modernization and globalization, television has rendered football (and sports more generally) less locally rooted.

Notes

1 "Grange Turns Professional," *New York Times*, 24 November 1925, 24. In a subsequent editorial, the *Times* singled out the *Harvard Crimson* and the *Yale News* as the leaders of the anti-Grange campaign and again defended him; see "Revolving Football," *New York Times*, 3 December 1925, 24.

2 In Atlanta, for example, the *Constitution*'s sports editor, H. C. Hamilton, repeatedly criticized the anti-Grange hysteria. Professional football could go its own way, Hamilton insisted; the college game was not threatened; see his columns in the *Atlanta Constitution*, 5 December, 6 December, 15 December, and 20 December 1925, for example. In Dallas, on the other hand, the *Morning News*'s Chauncey Brown was deeply critical of Grange's exploiting a fame that more properly belonged to his university, and he praised Andy "Swede" Oberlander of Dartmouth, who had refused professional offers and "thus will end a great career gloriously." Brown proved himself not much of a prophet when he added, "It is probable that the memory of Oberlander will remain fresh long after that of Grange has passed into the limbo of articles which looked like gold but turned out to be partially of inferior metal"; see "The Branding Iron," *Dallas Morning News*, 23 November 1925, 8.

3 See *New York Times*, 7 December 1925, 26; *Omaha World–Herald*, 8 December 1925, 20; *Los Angeles Times*, 11 December 1925, 1.

4   "Trying to Get Some of 'Red' Grange's Easy Money," *Seattle Post–Intelligencer, American Weekly,* 3 January 1926, 6.

5   Ibid.

6   Steven A. Riess, "A Social Profile of the Professional Football Player, 1920–82," in *The Business of Professional Sport,* ed. Paul A. Staudohar and James A. Mangan (Urbana and Champaign, 1991), 231.

7   Ibid., 223.

8   Ibid., 234.

9   See William Gudelunas and Stephen R. Couch, "The Stolen Championship of the Pottsville Maroons: A Case Study in the Emergence of Modern Professional Football," *Journal of Sport History* 9 (1982): 60.

10   Bill Cunningham, "Red Grange, on Trail of the Dollar, Has Lost His Campus Prestige," *Dallas Morning News,* 10 January 1926, 2: 4.

11   Grange's own account is given in his autobiography, *The Red Grange Story: An Autobiography, as Told to Ira Morton,* originally published in 1953 and reprinted in 1993 by the University of Illinois Press. My corrections of Grange's version, based on the local newspaper coverage, will be noted.

12   See "Grange's Gold Quest on for 6 More Weeks," *New York Daily News,* 19 December 1925. The *Dallas Morning News* had reported on 13 December that promoters in Houston feared they would be unable to meet the $25,000 guarantee demanded by Pyle and that a game was therefore likely to be played instead in Dallas, "where more patrons can be accommodated"; see "Red Grange's Team May Play in Dallas," *Dallas Morning News,* 13 December 1925, 2: 5. No further prospects were reported.

13   See " 'Red' Grange Leads Bears against All-Californians in San Diego Stadium Today," *Los Angeles Times,* 17 January 1926, I: 2.

14   The average salary figure comes from Riess, "Social Profile of the Professional Football Player," 223.

15   Ira Morton, "Introduction," in Grange, *Red Grange Story,* xiii. The figures on attendance and earnings cited here also come from Morton's introduction to this 1993 reprint.

16   Grange, *Red Grange Story,* 113. (Grange's estimate of 150,000 fans can also be found on this page.)

17   The *(Jacksonville) Florida Times–Union* (26 December 1925) put the Coral Gables crowd at 3,200, not the 8,000 claimed by Grange in his autobiography. Eight thousand saw the game in Tampa, according to the *New York Daily News* (2 January 1926), while 6,700 saw the one in Jacksonville, according to the *Seattle Post–Intelligencer* (3 January 1926). (Reports in most papers failed to give a figure.) The *Los Angeles Times* put the New Orleans crowd at 6,000 (11 January 1926), Los Angeles at 70,000 (17 January 1926), San Diego at 10,000 (18 January 1926), San Francisco at 20,000 (25 January 1926), Portland at 5,000 (31 January 1926), and Seattle at 6,000 (1 February 1926). Several of these figures are confirmed by other papers, which were probably served by the same wire services or special dispatches.

18   Attendance estimates of Grange's first eight professional games in the *New York Daily News* add up to 157,000 fans, exclusive of the Bears' rematch against the New York

Giants; the *New York Times* reported a crowd of 15,000 for that game. Combining these figures for 172,000, then adding to the 135,000 from the barnstorming tour, brings the total to 307,000.

19 See James Quirk and Rodney D. Fort, *Pay Dirt: The Business of Professional Team Sports* (Princeton, 1992), 334. Quirk and Fort used data apparently based on newspaper reports of a few games per team. An article in the *New York Times* claimed average attendance of 15,000 for the league, but my own investigations confirm Quirk and Fort's more conservative estimates; see " 'Pro' Football Is Coming in Favor," *New York Times*, 22 November 1925, 22. The *Times* figure may have been distorted by the local case: reports on the New York Giants' home games in 1925 put typical attendance in the 15,000 to 30,000 range. In Chicago, on the other hand, on those occasions when the *Chicago Daily Tribune* reported attendance at Bears or Cardinals games—at Wrigley Field or Comiskey Park, each accommodating a large crowd—the number barely reached 10,000. The Bears–Rock Island game on 1 November drew 8,000 (*Chicago Daily Tribune*, 2 November 1925, 29); while 6,000 saw the Cardinals beat Green Bay and 5,000 saw the Bears defeat the Yellow Jackets on 8 November (*Chicago Daily Tribune*, 9 November 1925, 23); the Cards drew 3,000, and the Bears 6,200, on 15 November (*Chicago Daily Tribune*, 16 November 1925, 25); on 22 November, the Bears drew 7,500, and the Cards 3,000 (*Chicago Daily Tribune*, 23 November 1925, 27), just before that Thanksgiving Day game in which Grange debuted with the Bears in front of 36,000 spectators. The fact that both the Cardinals and the Bears played regularly at home suggests that crowds were larger in Chicago than elsewhere—and that the estimates of 10,000 spectators per game for the Bears and 5,000 for the rest of the league may in fact be too high.

20 These figures are from the *New York Times*, 19 October 1925, 20 (27,000 for the Giants' home opener); 2 November 1925, 29 (18,000); 9 November 1925, 16 (4,000); 16 November 1925, 17 (20,000); and 23 November 1925, 27 (30,000).

21 "New York Pro Eleven Takes Opening Game," *New York Times*, 5 October 1925, 18.

22 "Professional Football," *New York Times*, 8 December 1925, 24.

23 The 371,000 total for Grange's college games was reported by the Associated Press (*New York Times*, 17 December 1925, 21), which also estimated a total of 223,000 spectators for Grange's eight pro games—50,000 more than a game-by-game accounting yields (a reminder to be cautious about accepting newspaper reports). But figures for college football crowds are more reliable because the game management was well organized and attendance closely monitored.

24 This account of Grange's Yankees is from Quirk and Fort, *Pay Dirt*, 336–37. Grange sat out the 1928 season with an injury, then played with the Bears from 1929 through 1934.

25 See the *Chicago Tribune*, 18 October 1926, 23; and 25 October 1926, 21. The *Tribune* reported the following crowd figures for subsequent Sundays: 31 October—Cardinals, 3,000; Bears, 6,500; Bulls, 4,000 (1 November 1926, 29); 7 November—Bears, 8,000 (or perhaps only 3,000—the microfilm is difficult to read); Bulls, 7,000; Cardinals, in New York against the Giants, 10,000, with Grange's Yankees drawing 30,000 (8 November 1926, 23); 14 November—Bears, 3,500; Bulls, 2,500; Cards game postponed because of mud (15 November 1926, 21); 21 November—Bears, 7,500; Bulls, 1,500 (22 Novem-

ber 1926, 27); and 28 November—Bears, 5,000; Cardinals, 14,000—a charity game for which 40,000 tickets were sold, but which only 14,000 attended (29 November 1926, 21).

26 This claim is made by Quirk and Fort, *Pay Dirt*, 337.

27 See Paul W. Ferris, "Jax All-Stars Have Full Strength in Stadium Workout," *(Jacksonville) Florida Times–Union*, 29 December 1925, 12.

28 See the accounts of 3 January 1926 in the *Los Angeles Times*, the *San Diego Union*, and the *San Francisco Chronicle*.

29 "Barron Outshines Grange, Nevers in Pro Contest," *Atlanta Constitution*, 3 January 1926, B: 3.

30 Pete Baird, "Chicago Bears Win 14–0; Grange, 'Brother' Brown Star," *New Orleans Times–Picayune*, 11 January 1926, 10.

31 See the coverage in the *Seattle Post–Intelligencer*, for example: "Wilson Stars as Grange's Team Wins, 17 to 7," 17 January 1926, 3: 1 (on the Los Angeles game); "Runyon Rates Wilson Greater than Red Grange," 18 January 1926, 3: 1 (on Damon Runyon's coverage of the Los Angeles game); "Wilson Outshines Grange; Tigers Win," 25 January 1926, 3: 1 (on the San Francisco game); and "Grange & Co. Swamp Local Gridders 34–0; Wilson Gets No Support from Mates," 1 February 1926, 3: 1 (on the Seattle game).

32 See "Tigers Defeat Grange's Bears, 14–9," *San Francisco Chronicle*, 25 January 1926, "Sporting Green," 1; and "Longshoremen out to Defeat Grange," *Portland Oregonian*, 29 January, 1926, 12.

33 "Grange to Display Wares Here Today," *Portland Oregonian*, 30 January 1926, 10.

34 See the *Omaha World–Herald*, 27 November, 8 December, 10 December, and 14 December 1925; and 1 January 1926.

35 Runyon's report was not carried by the *Los Angeles Times*, but it did appear in the *San Diego Union*, 14 January 1926, 16.

36 Braven Dyer, "Red Grange Arrives Today for Coliseum Game," *Los Angeles Times*, 14 January 1926, 3: 1.

37 For an account of Chandler's role in getting the Los Angeles Coliseum built, see Steven A. Riess, "Power without Authority: Los Angeles' Elites and the Construction of the Coliseum," *Journal of Sport History* 8 (1981): 50–65.

38 Braven Dyer, "Pro Football Not Startling," *Los Angeles Times*, 17 January 1926, 3: 1.

39 Braven Dyer, " 'Red' Receives Largest Purse," *Los Angeles Times*, 18 January 1926, 3: 1.

40 See "Promoter of Grange Game Makes Profit," *Los Angeles Times*, 28 January 1926, 3: 1.

41 Braven Dyer, "Bay City Gets Its First Look at Wheaton Ice Man," *Los Angeles Times*, 24 January 1926, 3: 1; and "Tigers Crush Grange Football Team, 14 to 9," *Los Angeles Times*, 25 January 1926, 3: 1.

42 See Braven Dyer, "George Wilson Gets Bids," *Los Angeles Times*, 27 January 1926, 3: 2; and "Grange Game Turnout Did Not Set Mark," *Los Angeles Times*, 29 January 1926, 3: 1.

43 See the *Los Angeles Times*, 22 November 1926, 3: 1.

44 Weekly pro games were first aired on radio in Omaha in 1946; in Dallas, in 1947; and in Atlanta, in 1949. Televised games soon followed in Omaha in 1951 (the championship game in 1950); in Atlanta, in 1952 (the title game in 1950); in Dallas, in 1953 (the

title game in 1952; segments or highlights of games had been aired since 1950); and in Portland, in 1953. (Weekly pro football games were televised in Portland without ever having been aired on local radio.) In each case, televised college football (starting in New York in 1941) had begun at least a year earlier: 1948 in Dallas; 1949 in Atlanta; 1950 in Omaha; and 1952 in Portland.

45   For an account of how the NCAA and the NFL came to terms with television in the 1950s, see Benjamin Rader, *In Its Own Image: How Television Has Transformed Sports* (New York, 1984).

Ann Fabian

Gamblers in the Garden:
The Political Consequences of the Fix

The fall I was studying for orals, I lived next door
to a man named Pete. That summer, Pete had
divorced a wife, gotten rid of a hardware store,
and like me, begun to spend the day at home.
Unlike me, Pete still had his high school friends,
including a group of small-time suburban bookies who volunteered to help him hide assets from
his wife. When the basketball season got under
way, Pete began to make his money by laying
off bets for one of his bookie friends. My academic life comes into the picture only because
Pete came over one afternoon to ask me what I
did. He figured he'd tell anyone who asked that
he did what I did, since I apparently supported
myself by doing nothing without arousing suspi-
cion. I was happy to think that studying for orals
might be a good cover for illicit activity, although
I had yet to discover that writing a dissertation
would offer even more time, enough to get an
illegal operation up and running.

If Pete was puzzled by what I did, I was clue-
less about him. I never learned what he actually
did or whether he had a chance to tell the neighbors about all the books he was trying to read. I

The *South Atlantic Quarterly* 95:2, Spring 1996.
Copyright © 1996 by Duke University Press.
CCC 0038-2876/96/$1.50.

thought of Pete and his bookie friends again in the spring of 1995 when references to the point-shaving scandals of the early 1950s appeared in the obituary columns. These scandals had erupted during a brief period when the operations of underground networks of gamblers were already attracting national attention. Nat Holman, the basketball coach at the City College of New York, suspended but reinstated, and Bill Spivey, the seven-foot Kentucky center, indicted but never convicted, were both dead.[1] When I went back over the story of basketball and betting, I was struck by what now seemed an excessive fuss over corrupted youth.

Many of you know this story. Like the Black Sox scandal, it is necessary to any list of bad moments in sports, a classic example of the disappointment that only errant athletes can deliver. We return to it not just because sports so often makes a fetish of its history, but because it contains particularly touching instances of squandered talent. Over the first ten months of 1951, investigators discovered that some thirty players from seven schools (Manhattan College, Long Island University, New York University, the City College of New York, Bradley University, the University of Toledo, and the University of Kentucky) had taken money from gamblers and played to their orders. There was enough action on college games to tempt gamblers, and these gamblers had found players greedy, dishonest, desperate, or stupid enough to believe that the fix was worth what little money they could get and squirrel away in the back of a closet.

The best accounts of these events appear in memoirs by those who grew up with the revelations about bribed players. The writer Stanley Cohen remembered the scandal at City College as a sad but instructive episode in the life of every New York Jewish boy growing up in the late 1940s. The story encapsulated for him the experience of a generation of young American men who had shared the sacrifices of war but then gone on to enact the ugliness of the 1950s. For Cohen, the players' shame and the public's shock over the scandal meshed with the private anguish of his own approaching adulthood. As other writers did with other sports stories, he used this one as a touchstone, finding private memories in public events.[2]

In contrast, my friend Pete's idea to use graduate school as a cover for gambling is the best I can do by way of any personal connection to the relationship between athletes and gamblers. This story has no emotional resonance for me, nor do I much care about the purity of college basketball. I come to this episode with only a cultural historian's interest in gambling and in the ways that several Cold War stories, unrelated to basketball but unfolding at precisely the same time, suggest that sports is sometimes (but not always) politics by other means. With this tangle of contemporaneous stories, and with these gamblers and players ensnarled at its center, I return here to the basketball scandal as something incomplete, investigating how those who followed the story as it broke in the press saw its plot cross and mingle with the bigger stories of the same months, with stories generated by the domestic Red Scare and produced on the battlefields of Korea.

We are used to the ways that fiction of the late 1940s and early 1950s worked in the twin themes of domesticity and alien invasion as the narrative logic for American society's postwar reorganization. Not surprisingly, the story of the basketball fixes conformed as well to the political logic of the Cold War. For several months, the story generated headlines; the public reacted with shock. If war and politics had impoverished language, the scandal at least gave people something to talk about. While those who reported it focused exclusively on basketball, others took the occasion as an opportunity to think about the place of sports in the university, about who should be included in a "student body," about the definition of amateurism, and about the roles of entertainment and commerce in athletic contests. But from the perspective of nearly half a century's distance, the scandal looks like one small piece of the public project of investigation, denunciation, and surveillance that dominated the early years of the Cold War. It offers us access to a cultural moment when subversives appeared everywhere, when rumor and gossip produced what was taken to be credible evidence in sports as in politics, and when increased surveillance promised to yield both a clean student body and a clean government.

The subversion that threatened college athletes came from gamblers. Evidence of corrupt gambling surfaces periodically in sports, and each generation seems to get the gamblers it deserves. While gamblers in general have been characterized as strangers, thieves, poor fools, gangsters, or renegade capitalists, in sports they are typically cast as sinners, profiteers, or sick men. (We treated Pete Rose like an inside trader, Art Schlichter like an addict beyond the help of twelve-step programs, and Michael Jordan like a rich man out for a good time.) But the gamblers of the early 1950s were subversives, and how they came to be defined as such is an interesting story.

The shady dealings of those gamblers and the ballplayers they subverted caught the attention of politicians, journalists, promoters, and college presidents—all men with a stake in protecting their authority by maintaining the amateur status of college athletics. The story involved congressional investigations, ruined careers, and the sense that innocent Americans were threatened by a vast, invisible conspiracy. It was perhaps just one more tale told in the paranoid style, but those investigators had the good fortune to find in college basketball a conspiracy, if not of immense proportions, at least large enough to be seen. Those conspirators—men who had corrupted youth and subverted sports—got caught, and when they did it became all the easier for those who watched those who tracked Communists to believe that, sooner or later, another Alger Hiss or a twofer like the Rosenbergs would be bagged as well. The conspiracy to subvert college basketball was neither earthshaking nor life-threatening. It was, however, precisely the kind of small domestic drama that ratified more destructive behavior on a larger scale.

The connection between sports and politics here, I think, was something more than a vague cultural ambience. Sometimes the events of the point-shaving scandal literally intersected with events in the hunt for Communists. At a single meeting of the New York City Board of Higher Education in 1952, for example, the City College basketball coach was suspended and three longtime teachers (one at Hunter and two at Brooklyn College), who had refused to answer the questions of the Subcommittee to Investigate the Administration of the Internal Security Act and Other Internal Security Laws of the Committee on the Judiciary of the United States Senate, were fired.[3] The stories overlapped in their means and their methods, the logic of one reinforcing the logic of the other. In each case an abstract concept—academic freedom, say, or amateurism[4]—proved difficult to define and, in its ambiguity, *dangerous* (dangerous, that is, in a university culture based on disinterest). In this respect, the amateur status of college athletics served as a figure for "pure" intellectual activity, a sort of advertisement for the disinterestedness of the university as a whole in the early 1950s. Professionals masquerading as amateurs threatened not only the lucrative college athletic programs but the very ground upon which the academic enterprise stood.

The basketball story opens in January 1951 with a 23-year-old, 6' 8" Manhattan College sophomore, Junius Kellogg, telling his coach, Ken Norton, that he has been approached by gamblers. Kellogg, one of eleven children and a World War II veteran whom the GI bill had transformed into a college youth, was the "first Negro who ever made Manhattan College's varsity basketball team."[5] He appears in this story as its first hero, the honest informer—not the man who confesses to Party membership and then must endure a ritual degradation, but the man who finds the idea of taking a bribe unthinkable and therefore nips conspiracy in the bud. According to Kellogg, Henry Poppe, the team's co-captain only a year before, had offered him a bribe to beat the point spread in a game against De Paul. Kellogg reported that he was "shocked" and that Poppe had never spoken to him before offering him the bribe.[6] The police and the district attorney, in collaboration with the coach and college officials, set up a small sting operation and, listening in at the switchboard, heard the fixer call the pivot man to tell him to forget the "rah rah stuff."[7]

Once the plot was exposed, everyone—coaches, players, students, fans, and reporters—expressed "shock." And how useful that shock must have been in rehabilitating the innocence of postwar New Yorkers, who, then as now, probably considered themselves unshockable. Poppe's wife was shocked when detectives arrived to take him away at one o'clock in the morning.[8] Coach Norton "was shocked to hear that gamblers had got to my kids." But, he added quickly, "if our boys were approached, certainly boys were being approached all over the country. There must be a national syndicate."[9]

The events at Manhattan served as a prologue to the bigger scandal that would break a month later at City College. Sports columnists blamed the sordid air of Madison Square Garden and encouraged coaches to play their games on campus. Several reporters also confessed to their own complicity in corruption, admitting that published point spreads had increased betting on college games. In the aftermath of the Manhattan College story, reporters acknowledged that for the last decade honest bookies had used point spreads to balance their books by attracting bets on both sides of a contest. But honest bookies were peripheral to the story, which revealed just how point spreads worked for the less than honest. A point spread could be manipulated, enabling "sure-thing" gamblers to finesse what would otherwise have been obviously unethical. They did not ask players to throw a game. By beating a point spread (i.e., winning by less than the oddsmakers had predicted), players could win money without losing a game. As one gambler put it, "Now technically, I suppose a young boy was able to assuage his conscience with the thought that he was not throwing his dear ole Alma Mammy to the winds, that he was going to win the game, so what difference did it make whether his team won by 5 or by 14?"[10] Moreover, gambling "was rampant," as the judge noted at the players' sentencing. "The point spread was shouted from one end of the arena to other. Very few of the thousands of spectators were interested either in the college or the players."[11]

The City College scandal broke in February with high drama. Among the elements that made it far richer than Manhattan's little brush with sin was City College's identification with New York and its immigrant families. (It had also housed a large and disciplined academic unit of the Communist Party in the late 1930s.) Now, for those who followed basketball, City College was a great power unexpectedly taking a great fall. In 1950, its basketball team had won both the NCAA tournament and the National Invitational Tournament (NIT), the first team ever to do so in the same year. The campus celebrated; the city celebrated, and the mayor entertained the team. *Ebony* ran a feature on one of the co-captains, Ed Warner, "a Harlem kid who came up the hard way."[12] A *Life* photographer posed the team in front of a bust of Lincoln, and the magazine congratulated the players on their surprising victories over Kentucky and Bradley. Describing the school as "a free-tuition college," *Life* praised its "earnest, hardworking student body of 34,000, all from New York City, who need good grades to get in and good grades to stay in." The reporter concluded by noting that, with "no athletic scholarships to lure high school stars," the team's working-class players had to take summer jobs.[13] The best of them played for resort teams in the Catskills, and *Life* followed them there during the summer of 1950. Working as bellhops, waiters, and lifeguards, these players—some Black, some White—also made money by playing ball and entertaining guests, staying in shape while maintaining "their amateur standing."[14]

But the "borscht belt," like Madison Square Garden, harbored an unsavory element, and the happy world of post-Harlem success, good grades, and wholesome summer jobs was to be blown apart by the scandal. William Randolph Hearst's *Journal–American*, New York's loudest organ of the Right, broke the story of the City College fixers on 18 February 1951. Max Kase, the paper's sports editor, would win a Pulitzer Prize as much for what he did not do as for what he did. In January, Kase had gone to Manhattan District Attorney Frank Hogan "with vital information about college basketball fixing in New York's Madison Square Garden," but at Hogan's request he had agreed not to run the story until the DA had enough evidence to indict the players and the fixers. Kase's cooperation (much celebrated in the columns of his paper) not only netted him a Pulitzer, but also enabled him to settle a personal score. A few years earlier, Kase and the Garden's Ned Irish had been rival bidders for the Basketball Association of America's New York franchise. When team owners awarded the franchise to Irish, who had Madison Square Garden and deep pockets, he also acquired the enmity of Kase.[15]

The first five players to be arrested were Ed Warner, Alvin Roth, and Ed Roman of City College; Eddie Gard, a Long Island University senior; and Harvey Schaff, who had played for New York University, then graduated to become the gamblers' agent among the players. Within a few days of these arrests, Hogan booked four more LIU players—Sherman White, Al Bigos, LeRoy Smith, and Nathan Miller—as well as Floyd Layne of CCNY. He also arrested a fixer, Salvatore Tarto Sollazzo, a 45-year-old Manhattan jeweler and ex-con who was married to a "svelte former model." Sollazzo and his wife were perfect figures of scandal: she draped in mink and sporting a poodle, he vaguely linked to Frank Costello and other mobsters.[16] (Sollazzo also scandalized New York by spending more money on his second wife's poodle than on his son by a previous marriage.[17]) Over the next few weeks, the DA's office continued to arrest players who were allegedly in on various fixes; by March, Hogan had indicted seventeen former or current students of New York colleges or universities. As the private anguish of the players became public property, their arrests and confessions were woven into a narrative much like other stories of the early 1950s.

Eddie Gard, the *Journal–American* reported, had cooperated, taking Hogan's advice "to talk cold-turkey and name names of all involved."[18] Others cooperated too, and, over the following summer, the scandal spread to Bradley University and the University of Toledo. Then, in October, the University of Kentucky team was investigated, and two former players, Ralph Beard and Alex Groza, who had gone on to play for the Indianapolis NBA franchise, were implicated, as was Kentucky center Bill Spivey. A few of the New York players went to jail, several others received suspended sentences, and the remorseful got off, but all were barred for life by the NBA. Like some of their professors who became embroiled in the Red Scare, the players were effectively fired and blacklisted. Although none of these distinctively lanky men could reappear on the court even under a pseudonym, several players made careers for themselves on the periphery of basketball. Over forty years later, Spivey went to his grave still believing that he could have been a contender: "I would have had an era all my own in the N.B.A. . . . George Mikan was near the end of his career and Wilt Chamberlain hadn't started. I was the biggest and best in the country. I think I would have dominated the game like those two did."[19] So, after a fashion, must have run the regrets of many more innocent men and women whose careers withered on the blacklist.

From January to March 1951 at least, the basketball scandal was a New York story. During February and March, however, it competed for attention with the Rosenberg trial, the hearings on the Reconstruction Finance Corporation, Estes Kefauver's Senate hearings on organized crime, the renewed HUAC investigations of Hollywood, the imprisonment of Alger Hiss, and allegations of corruption among New York City firefighters. The basketball story shared method and metaphor with all of them. To the rest of the country it looked as though the ethnic, interracial world of New York's college athletic programs displayed the pattern of corruption that characterized the city more generally. Many Americans reassured themselves that, whatever they were, they were not New Yorkers. Such was the attitude of Phog Allen, basketball coach at the University of Kansas, who declared: "Out here in the Midwest this condition, of course, doesn't prevail, but in the East the boys, particularly those who participate in the resort hotel leagues during the summer months, are thrown into an environment which cannot help but breed the evil which more and more is coming to light."[20] In August 1951, Kentucky coach Adolph Rupp boasted that "gamblers could not touch my boys with a ten-foot pole," a claim that was quoted repeatedly after the scandal spread to Kentucky.[21]

In their first expressions of shock and horror, people blamed the Garden, the Catskill resorts, and pro sports, which had corrupted amateur athletics. The New York story was set in penthouses, nightclubs, restaurants, resort hotels, Madison Square Garden, and, most important, in the city's public university. Each place housed one or more elements of the new social mix that characterized the postwar United States. Several versions of the story, like Phog Allen's, traced the corruption to the borscht belt, where ethnic figures from the upper circles of the underworld allegedly mingled with middle-class vacationers. With this setting, the story could weave anti-Semitic and anti-Italian prejudices together into a regional bias against New York. For some, the ethnic lifestyle of the Catskill resorts was perhaps paralleled by the ethnicity of leftist academics. Warner and Spivey had worked for Grossinger's in the summer; Gard had met Sollazzo in the Catskills, where they made deals around the summer leagues that carried over to the serious business of the regular season.[22] The hotel owners, of course, denied the allegations; they blamed the colleges. "Isn't competitive bidding for playing talent by the colleges, with free scholarships [*sic*], boondoggling campus jobs and other inducements a more pointed signpost toward 'easy money'?" asked the president of the Mountain Hotelmen's Federations of Sullivan and Ulster Counties.[23]

And he was right to ask about such practices, for the scandal led to accusations of recruiting violations.[24] In the meantime, however, the press, the public, and academic administrators found an easier target in Ned Irish's Madison Square Garden. A successful promoter but a man loved by few, Irish controlled New York's only commercial arena, a lucrative venue for the colleges and a place where gambling went on openly. One man who made his living by betting on basketball told a congressional committee that honest gamblers avoided the Garden because "abnormal" fluctuations in the point spread suggested that the games played there might be fixed.[25] According to the DA, the Garden provided an "unwholesome atmosphere for college basketball," and the NCAA responded to initial reports of the scandal by suggesting that teams play all games either on campus or in arenas under the direct supervision of college officials. Indeed, the scandal offered the NCAA an opportunity to consolidate its authority, and it was during the late 1940s and early 1950s that the association, by defining unfair practices, devising rules against them, and promising to enforce those regulations, began to exercise control over college sports.[26]

The opposition between Garden and campus, like the opposition between New York and the rest of the country, was a useful fiction. But many, particularly those who recognized the potential impact of television on college sports, knew that there was already too much money involved to simply move basketball back to campus, so they used the scandal to create a new consensus on the place of sports in the academy. What had to be addressed first were the newly exposed (and still unresolved) contradictions of amateurism: How was the amateur to be accommodated in money-making sports? How was the profitable athlete to be accommodated in the university? How were sports as commercial entertainment to be balanced with sports as purely athletic competition? And here those studying the role of sports adopted the language of ethical hygiene (the quest for clean players), which had already been perfected in the rooting out of political heretics. Players tried to explain themselves. Some said they had succumbed to temptation because they knew that the colleges were profiting from their playing. Bradley's Gene Melchiorre confessed, "We justified ourselves, I guess, by saying the colleges were making plenty out of us."[27] The fixers had in effect offered to pay them wages, and the athletes had simply acted like employees but of the wrong boss.

For a number of the players, amateurism was a kind of regression. Several were men in their early twenties who were matriculating on the GI bill. They had enlisted after graduating from high school, joining up in the last few months of the war. During the late 1940s, they took advantage of the benefits available to veterans. This was the case not only with Junius Kellogg, but also with Gene Melchiorre, Louis Lipman, Henry Poppe, Richard Feurtado, Nathan Miller, and Aldoph Bigos—a favorite of the press—a decorated war hero whose widowed mother ran a meat market in Perth Amboy, New Jersey.[28]

The press projected an image of quasi-innocent haplessness by reporting where each player's small cache of unspent money had been hidden. Bigos sewed $5,000 into the lining of a sports coat and hid it in the back of his closet; White taped an envelope containing $5,500 to the back of a dresser drawer in his room at the Brooklyn YMCA; Smith hid $1,030 in the toe of a shoe in the closet of his room at the Newark YMCA; Layne buried $2,890 in a flowerpot in his bedroom; and Warner left $3,050 in a shoe box in the basement of his aunt's house.[29] Some players, such as LeRoy Smith, were just too poor to explain a sudden influx of cash to friends and family. (Smith told a reporter that he still remembered his high school teammates buying him his first new pair of sneakers.[30]) Others, like Al Roth, the son of a soda-truck driver from Brooklyn, insisted that they had been trying to get enough money together to set themselves up after school. Some saw gambling as part of the wild life of the streets; as Sherman White's father put it, "It would have been different if he was raised on the street, but he had to go to college to learn something he was never taught at home."[31] But players like Roth saw gambling as a backdoor means of access to middle-class, responsible, male adulthood. Their hidden money suggested both a sense of guilt and a naiveté or innocence on the part of the players; like countless boys before them, they had been seduced by cunning gamesters who used them as pawns in a dirty game. The story also reinforced a familiar moral of oft-told gambling tales: not all gamblers actually gamble. Sollazzo, the press reported, bet $8,000 a day on sure-thing gambles, and, like other pseudo-gamblers, he had used his beautiful wife and his fancy penthouse to lure college boys into his clutches—not boys with money to lose, but those who were both talented enough to make him some money and hungry enough to be tempted by the promise of unearned wealth.[32]

The authorities did not buy the criminal-seduction story, and they punished all of the athletes implicated in the fixes by banning them from basketball for life. Four New York players actually went to jail. Prior to their sentencing in November 1951, Judge Saul S. Streit ordered their female relatives removed from the courtroom, to "prevent any possible hysterical outburst." (And there they stayed, where they had been all along, on the periphery of the story.) Drawing an analogy to the Rosenberg case, Judge Streit warned college administrators and coaches that this case had the potential explosiveness of an "atomic athletic scandal," and he chastised those who recruited players with promises nearly as inflated as the fixers'. It was apparent to Streit that the hypocrisy and fraud practiced on the Garden court was matched by the bad faith displayed in academic offices.[33]

Politicians jumped on the scandal. Sports, as usual, offered them an opportunity for moralistic posturing and pious rhetoric. Governor Dewey suggested moving the games out of the Garden to keep the "lice from corrupting those boys," while Senator Fulbright went after college alumni who promoted the "cynical immoral doctrine that one must win at all costs."[34] And, in a rambling statement to the Senate Appropriations Committee in which he deplored the basketball fixes while celebrating the success of government loyalty checks, J. Edgar Hoover laid the blame on the "hypocrisy and sham" of college athletic codes, the lax supervision of athletes, and a growing public taste for spectacle that made good entertainment seem more important than a clean contest.[35]

The scandal came under federal scrutiny during Senator Kefauver's hearings on organized crime, an "industry" that in the late 1940s was no longer driven by liquor sales and not yet by drugs, but one that depended on the billions of dollars generated by illegal gambling. The mob skimmed profits from casinos, tracks, and numbers games. During the Kefauver hearings, the discussion of Sollazzo's sure-thing betting system revealed one of the finer ironies of the scandal: it had led officials to devise a set of regulations that assured the integrity of college sports not just for fans and players but also for professional gamblers. These gamblers welcomed the move to put dishonest bookies out of business, at least with respect to college sports. In many ways the elimination of open gambling from the arena resembled nothing so much as the nineteenth-century purge of prostitution from the theater. College basketball was to provide well-ordered entertainment to a public whose interest might be emotional, intellectual, aesthetic, or even erotic, but not financial—or at least not openly so. Gambling was either atavistic or corrupt, and figures like Sollazzo belonged either on Broadway or at the track, but not at a college game.

After questioning a spate of reluctant criminal witnesses, the Senate committee heard the testimony of a friendly witness, a "million-dollar-a-year" Milwaukee gambler named Sydney Brodson. Brodson said he was happy to appear before the committee (and before the large viewing audience of the first congressional hearings ever to be televised).[36] Like the senators, Brodson was a professional man, a lawyer who happened to have chosen to make his living by betting on college basketball games. Brodson explained to the committee how an elaborate world of fictitious businesses operated as fronts for gambling. The senators, with Brodson's phone records before them, interrogated him about calls to the "Get the Vote Committee," "Acme Construction Co.," "National Union of Government Workers," "United Lumber Co.," "Tip-Top Smoke Shop," and "Atlantic and Pacific Cleaning & Dyeing." The benign faces of small businesses and local political organizations, he admitted, served gamblers well. But while Brodson was forthcoming about his own practices, he resisted the committee's efforts to push him into naming names, refusing to identify his contacts or to answer any questions about his friends and acquaintances. "It is unfortunate," he told the senators, "that you have gotten people in here who are in no way implicated."[37]

Brodson's candid testimony supported one theme of the story in particular: the common interest of all legitimate parties in an honest game. The "loudest screams of anguish" over the betting scandal, one sports columnist wrote, came "from the vast army of bookmakers, the fellows who book the bets," for "a scandal louses up their business something dreadful."[38] The committee erred in regarding all gambling as evil, suggested Brodson; there was a real difference between his own honest enterprise — that of a family man, a Midwesterner, a businessman who subscribed to hundreds of newspapers, supported a full-time employee, and was widely respected for his skill—and the lowlife scum who would simultaneously ruin an honest bet and the morals of a college basketball player.[39] It is difficult to believe that the senators were truly unaware of this difference, for betting was common and both pro-team owners and college officials organized their leagues and athletic programs to keep gambling at a distance, precisely the remove at which Brodson said he operated. It was that distance, however, that kept the money Brodson could make out of the hands of college officials and promoters.

Brodson testified that he counseled his betting friends to avoid games played in Madison Square Garden; his own interests and those of all honest bookmakers, he assured the committee, would be served by the new NCAA regulations, by increased surveillance of players, and by legislation to penalize those who tried to bribe players. He knew that, the pious rhetoric of amateurism notwithstanding, anything that regulated college basketball as a commodity would ensure its integrity for gamblers. Brodson not only supported regulations that distanced him from the players, but testimony like his helped administrators devise rules for commercialized sports within the academy. These rules were about money, but they also concerned such issues as race, class, talent, and entertainment. In the 1940s, African Americans playing for New York schools had changed college basketball. The integrated New York teams were good, but they played in a world where racism was still common on and off the court. Before LIU could play Arizona, for example, the New York school had to be "reassured [that] there would be no discrimination against or hostility to its Negro players" and that they would be offered the same accommodations as their White teammates.[40] And when (White) Kentucky players were implicated in the fixes, the African American New Yorkers who had been shunned by Rupp and his team must have relished the exposure of this smug coach and his racist players.[41]

As the scandal spread from New York to the Midwest and the South, scrutiny of City College shifted from the basketball court to the classroom, and a committee was appointed by the Board of Higher Education in April

1951 to investigate recruiting. The question addressed by the Committee on Intercollegiate Basketball concerned neither what the players had done nor where basketball fit into the university, but how college basketball players fit into the student body. The committee concluded that, while "all of us who failed to speak or act in time share the blame," the primary responsibility for the players' corruption rested with the individuals themselves: "They will remember forever that if they had taken the simple step, had said NO at the instant of the offer and had gone directly to their coaches and had told them the story, they and the sport they betrayed would have been spared dishonor." [42]

But City College's internal investigation continued, and investigators implicated coach Nat Holman in the fixes. His case coincided with those of three New York college faculty members who refused to tell a Senate subcommittee whether they had had any contact with the Communist Party. The City College committee reported to the Board of Higher Education that it had found Holman and two of his associates guilty of "neglect of duty, conduct unbecoming a teacher, and disobedience of a direction of this Board and this Committee." At the same meeting (17 November 1952), the board charged the three teachers—Henrietta A. Friedman, Melba Phillips, and Sarah R. Reidman—with violating Section 903 of the New York City Charter, which required public employees to cooperate with legislative investigations and congressional committees. [43]

On looking into the records of its athletes, the City College committee found that the high school transcripts of fourteen of the 300 athletes admitted between 1945 and 1951 had been altered. Moreover, Warner and Layne, students with poor high school grades, had apparently done college work with no difficulty and had transferred with surprising ease from night classes to the more competitive day-student program. The committee also discovered that the assistant basketball coach, Harry Sand, who was granted tenure shortly before the November 1952 board meeting, had written to Warner, promising to pay him to play on a team that would tour South America to raise money for sports in Israel. [44]

Holman, pleading ignorance, denied the charges and appealed his suspension. [45] The board, countering that he either knew what was going on or was so naive that one would question his fitness to teach, nevertheless appointed a subcommittee to continue the investigation; sixteen months later, the subcommittee recommended that the charges against Holman and Sand be dismissed. In Holman's case, however, the board overruled its own subcommittee. While Sand had cooperated with the investigation, admitted his guilt, and expressed his "repentance," Holman had been "'uncooperative' in his testimony before a special investigating committee and had answered only those questions put to him, without availing himself of opportunities 'to volunteer information.'"[46] Here again, the attitudes and expectations of the Red Scare informed the college sports story. The methods and idioms of humiliation, degradation, and recantation so carefully developed by and for congressional committees had become standardized for investigations of matters that bore little or no relation to political subversion.

Students, alumni, and friends organized in Holman's defense, and he was reinstated with back pay in August 1954.[47] New York basketball, however, was not the same. The City College team never regained its Division I status, while St. John's (protected, some said, by Cardinal Spellman) and Seton Hall emerged as metropolitan basketball powerhouses. New York's Black players began to go to colleges outside the city, changing the style of play across the country.[48]

The story spread too, taking on an odd life of its own and offering a variety of lessons in a variety of contexts. From today's perspective, the most important lessons seem to be those we can draw from the early 1950s politics of surveillance, but for the New Yorker Stanley Cohen and the great Trinidadian intellectual C. L. R. James, who were both much closer to the scandal, it revealed something important about national character as well. Cohen remembered the story's circulating throughout his youth. For him it represented the experience of a generation torn between the confining middle-class morality of striving immigrant parents and the lure of a looser life of the streets. On the court, two different styles of masculinity met, and college authorities saw to it that some version of middle-class responsibility appeared to dominate the expressive world of working-class youth, White and Black. The scandal also seemed to Cohen to be a perfect figure for the United States in the 1950s, a nation shaped by warring impulses — a people capable of "profound largesse and the pettiest recriminations," athletes capable of high art and low tricks.[49]

For James the issue was loyalty to the integrity of sport itself. He remembered expressing his "horror to . . . friends with an unaccustomed freedom that astonished them":

> Before I could choose my words I found myself saying that adults in Trinidad or in Britain, in the world of business or private life, could or would do anything, more or less. But in the adult world of sport, certainly in cricket, despite the tricks teams played upon one another, I had never heard of any such thing and did not believe it possible. That young men playing for school or university should behave in this way on such a scale was utterly shocking to me.[50]

James confessed that as "shock succeeded shock," he was most shocked by his American friends' lack of shock. They were "chiefly political people," honest people who had rejected the "bribes offered by wealthy parents to return to the fold of Democrats or Republicans." But they were not shocked by players who took bribes. Their wealth had made them indifferent to the moral dilemmas besetting their working-class countrymen. Sophisticated and cynical, part of the besieged Left, they viewed the manipulation of college sports with indifference. The story revealed how wide a gap existed between James's sense of loyalty and that of his American friends. He had never held Americans to an artificial English measure, so it was not disappointment on that front which came into play, but rather something he learned about the American character from the scandal: his friends had no loyalties to the players themselves, but, like the bribed players, they were caught in a kind of individual selfishness. They seemed to have "no loyalties to anything. They had a universal distrust of their elders and preceptors, which had begun with distrust of their teachers. Each had to work out his own individual code."[51]

James perhaps ignored the controversy surrounding the very meaning of "loyalty," for individual codes could have different consequences in politics and in sports. The players' codes seemed far less principled than those of Americans who refused, on principle, to sign loyalty oaths. For most commentators, the players who took bribes did not exemplify an American type but an aberration, a deviance that demanded explanation. The shock that seemed at first to beggar understanding soon gave way to a flood of interpretations, many of which endeavored to construe innocence in what must have seemed a world beyond redemption. While the Red Scare left many baffled, tongue-tied and inarticulate, especially those who were subjected to the aggressive tactics of Communist-hunters, few were shocked into silence by the revelations of corruption in college basketball. The profound political silence notwithstanding, there was always something to be said about sports. Expressing shock in this context was equivalent to demonstrating loyalty and patriotism, doing one's bit to reconstitute innocence in a fallen world corrupted by war and by witchhunts.

The story of the point-shaving scandals was so clear and easy. There were villains; there were victims — boys susceptible to corruption. And the scandal proved just how a secret agenda could be hidden behind the surface of healthy sports. Ellen Schrecker has pointed out that congressional investigators never seemed concerned with exactly what was being propounded by Communist ideologues in the classroom; it was enough, as Sidney Hook argued, to have been a member of the Party.[52] Sure-thing bettors and bribed athletes played the same kind of invisible game that Communist teachers supposedly did with students; what was never demonstrated in the classroom, however, was exposed on the court. Investigators suspected teachers of inserting a Communist agenda in the materials they taught, even if no one could say precisely how or where. The sports scandals served those who hunted political subversives by illustrating precisely how a hidden agenda could lurk where one least suspected it; thus the investigations of basketball fixes led to mini–show trials. Like the Hunter College students who for twenty-five years had sat in classics courses taught by Henrietta A. Friedman and the Brooklyn College students who had studied physics with Melba Phillips and biology with Sarah R. Reidman, fans missed the deeper game organized by gamblers and the players who were in on the fixes.[53] Fans saw a charade, a performance, a fiction — as Hoover pointed out, a spectacle that substituted for an athletic contest. What the spectacle on the court obscured was a game subverted by a cast of players who took their orders not from their coaches but from crooks like Sollazzo. This "entertainment" was surely unfit for television's emerging audience, let alone the sponsors who would underwrite its programming.

In order to win back the loyalty of its fans (and of honest gamblers like Brodson and those whose bets my neighbor Pete would take some thirty years later), basketball had to become clean. Throughout the 1940s, college teams had achieved thrilling victories, just as college students had mastered classics, physics, and biology, among other subjects taught by Communist and ex-Communist professors. But for those bent on purging the college classroom, the basketball scandals stood for the corruption hidden from innocent eyes. Neither students nor fans, academic authorities announced, had seen the whole game. The sports story delivered what the political story could not: proof that "innocent" Americans could be subverted by forces of corruption so cunning that they could evade for a time even the most probing reporters and the most zealous investigators.

The connection between sports and politics appears strongest when their stories intersect and overlap. In the first chapter of *Moby-Dick*, Ishmael remembers his whaling voyage as "a brief interlude and solo between more extensive performances: I take it that this part of the bill must have run something like this: '*Grand Contested Election for the Presidency of the United States.* Whaling Voyage By One Ishmael. BLOODY BATTLE IN AFGHANISTAN.'"[54] For Ishmael, life unfolded in a series of dramatic acts. But if we take the acts on Melville's stage bill and turn them into newspaper headlines (which is what Ishmael's list has always seemed to me to be), sequence becomes simultaneity.

It is this logic of simultaneity, I would suggest, that binds the story of the basketball fixes to that of the anti-Communist witchhunts. Stories in a newspaper are joined, as Benedict Anderson has pointed out, by an implicit "meanwhile."[55] They are rehearsed not as separate acts on the stage but as a full-length drama slowly unfolding for the reading public. And in their unfolding, such dramas accumulate meanings—the meanings of a larger cultural moment as well as idiosyncratic private meanings. The language of cleanliness versus corruption, subversion, and confession—the exposés of fronts, double lives, and secret deals—that suited the hunt for political subversives informed the story of the basketball fixes as well. Like so many sports stories, this narrative seemed to provide a particularly fertile ground for transplanted meanings. It mixed personally for some with the theme of innocence, youth, and promise destroyed, but it also mixed more publicly with the narrative ends of the stories of domestic subversion that were so crucial to the early battles of the Cold War. It was a story in which the apparent absence of politics served political ends.

The episode of the basketball players bribed by sure-thing gamblers fits somewhere in our national epic between the allegory of a great political battle over the American soul and the bloody war story set in Korea. The university—where some lost their jobs while others avoided the draft—was the setting for the sports story. Such a context should remind us that the much-vaunted innocence of the 1950s, still proving useful to political speech writers, was a carefully maintained artifice. This story of innocence corrupted was the product of an odd collaboration among the college athletes who fell from grace, the investigators who exposed them, the reporters who told the story, and an American public who learned to believe in the efficacy of investigation and surveillance, in the "amateurism" of college sports, and in what passed for disinterested academic inquiry. This forty-year-old compromise between public virtue and private vice in sports is compromising indeed. It may even allow us to yield to pressures from taxation opponents who would exploit the private pleasure of gambling to minimize public obligation. Meanwhile, we will go on questioning the amateur status of college sports, rooting out corruption, and pondering the costs of gambling, but perhaps we will also one day be able to welcome the loud gamblers back into the Garden.

Notes

1 Sam Goldaper, "Nat Holman Is Dead at 98," *New York Times*, 13 February 1995, B: 7; Frank Litsky, "Bill Spivey, 66, Kentucky Star Implicated in Scandal of 1950s," *New York Times*, 10 May 1995, D: 22.

2 Stanley Cohen, *The Game They Played* (New York, 1977). The scandals were also the subject of a novel; see Leo Rutman, *5 Good Boys* (New York, 1982). In the mid-1970s, Charles Rosen tracked down several players who were implicated in the point-shaving schemes; some talked to him, others refused; see his *Scandals of '51: How the Gamblers Almost Killed College Basketball* (New York, 1978).

3 Board of Higher Education of the City of New York, *Minutes of Proceedings*, 17 November 1952, 617–23, New York Municipal Archives.

4 On efforts by the Association of American University Professors (AAUP) to define academic freedom, see Ellen Schrecker, *No Ivory Tower: McCarthyism and the Universities* (New York, 1986), 12–13, 105–11. On efforts by the National College Athletic Association (NCAA) to define amateurism, see Arthur A. Fleisher III, Brian L. Goff, and Robert D. Tollison, *The National College Athletic Association: A Study in Cartel Behavior* (Chicago, 1992), 46–48.

5 "Gambler Is Sought in Basketball 'Fix,'" *New York Times*, 19 January 1951, 26; see also Arthur Daley, "Sports of the *Times*," *New York Times*, 18 January 1951, 34.

6 "Cage Star's Story of 'Fix': More Players in Payoff Link," *New York Journal–American*, 18 January 1951, 1.

7 Ibid., 13. Junius Kellogg, the informer–hero, was feted by his classmates, by the Chicago Catholic Youth Organization, by the Portsmouth (Virginia) City Council, and by the New York City Police Commissioner; see the *New York Times*, 1 February 1951, 18; 7 February 1951, 30; and 14 February 1951, 23. In March of that year, Kellogg left school and reenlisted in the army. Stanley Cohen found him working for the City of New

York in the mid-1970s; a car accident on a barnstorming tour with some of the Harlem Globetrotters had left him paralyzed. Kellogg went on to coach wheelchair basketball in the Bronx; see Cohen, *The Game*, 87–88.

8   See Cohen, *The Game*, 1. Or perhaps they had all been remembering *Casablanca*.

9   "Two Ex-Stars Held in Basketball 'Fix' at $2000 a Game," *New York Times*, 18 January 1951, 23.

10 Sydney A. Brodson testimony, U.S. Senate Special Committee, *Hearings before the Special Committee to Investigate Organized Crime in Interstate Commerce*, 81st Cong., 2d sess., and 82d Cong., 1st sess., 12 March 1951, pt. 12, p. 468.

11 "Excerpts from Judge Streit's Comments on College Basketball Fix," *New York Times*, 20 November 1951, 26.

12 "Ed Warner: All-American," *Ebony* (January 1951): 76–79; quotation from 79.

13 "*Life* Congratulates . . . C.C.N.Y. and Joins in 'Allagaroo' for Its Basketball Champs," *Life*, 10 April 1950, 42; see also Schrecker, *No Ivory Tower*, 42, 46–47.

14 "Borscht Basketball," *Life*, 28 August 1950, 66–68; quotation from 66.

15 See "Max Kase Wins Pulitzer Citation," *New York Journal–American*, 5 May 1952, 1; and Roger Kahn, "Success and Ned Irish," *Sports Illustrated*, 27 March 1961, 39–46.

16 Mink was doubly coded for scandal that spring with the Reconstruction Finance Commission corruption story featuring a mink-coated secretary. Sollazzo lived in a penthouse at 115 Central Park West, an address he shared with Costello.

17 "Say Fixer 'Schooled Pet—But Ignored Son,'" *New York Journal–American*, 3 March 1951, 3.

18 "2 More Arrests Due in Cage 'Fix,'" *New York Journal–American*, 1 March 1951, 10.

19 Litsky, "Bill Spivey," D: 22.

20 As quoted in "Hogan Questions Three L.I.U. Stars in Basketball 'Fix,'" *New York Times*, 20 February 1951, 1.

21 See, for example, "3 Basketball Aces on Kentucky Team Named in '49 Fix," *New York Times*, 21 October 1951, 1; and Alfred E. Clark, "Judge in Fix Case Condemns Kentucky Teams and Coach," *New York Times*, 30 April 1952, 1.

22 See Alexander Feinberg, "3 Players at L.I.U. Admit Collecting $18,500 Cash Bribe," *New York Times*, 21 February 1951, 1.

23 Armand Schwab, Jr., "Basketball in the Summer Resorts," *New York Times*, 25 February 1951, 2: 17; see also Alexander Feinberg, "Government Files $1,128,493 Tax Lien against Sollazzo," *New York Times*, 24 February 1951. Gene Melchiorre remembered Greek gamblers striking up an acquaintance with a Greek kid on the Bradley University team, in "How I Fell for the Basketball Bribers," *Look*, 13 January 1953, 62–64.

24 See "4 'Fixers' Sought in Florida Resorts," *New York Times*, 29 March 1951, 23.

25 On professional gamblers and the Garden, see Brodson testimony, Senate Special Committee, *Hearings . . . to Investigate Organized Crime in Interstate Commerce*, 464.

26 See Fleisher, Goff, and Tollison, *National College Athletic Association*, 46.

27 Melchiorre, "How I Fell," 63.

28 See "Who's Behind the Cage Fixer?" *New York Journal–American*, 21 February 1951, 8.

29 See "4 L.I.U. Stars Admit $19,000 Cage Bribes," *New York Journal–American*, 20 February 1951, 1; Feinberg, "3 Players at L.I.U.," 1; and "Hogan Questions Three L.I.U. Stars," 1.

30 See "L.I.U. Star Still Has Pals in Newark," *New York Journal–American*, 22 February 1951, 4.

31 "Dumping Scandal Spreads," *Life*, 5 March 1951, 38.

32 See "Hogan Bares $8,000-a-Day Sollazzo Bets," *New York Journal–American*, 24 February 1951, 1.

33 See "Excerpts from Judge Streit's Comments," 26.

34 Feinberg, "Government Files . . . Tax Lien," 1; "Mockery of College Sports," *New York Journal–American*, 27 March 1951, 25.

35 See "J. E. Hoover Scores Colleges on 'Fixes,'" *New York Times*, 10 April 1951, 18.

36 See Estes Kefauver, *Crime in America* (Garden City, NY, 1951).

37 Brodson testimony, Senate Special Committee, *Hearings . . . to Investigate Organized Crime in Interstate Commerce*, 458, 462, 481, 489.

38 Arthur Daley, "Sports Are Honest: A Defense," *New York Times*, 4 March 1951, 6: 20.

39 See Brodson testimony, Senate Special Committee, *Hearings . . . to Investigate Organized Crime in Interstate Commerce*, 449–51.

40 "L.I.U.–Arizona Game On," *New York Times*, 20 January 1951, 11.

41 See Nelson George, *Elevating the Game: Black Men and Basketball* (New York, 1992), 79.

42 Board of Higher Education of the City of New York, "Report of the Committee on Intercollegiate Basketball," *Minutes of the Special Meeting of the Board of Higher Education of the City of New York Held April 30, 1951*, 232, 228, New York Municipal Archives.

43 Board of Higher Education, *Minutes of Proceedings* (17 November 1952), 617–21; quotation from 617.

44 See Schrecker, *No Ivory Tower*, 79.

45 "Holman Suspended," *New York Times*, 18 November 1952, 1.

46 "Holman Ousted at City College," *New York Times*, 4 March 1954, 1; see also "Excerpts from Judge Streit's Comments," 26. Streit noted that several of the players had low IQs and ranked near the bottom of their high school classes. Like Shoeless Joe Jackson, these were poor and poorly educated young men.

47 See "Holman Reinstated," *New York Times*, 28 August 1954, 1; and Goldaper, "Nat Holman," B: 7.

48 See Cohen, *The Game*, 153; and George, *Elevating the Game*, 80.

49 Cohen, *The Game*, 160, 51; see also Barbara Ehrenreich, *The Hearts of Men: American Dreams and the Flight from Commitment* (New York, 1983), 14–41.

50 C. L. R. James, *Beyond a Boundary* (London, 1963), 52–53.

51 Ibid., 53.

52 See Schrecker, *No Ivory Tower*, 108. Louis Francis Budenz, who made a career out of being an ex-Communist, took up this issue in "Do Colleges *Have* to Hire Red Professors?" *American Legion Magazine* (November 1951): 11–13, 40–43.

53 See "CCNY Suspends Coach Holman," *New York Times*, 18 November 1952, 1. Reidman was one of ten teachers whose pensions were restored by the city in 1982; see "10 Teachers Ousted in '50s Given Restitution from City," *New York Times*, 29 April 1982, B: 3.

54 Herman Melville, *Moby-Dick or, The Whale* (Indianapolis, 1964 [1851]), 29.

55 Benedict Anderson, *Imagined Communities: Reflections on the Origin and Spread of Nationalism* (London, 1983), 28–37.

James T. Fisher

"The Great Beader": Pete Axthelm and the
Bonds of Tradition

At Monmouth Park, a thoroughbred racetrack
in Oceanport, New Jersey, there is a dark bronze
plaque mounted on a brick wall just behind and
slightly to the left of an outdoor bar as one
faces east, toward the track itself and the Atlantic Ocean four miles distant. The inscription on
the plaque, barely discernible from more than a
few inches away, reads simply "The 'Ax.'"

During his lifetime, most of the friends and
colleagues of sportswriter, essayist, and television commentator Pete Axthelm paid homage
to his legendary informality by going the simple
plaque one better; to them he was always just
"Ax." Yet the sobriquet winked at the complex
history of one Peter M. Axthelm, whose collegiate senior-year essay on *The Modern Confessional Novel* had been published by Yale University Press in 1967 when its twenty-four-year-old
author was already a veteran reporter, columnist,
and turf authority on two storied, though now
defunct, newspapers. Then there was the Pete
Axthelm who, dying prematurely in 1991, made
a widow of the woman he had married just the
year before and left behind a daughter from a pre-

The *South Atlantic Quarterly* 95:2, Spring 1996.
Copyright © 1996 by Duke University Press.
CCC 0038-2876/96/$1.50.

vious marriage as well. The facts of that life must for now be largely confined to what Jack Beatty — biographer of James Michael Curley, the kind of
character Axthelm loved telling stories about — called "the hidden history
at the edge of the page."[1] Our focus will fall somewhere between the person and the persona, on the place that Axthelm crafted for himself within
a tradition of urban sports journalism whose irresistible spell abided until
what seems like just moments ago.

With Pete Axthelm, you must always begin at the track. No respecter of
social hierarchies, he loved above all the promiscuous tableaux enshrined
at race plants across North America. Take, for instance, the area surrounding his plaque on the brick wall at Monmouth Park. The bar it decorates
serves the "Lady's Secret Café," a patio with umbrella tables overlooking
the walking ring where prospective bettors examine the horseflesh about
to be led onto the track for the next race, yet just across the bar and along
the same brick wall a wooden board inelegantly inscribed "Paddock Bar"
indicates the existence of an entirely different facility — but where is it?

The Ax's plaque is suspended in an indeterminate zone between the
Jersey elegance of the Lady's Secret Café (the kind of setting Hunter S.
Thompson envisioned when he wrote that Axthelm "loved the sound of
ice tinkling in tall crystal glasses in clubhouse tents") and the smoke-filled,
paper-strewn Paddock Bar, which, upon further inspection, can be found
trackside of the redbrick wall (the sort of place where Axthelm, according
to the *Thoroughbred Times*, "enjoyed life as a common, ordinary racetrack
degenerate").[2] At racetracks the social boundaries signified by café versus
bar tend to be increasingly breached as the day's card is filled in with an
infinite variety of narratives, equine and human alike, but few people have
ever been so much at home in each precinct of the track as Axthelm always
was. He would have appreciated the setting for his plaque, but even more
so the bartender's smile when I asked why his name was on the wall in
the first place. "He came here a lot," she casually replied, adding after a
moment's reflection, "He was a horseperson."

Since Pete Axthelm died at the age of forty-seven from drinking too
much in too many racetrack bars — without having had a chance to publicly apologize like Mickey Mantle, in whose company he no doubt enjoyed
a cocktail or two — there is ample reason to eschew the celebratory mode
in assessing his career. To borrow some racing lingo, the "coupled entry"
of his literary gifts and fragile character found its complement — and true

subject—in the flawed beauty of thoroughbred racehorses and the two-legged "sports" they enticed and tormented. Was that a meaningful vocation in this world? It depends on what you look for in stories.

═══════

The Lady's Secret Café was the namesake of a stout grey mare owned by Eugene Klein, ex-proprietor of the San Diego Chargers. Klein entrusted the care and handling of his racing stock to trainer D. Wayne Lukas, a former Wisconsin high school basketball coach who, following a successful stint racing quarter horses, parlayed a confident manner and a keen eye to position himself as head of the most powerful North American thoroughbred stable of the 1980s. Lukas specialized in acquiring well-bred yearlings for his wealthy clients and racing them early and often during the following season, when they would net him many of the handsome purses offered in races restricted to two-year-olds, or "juveniles." His handling of these young equine athletes generated even more controversy than his unhorseman-like self-presentation. (*New Yorker* writer William Murray described Lukas as a "tall, permanently tanned, expensively dressed, supremely personable man with a sculpted hairdo, a gleaming smile, and eyes hidden most of the time behind designer shades."[3]) A familiar joke of the time began "What's the rarest thing at the racetrack?" Answer: "a four-year-old trained by Wayne Lukas."

Lady's Secret, however, had silenced many of Lukas's critics by improving dramatically with age: named Horse of the Year as a four-year-old in 1986, at the age of five in July 1987 (for racing purposes, all thoroughbreds celebrate their birthdays on 1 January), she became the richest mare in racing history after winning at Monmouth Park. Less than three weeks later when she faced a weak field at the venerable Saratoga Race Course, she was inevitably bet down to odds of one-to-five, meaning that each two-dollar ticket to win on Lady's Secret would return a paltry $2.40 (providing, of course, that the champion did make it into the winner's circle).

Enter the "bridgejumpers," a tiny but oft-ridiculed cohort of horseplayers who specialize in locating an "unbeatable" favorite and betting it neither to win nor even to "place" (come in second), but to finish third, or "show." The mathematics of the game is not my forte; suffice it to say that if you bet a horse to show and she finishes first, second, *or* third, you collect something for your handicapping efforts, unimaginative though they may be. (The great majority of bettors don't even bother with the win, place, or show pools anymore, but focus instead on "exotic" wagers such as the exacta, in which both the first- and second-place finishers in a given race must be predicted.) The bridgejumper's theory holds that an overwhelming favorite like Lady's Secret represents a terrible risk value as a win bet since the payout, if she does indeed finish first, will reflect the horse's true payout odds—as determined by the amount of money wagered—minus various punitive taxes known as the "takeout." Pete Axthelm liked to quote an old racetrack maxim that goes something like "there is nary a man alive who pays his rent on three-to-five"; over the grinding long run, too many of these favored animals will "bobble at the start," "jump shadows," "fail to menace," "forget to switch leads," or otherwise earn one of the many colorful euphemisms for "lose" employed by racing people.

Seekers of the "sure thing" will sacrifice twenty or thirty cents on the dollar for the security cushion of the show bet. With this hedge against the horse's failure to place first or second comes another equation, based on the track's obligation to return at least a dime in profit on each successful two-dollar bet even when so much has been wagered on a single horse's showing that a finish "in the money" (first, second, or third) yields a "minus pool." Without that provision, a minus pool would be self-defeating for the betting public because, with so much cash dumped on one horse, there would be insufficient funds left in the pool after the takeout to redeem all the winning tickets. But in the very act of accepting the public's wagers, the track guarantees that it will return at least the minimum profit on each "live" ticket. The house takes a beating, then simply finds another way to get its money back and a few dollars more.

Some tracks, faced with the prospect of an overwhelming favorite in a big race, simply prohibit show-betting altogether. Yet that is hardly the kind of sporting gesture that made the Saratoga Race Course home to the "sport of kings" every summer for well over a century. So the bridgejumpers were all over Lady's Secret as the horses came onto the track for the first race on 10 August 1987. As post time approached, it took just two plungers with deep pockets to inflate the already swollen show pool by $100,000. Then the starting gate burst open and "Lady's Secret broke to the front as usual. Instead of leaning to her left as she approached the first turn, though, she drifted wider and wider towards the outside fence, in the direction of the stables." Her celebrated jockey, Chris McCarron, "tried for a few seconds to get her back into the race, then pulled her up." Spectators gasped at the prospect of a career-threatening or even fatal injury to the champion thoroughbred, but within moments "the gray mare was feistily trotting back to be unsaddled, apparently sound and healthy."⁴ As there are no refunds on horses who fail to even break a sweat for their present investors, an alert went out to the many bridgekeepers along the Hudson just to the east of Saratoga Springs.

"It appears she's not interested in racing," McCarron later calmly explained, in the patented understatement of a jockey who—even as one of the "greats"—could expect to lose at least eight of every ten races in which he rode.⁵ Meanwhile, the intrepid few who had placed show bets on horses other than Lady's Secret gleefully reaped the windfall fruits of their fellows' overconfidence. (Suddenly, everyone recalled her spotty form in races earlier that season.) With all that cash in the pool, a modest two-dollar show wager on each of the other four contestants in the race yielded a tidy profit of $47.80, or a 600 percent return. All of this transpired in less than five minutes: the thunder of hooves, the heart-stopping drama, the torn pari-mutuel tickets fluttering down from the grandstand, and finally, the jubilant human "connections" of a long-shot winner having their picture taken in the storied winner's circle at Saratoga.

Pete Axthelm was no bridgejumper: as the self-designated "Great Beader," he preferred to bet on a long shot whose apparent readiness for the top that day—signaled by certain features of the animal's appearance not readily evident to the untrained eye—propelled him to the betting windows with a gnomic smile. (His friend Andy Beyer, the legendary handicapper and *Washington Post* racing writer, fondly recalled Axthelm's boasting "for years how he 'beaded' and bet the two horses that produced a $7,000 exacta payoff that remains the largest in Gulfstream Park's history. His friends debunked this achievement by pointing out that Pete always liked the looks of horses whose jockeys wore yellow silks, and both horses in the exacta were carrying his favorite color."⁶) Axthelm never tired of admonishing overconfident horseplayers: "The Goddess must be appeased, soothed, tithed. She must never be affronted by statements hinting that a gambler has taken fate into his own firm grip." But Axthelm himself, as Beyer sadly noted, had long since "clearly chosen" to relinquish "his own firm grip" on fate, which is not the same as saying that he had lost faith.⁷

When Pete Axthelm entered Yale College in 1961, the all-male student body attended classes six days a week, attired in the crisp Ivy League uniform supplied to generations of Yalies by the J. Press Company. Axthelm was far from unprepared to thrive in his new environs. He had compiled a stellar record at the Marianist Chaminade High School in Mineola, New York, a Long Island bastion of upwardly mobile Catholicism. (Senator Alfonse M. D'Amato attended Chaminade in the mid-1950s.) Axthelm's class was a hotbed of aspiring broadcasters: his debate team co-captain, Robert Wright, later became president of NBC (following Axthelm's own stint as a football tout on the network's NFL pregame show), while another classmate, Peter Desnoes, went on to become managing general partner of a major television conglomerate.[8] By the time he got to Yale, Axthelm (who, like most New York area Catholics born after 1940, was of mixed ethnic ancestry) was anxious to enlist in a tradition that had inscribed a new form of personal identity—"New York journalist"—on a variety of urban-tending Americans. The ethnocultural matrix of this tradition, prefigured in sports pages and entertainment columns earlier in the century (when, for instance, "Irish" had been recoded as a synonym for "street-smart realist" and "cultural democrat"), was fluidly ecumenical: the avatar of "New York journalism" was Damon Runyon, a Huguenot from Manhattan—Manhattan, Kansas.

This tradition imbued its initiates with an ethic—a duty and a spirituality—part of which seemed to entail the role, however honorary, of a lovable, if gruff, Irish ward heeler/horseplayer. Pete Axthelm thus faced a potential conflict of interest in matriculating at the college of his choice. While he was still a junior at Chaminade, a riot had broken out during New Haven's 1959 St. Patrick's Day parade after a large group of Yale students pelted cops and marchers from Catholic schools with snowballs. The names of most of the sixteen students arrested in the fracas evoked Congregational divines of the eighteenth century, while the seven New Haven police captains in charge at the riot scene were named Dinnan, McSherry, McGuire, Scanlon, McCarthy, Hallisey—and Fred J. Esposito. After an unnamed university official blamed the debacle on "the gross stupidity of the police," a spokesman for an Irish Catholic fraternal group admonished Yale President A. Whitney Griswold: "It is extremely regrettable that it should be the students of Yale who participated in manifesting the fact that there is still a great deal of underground and latent bigotry in America."[9] Although the world had changed considerably in the two short years between 1959 and 1961, the Ivy League had certainly long been hospitable in any case to those alumni of schools like Chaminade who could run while carrying an oblate spheroid or skate while holding a curved stick. Now, in Pete Axthelm, Yale had a Chaminade graduate who could write with real flair of football and hockey as well as of politics and post parades at Churchill Downs. (Axthelm's writing, like his public persona, would always convey an effortless, natural quality that seemed to defy facile analysis; that's what being "The Ax" was all about.) In the summer of 1964, for instance, he would conduct an exclusive interview for the *World–Telegram and Sun* with Rita Schwerner on the day her husband's body was found, together with those of two other slain civil rights activists, in Mississippi. Axthelm's practical liberalism (such as his early and vocal advocacy of gender equity in sports) seemed to flow as naturally from his experience as any of his other commitments.

As a child growing up within a family that, by Thompson's slightly delirious account, "openly worshiped gambling and had no regard for money," Pete was taken along on pilgrimages to Roosevelt Raceway, a dingy, raucous harness-racing track on what is now the site of a Long Island shopping mall.[10] Once he was old enough to make solitary journeys to nearby Belmont Park, a venerable thoroughbred plant, he would peer into the winner's circle from the grandstand, catching his first glimpses of the patrician sportsmen whose surnames he would later find adorning the halls of Yale. Among the most prominent of these gentlemen was John Hay "Jock" Whitney (Yale '26), owner of Greentree Stable—and the *New York Herald–Tribune*. Whitney would later be so taken with Axthelm's racing stories in what Yalies refer to as the "oldest college daily" that he would hire him, inadvertently for not one but two positions at the paper, both of which Axthelm filled with distinction.[11]

"Ax must have passed through Yale in a blink," wrote sports columnist Tom Callahan, "because he made it to the *New York Herald–Tribune* under the wire."[12] Timing was indeed a major issue in Axthelm's career: he entered college at the dawn of a new era and then joined the *Trib* just in time to witness the demise of a journalistic tradition with powerful claims on his own worldview. While signs of "creative tension" are often sought in the work of writers who cross various boundaries, Axthelm's writing was seamless and wholly lacking in irony—apart from what was built into the style of sports journalism that he proudly inherited from the likes of Red Smith and Jimmy Cannon, as well as Joe Palmer, his legendary predecessor as turf columnist for the *Herald–Tribune.*

He was no less thoroughly schooled in the discourse of postwar urban populism that saturated metropolitan New York. In the first decade of the television era, newspapers had successfully competed with the new medium, and they would continue to shape programming so long as columnists like Dorothy Kilgallen, Walter Winchell, and Ed Sullivan also remained dominant figures in the entertainment business. (All three disdained TV yet were quick to scramble aboard.) Pete quickly mastered the intricate codes through which New York journalists and their various employers communicated to an extraordinarily diverse audience. In a haunting essay, another product of this milieu, the late James E. B. Breslin (biographer of Mark Rothko and not to be confused with Jimmy Breslin, Axthelm's mentor and friend), invoked the titles of some New York newspapers from the early 1950s to distinguish the various guises of his "conservative, frustrated, alcoholic," Irish Catholic father, who died of a heart attack in 1953, "reading the *Herald–Tribune* while seated on the Flatbush Avenue IRT on his way to work." That paper, boasting what its historian, Richard Kluger, called a "national and international standing and literate, sophisticated style," was the ideal accessory to the "elegant three-piece suits" that Breslin's father sported, "as if he were an executive," while commuting daily from his working-class Brooklyn neighborhood.[13] On weeknights in the privacy of his home, however, Breslin's father had "intently read the *World–Telegram*," a moderate Democratic organ whose lower-middle-class focus and emphasis on local issues contrasted sharply with the prestigious, Republican *Herald–Tribune*. Perhaps the only thing the papers shared was a decent reputation among Catholic readers of most classes, especially when compared with the *New York Times*, the appeal of which to Breslin's father was apparently limited to its Sunday crossword puzzle. On weekends, Breslin wrote, his father careened through the house "in his undershirt, suit pants, and socks"; when a Dodgers game was televised, he would engage his son in "nine innings of empty dispute" while sitting in front of "a small Philco television set," with "a can of beer in his left hand and a Lucky Strike in his right."[14]

Breslin's essay, which traces the process by which his Rothko biography became a "monument . . . to preserve the memory of my father's substitute," does not concern itself at all with the ethnoreligious politics of cultural literacy outlined above, and some readers would undoubtedly view his litany of newspapers as merely so much "period" detail. But just as Breslin's study of Rothko was "built carefully, with abundant particularity and with some irony," his rendering of a deeply painful relationship with his father was refracted through media artifacts that evoked a whole lost world, one which was reconstructed only to be consumed in a smoldering, eloquent anger.[15] While Breslin and other writers of his generation channeled their fury into self-immolating narratives of ethnoreligiosity, Pete Axthelm reserved *his* for thieving horse trainers and corrupt sporting moguls, influenced in that way, as otherwise, by another writer named Breslin. Rockville Centre, where Axthelm grew up, was essentially an extension of Queens County, home to a number of exemplary New York journalists, such as A. J. Liebling and Jimmy Breslin, and to such characters as the basketball- and horseplaying McGuires (Al, Dick, and John), who would provide him with enough sporting lore of the city's urban outer boroughs to last a career.

Early in Axthelm's junior year of college, the *Yale Daily News* ran his page-one requiem for a New York newspaper on which few, if any, veterans of the country's "oldest college daily" had ever toiled. In quoting a cartoonist who likened the demise of the *New York Mirror* to "a death in the family," Axthelm did not exaggerate the emotional cost of the tabloid's recent closing. "It'll be a tough adjustment for these people," he wrote of the *Mirror*'s staffers; "it may prove just as tough for the readers." They would "miss the vigor and life of a paper that, written for the 'straphangers' of the New York subways, managed to capture much of the spirit of the big town itself." He invoked some of the great names associated with the *Mirror*: Walter Winchell, who "may never seem the same as he did when he fed early-risers a lively diet of glamor and gossip"; the "vivacious society gal 'Suzy'"; Drew Pearson, who "kept his readers 'inside' everything"; and Art Sloggatt, who "chipped in with probably the city's best conservative editorial cartoons." In the midst of this litany, Axthelm also paid tribute to labor union gadfly Victor Reisel, whose columns not only took on the mob, but also "waged a colorful war with Communists in labor"—a phrase resonant with the counterideological tone of much popular New York journalism of that era.[16] What Axthelm would especially miss, however, was "the city's most light-hearted racing staff," especially Ken Kling, whose blend of good-natured satire and moral indignation — Kling "was unabashed about accusing trainers of sending lame horses to the post" — would be echoed in his own subsequent racing journalism.[17]

Another, inevitable model for Axthelm was the Queens Irishman Jimmy Breslin, whose Ozone Park high school stood "about a furlong from the place where wallets die, the last turn at Aqueduct Race Track."[18] In a 1964 *Yale Daily News* column, Axthelm described a long day spent in the company of the "boyish-looking, ebullient writer" and star columnist of the *New York Herald–Tribune*, as Breslin shared his views of the writing trade while nursing "a persistent hangover." ("Sportswriting is great for openers in this poker game," he assured his young admirer. "Underplay, underplay everything.") Axthelm appreciated Breslin's versatility, above all: he could produce a story on "Junior, the unlucky bookie," then "rush directly from the Back Street to Dallas to produce his widely-reprinted masterpiece on the assassination of President Kennedy ('I hope that one wins a Pulitzer Prize or something,' he confessed, 'just to show up the phonies')." Jimmy Breslin was no phony but a man who could "handle with equal facility the worlds he [lived] in — the world of broads, booze and bookmakers — and the world of international news."[19]

At Yale in the early 1960s, such attributes in just the right casual balance could still assure one the Big Man on Campus role that Axthelm enjoyed. (He described attending a post–football game party with his girlfriend that had made it "very hard to think about writing anything. I ordered four drinks for the two of us — one for each hand — and we could have forgotten all about this column."[20]) Yet for someone who frequently wrote of drinking in the shadowy realm of bookmakers, Axthelm spent his Yale years in remarkably illustrious company: his roommate in Ezra Stiles College was an aspiring journalist from the Midwest named Bob Woodward, while Joe Lieberman, currently a U.S. Senator from Connecticut, was both his friend and, as editor-in-chief of the *Yale Daily News*, his boss. And Axthelm was certainly a much less volatile personality than David Milch, who succeeded him as Yale's champion undergraduate gambler long before he launched such television hits as *Hill Street Blues* and *NYPD Blue*. Milch was a familiar figure within New Haven's rather extensive "action" community. Like Axthelm, he preferred wagering on the sport of kings, which in those pre-offtrack-betting days meant doing business with one of the many bookmakers who operated openly, if subculturally, in New Haven.[21]

Milch was also a bona fide intellectual and literary light whose admirers included Robert Penn Warren and R. W. B. Lewis, while Pete Axthelm was simply a very good student, an English major whose senior essay was good enough to be published in the Yale University Press series featuring "some of the best work by the Honors majors in the Senior Class." Thirty years later, one member of the selection committee, the literary scholar Eugene Waith, still recalled both the essay and Axthelm's outstanding reputation among the faculty, although Waith was unaware of Ax's extracurricular pursuits at Yale and his subsequent career in journalism. Yet *The Modern Confessional Novel* is surprisingly standard, smoothly written, Yale senior-essay fare, conveying the tone of modern literary scholarship but offering few original insights.[22] In his section on Dostoyevsky, for example, Axthelm failed to discuss *The Gambler*, perhaps because, unlike David Milch, he was so far from being a Dostoyevskian character. Again unlike Milch, Axthelm had never received mixed messages as a boy about the propriety of gambling. Even at the time of its publication, *The Modern Confessional Novel* was considered "a bit disappointing in its orthodoxy,"[23] but few would be subsequently disappointed by Axthelm's orthodox allegiance to another tradition that he was even better equipped to serve.

═══════

I have an image from the early 1960s of my grandfather sitting in our living room—a highball glass listing perilously on the wing of his armchair—speaking animatedly of Kelso, the wondrous gelding that earned Horse of the Year honors an incredible five consecutive times (1960–64), the fifth year at the age of seven. As a kid I was mystified by the fuss over Kelso since, then as now, television coverage of racing was largely confined to the Triple Crown, races restricted to three-year-olds. Kelso, I must have believed, was an old horse for even older people, although at seven he still could have dusted the best three-year-olds of his era.

My grandparents enjoyed going to Belmont, Aqueduct, and Jamaica—the latter a racetrack once located not in the Caribbean but in the Borough of Queens. My grandmother enthusiastically worked the place pools, perhaps in the belief that betting on a second-place finish split the difference between the excessive optimism of win bettors and the stolid caution of punters who wagered strictly to show. The people on that side of my family were brash and brassy in the manner of those snappy characters found in Damon Runyon stories. They were originally from the tough little Irish city of Cork, but, as I grew up, it was sometimes darkly hinted that I more nearly resembled the vaguely hapless, if sympathetic, figures from my mother's family — the New Jersey side — souls bred in the bogs of Clare, who (I discovered only much later) had proved ill-suited for the action life that lured them nonetheless.

Before she was married my mother had worked as a secretary at 1440 Broadway, the fabled headquarters of the Mutual Broadcasting System in the last heyday of American radio. (She worked for a time on Jack Bailey's *Queen for a Day* radio program just prior to its switch to the new medium.) In remaining a most faithful listener to WOR regardless of where we lived, my mother provided all the cultural literacy to be found in a house without books, courtesy of an Irish American battalion of talk-show hosts. I grew up on the domestic chatter of Ed and Pegeen Fitzgerald, the witticisms of Peter Lind Hayes and Mary Healy, and the "Voice of Broadway," Jack O'Brian, a scrappy protégé and crony of Walter Winchell.

The *New York Herald–Tribune* began appearing in our mailbox, a day late, around 1965, just months before the paper would expire after its last, desperate incarnation as the *World–Journal Tribune*, the result of the *Trib*'s doomed merger with the *Journal–American* and the *World–Telegram and Sun*. My mother longed for a newsprint accompaniment to such WOR programs as O'Brian's *Voice of Broadway*; although she rarely got to see a show in New York, she particularly enjoyed the theater reviews of Walter Kerr (a former drama professor at Catholic University, where Ed McMahon had been among his star pupils). Years before seminars would be offered on the New Journalism (the work not only of Jimmy Breslin but of Tom Wolfe, Gail Sheehy, and Dick Schaap as well — *Herald–Tribune* compatriots all), she had read excerpts from Breslin's columns over the telephone to her perplexed friends. Breslin himself always insisted that his writing style grew naturally out of journalism's long-established tradition of spontaneity and immediacy — "like you were covering the eighth race at Belmont." "But no one was doing it when I started. That's why everyone thought it was new. . . . We were ahead of everybody in bringing back the past," he explained, invoking such fabled predecessors as John McNulty, Paul Gallico, and Red Smith, each of whom had employed similar techniques.[24]

Red Smith was still plying his craft when Pete Axthelm joined the staff of the *Herald–Tribune*. After Smith was belatedly awarded the Pulitzer Prize in 1976, Axthelm wrote in tribute: "Like almost every sportswriter of my generation who had any sense, taste, and larceny in his soul, I didn't just emulate Smith. I stole from him liberally."[25] I was reading the *Trib* devotedly every afternoon in 1965 for news relating to my two sporting loyalties, the Pittsburgh Pirates and the Notre Dame football team, but I was startled to discover in researching this essay that my family's subscription to the *Herald–Tribune* coincided almost exactly with Axthelm's tenure at the paper. I vaguely recall being disappointed whenever Red Smith's column was devoted to horses, and I know I ignored the broadsheet pages at the back of the sports section where Axthelm's brisk racing reports appeared, along with the regular column he had taken over at the age of twenty-two as the designated heir to the *Trib*'s erudite racing writer, Joe H. Palmer, whom Red Smith described as "the best writer I ever knew."[26]

In June 1965, at baccalaureate services, Yale President Kingman Brewster rebuked the "new radicals" among Pete Axthelm's graduating class. Comparing the young militants to Mussolini, whose "proud boast" had been "action first, doctrine second," Brewster voiced his grave concern that "the passion of self-indulgence and involvement" might "override all counsel of self-restraint."[27] Although Axthelm was clearly devoted to "action first," he had exhibited his own, more conventional liberalism two weeks earlier in lauding a hard-earned victory by a horse named Gun Bow in the Memorial Day Metropolitan Handicap at Aqueduct: "With no racing luck at all, the big horse still managed to show his class to a crowd that was Aqueduct's version of the Great Society—73,375 people who produced the first six-million dollar betting handle in racing history."[28] As Red Smith noted in his *Herald–Tribune* column of 2 June, thoroughbred racetracks across America had attracted "468,707 selfless sportsmen" on that Memorial Day, "who bet $30,797,603 over and above what they paid for admission, transportation, whiskey and other necessities of gracious living." The five largest tracks had drawn nearly as many paying customers as the ten major-league baseball stadiums where games had been played that same day. "Gun Bow is handsomer than Mickey Mantle," Smith concluded. "He hits harder than Roger Maris, and Sonny Liston should have his class."[29] Thirty years later, when Steven Crist—a distinguished racing writer and world-class handicapper—was named "director of communications and development" for the New York Racing Association, he acknowledged that it would be "unrealistic" to expect "to go back to the days when 25,000 guys in hats would come out to Aqueduct every day."[30] Crist's understatement of the numbers reported by Axthelm and Smith in 1965 confirmed that in the case of thoroughbred racing, one of the few American institutions whose "stories of decline" (Carlo Rotella's term for the central narrative mode of postwar urban America[31]) are not mythical, grim fact had actually outpaced narrative figure. In 1965 Red Smith turned sixty. Having already weathered television's first-wave invasion of American sports, he would, unlike his young acolyte, at least be spared the temptation to court the new medium "for money and fame."[32]

───

Pete Axthelm's approach to journalism was as simple as a maxim: "Any bettor's statement about racing, sports or life is likely to be accompanied by the phrase: 'And a story goes with it.'"[33] The races he covered resembled short stories whose reading took roughly one to two-and-a-half minutes, depending on the "distance of ground" the horses were asked to cover. Like well-crafted stories, good races must start with an "honest pace": two or more "speedballs" vying for the lead often "set up" a dramatic finish by other horses whose jockeys, having taken the measure of the early leaders, rally furiously as they turn for home. But some races, like some stories, "fall apart": the early pace is either dawdling or suicidally quick, the animals career into each other, or a horse gets "loose on the lead" and coasts home, a wire-to-wire victor. Axthelm's favorite horses were the kind whose "running style" dictated a late move from well off the pace. He also preferred grass (or "turf") races to those run on dirt. While most European racing is conducted on grass, dirt strips predominate in America, although turf racing is a staple of the classier tracks in Florida and the Northeast, weather permitting. Turf races typically produce the best story lines because strategy, positioning, and the jockey's timing are usually more important than the raw speed that is often crucial in races over "the main track."[34]

Races commonly fail to unfold as expected—and for Ax a story went with that, too. Reporting on the Bowling Green Stakes of 19 June 1965, a turf race contested at Aqueduct, Axthelm described how, throughout most of the race, "people were watching the come-from-behind horses" favored to win:

> Baitman was in front and Or et Argent was close to the pace, but everyone was waiting for Hot Dust and Tenacle and Knightly Manner to make their big moves from far back. Then time ran out and Or et Argent, with Walter Blum riding, was across the finish line. Hot Dust was second, three-quarters of a length behind, and Prince O'Pilsen was third. Knightly Manner, the 2–1 favorite, was nowhere.[35]

Axthelm then shifted the point of view to jockey Walter Blum, astride Or et Argent, the stalking-horse who forgot to quit:

> Blum had a bad moment near the half-mile pole, as several horses moved from behind him. . . . "For a minute, the three horses were outside me," Blum said. "I was on the rail behind Baitman and I was afraid they would bear in and box me in. So I had to move a little earlier than I wanted to. I got clear position, and from there on, there wasn't too much to it." The horses outside Or et Argent fell back around the turn. Then he took his shot at Baitman, and went past him at the head of the stretch. At the same time, Braulio Baeza rushed Hot Dust into contention along the rail. Hot Dust ran willingly in the stretch, but he wasn't gaining very fast on the winner.[36]

Noting that Or et Argent's sire was French and his dam English, Axthelm also remarked on the mixed background of the horse's trainer, Wayne Stucki, "who . . . came to racing after driving chariots at rodeos in Idaho and California."

Like his idol Red Smith, Axthelm loved racehorses, but never so much as he loved the people who loved them. He was, above all—as Smith wrote of another newspaperman—"a collector by grace of Providence. He has no special enthusiasm, however, for rare stamps or first editions or old masters or antique shaving mugs. He collects characters."[37] In Axthelm's racing stories and columns alike, the equine angle served primarily as a foil for his colorful accounts of bettors, jockeys, trainers, and grooms, whose endless efforts to beat the racing game were as humorous as they were quixotic. His fascination with racetrack folklore sometimes strained the limits of his genre. In a July 1965 *Herald–Tribune* story, for example, he reported on a conversation in the paddock at Aqueduct between a young trainer, Howard "Buddy" Jacobsen, and track veterinarian Manuel Gilman, who joked about various illegal ploys to inspire more effort from a floundering four-year-old gelding named Nopal.[38] In response to the ensuing uproar among literal-minded, non-sporting readers—"the only people who didn't pay any attention were the horseplayers"—Axthelm wrote in the following day's edition, "Horseplayers have been looking for larceny in racing since the first Roman chariot driver got boxed in in a Forum stakes race."[39]

While racing journalism did not have *that* venerable a tradition, it had been practiced in America for well over a century by the time Pete first began to read the *Daily Racing Form* as a child. Racing news had dominated the *Spirit of the Times* ("A Chronicle of the Turf, Field, Sports, Aquatics, Agriculture and the Stage"). A New York "gentleman's" newspaper that was published interminently beginning in 1831, the *Spirit* ran theater reviews alongside stories that chronicled, in ornate detail, "the most glorious pastime of a civilized people."[40] The inaugural issue of the *Daily Racing Form* appeared on 17 November 1894. The first newspaper "dedicated exclusively to racing," it coexisted with a sister edition, the *Morning Telegraph*, until chronic labor troubles in New York forced the "Telly's" closing. (The *Racing Form* lives on.) The "Telly" coupled entertainment and gossip columns by the likes of Louella Parsons and Walter Winchell with the elegant racing journalism of Charles Hatton (whom Red Smith called "the last of the graceful writers") and Evan Shipman, whom drinking buddy Ernest Hemingway recalled as "a fine poet," one who "knew and cared about horses, writing, and painting." New York journalist Joe Flaherty wrote that "Shipman liked to fill his glass at the bar and empty his pockets at the windows. He was so obsessed with the game that he often sat in restaurants writing horses' extended pedigrees on tablecloths."[41] The best racing writers were permitted to be as sophisticated and "literary" as they wished so long as they conspicuously bore the gambler's mark of original sin, preferably on their sleeves. As Hunter Thompson wrote in eulogizing Axthelm, "He would gamble on anything, especially horses. . . . He also loved football, whiskey, and fine chamber music."[42]

From the 1920s until well into the 1970s, thoroughbred racing consistently boasted the highest attendance figures of any American sport, but the pervasive influence of racing in popular culture can hardly be measured by the click of turnstiles alone. Hollywood fell hard for the thorough-breds: the Santa Anita Race Course was built near Pasadena in 1934 on property owned by producer Hal Roach; three years later Bing Crosby and Pat O'Brien—with additional backing supplied by Oliver Hardy, Gary Cooper, and Joe E. Brown—founded the Del Mar Turf Club just north of San Diego. Featuring impromptu entertainment by the likes of Al Jolson, Danny Thomas, and Jimmy Durante, Del Mar has been aptly described as "the most relaxed and enjoyable place to go racing in America."[43] Holly-wood's romance with the turf also made for serious business: Louis B. Mayer and Harry Cohn were only two of the movie magnates who occa-sionally invested some of their profits in racing stables—or simply went on betting jags. (Robert Towne's screenplay for the 1974 film *Chinatown* wonderfully captured the racing subtext that underwrote Hollywood, as it did much of urban America, for several decades.)[44]

≡≡≡

The first time I went to the races, I left without witnessing even a single thoroughbred up close and personal. I had just finished college and was well into the second or third season of a farewell tour celebrating my career as a country club caddy, or "looper." Although I still had over a de-cade of part-time looping ahead of me, I was already viewing my position at a comically understated, if ultra-exclusive, Central Jersey club as more in the realm of consultancy than the regular sweaty grind which had en-dowed me with a closet full of tattered shirts and mossy sneakers, and a set of rounded shoulders. All tradition-bound country clubs employ a "caddymaster," a member of that dying breed obligated, by ancient cus-tom, to provide green youths with disinformation on matters of sex and hygiene, as well as a model of mock obsequiousness toward the member-ship adapted from old movies depicting royal courts of the fifteenth cen-tury. Caddymasters are also expected to demonstrate an ardent devotion to gambling, which is how I came to serve as a courier for an ad hoc syn-dicate of heavy hitters clustered around a gentleman known as "Peewee," the finest caddymaster of my acquaintance.

Peewee and his various non-looper buddies liked to joke about the horses owned by some of the club's more prominent members, steeds bred to the purple, just like their human connections, that competed regularly at Monmouth Park and always seemed to lose. So I was surprised to learn—

hanging around the caddyshack one desultory Saturday afternoon—that Peewee and the boys were onto a live number running down at the shore later that day. This time, however, the owner was not an elderly sportsman content to occasionally visit the shed row, bearing carrots, but the "Pepsi Man," who (in lucrative collusion with Peewee himself) operated the caddyshack's soda machine concession. This tip was strictly about business. Peewee dispatched me to the track, after some failed negotiations on my part over the use of his late-model red Eldorado. (When one of the club's elderly members—who generally piloted battered Chevys—first saw Peewee in his Caddy, she exclaimed, "I'm all for it!") On my way to the shore I stopped in New Brunswick to pick up a young woman with whom I was very close; her father had been a bookmaker and she seemed to know all about affairs of this kind. Naturally, we added a small portion of our own cash reserves to the thick packet of large bills getting damp in my pocket. As we tooled down Route 18 in quiet anticipation, my friend thought to ask what time the races began; when I replied, "He said around three," she inquired, in a tone of growing alarm, "The first race, or our race?"

All the talk about the mighty Kelso I had absorbed while growing up had not sufficiently schooled me in the first law of racing: you must get your bet down before the horses start running. The first race, it turned out, had gone off at one o'clock; our own four-legged hope, a cheap and thoroughly undistinguished "claiming" animal called Power of Choice, was due to enter the starting gate momentarily at some racetrack in a town I had never heard of until a couple of hours earlier. "Claiming races" comprise the substantial majority of contests among thoroughbreds: each horse is entered "for a tag," or the price at which it may be "claimed" by a licensed trainer (acting on behalf of a prospective owner) up until just moments before post time. The purpose of claiming races is to ensure a rough equality among the competitors. Say you had a horse whose value—determined less by bloodlines than its form in recent races—was around $50,000. A trainer would rarely risk "dropping" a horse of that caliber into a race featuring cheaper horses just to cash in on a purse or a bet because the animal would almost surely be claimed, provided that it appeared to be physically "sound." And that, of course, is the rub. When an animal with "back class" is dropped precipitously through the claiming ranks, prospective owners and members of the betting public alike must ask whether the horse's connections are merely hoping that someone will claim their ailing charge or if the beast is indeed "well-meant" for that particular race.

Whatever chicanery exists in racing primarily involves claiming events, which offer smaller (often dramatically so) purses than "allowance," "handicap," or "stakes" races, in which the horses are not for sale and thus are all presumably well-meant. Yet even at the highest levels of racing, a horse may be entered in a contest because it "needs a race" as preparation for a more serious effort down the road. Very few races are "fixed" in the film noir sense; what happens instead is that a trainer may tell his jockey his horse will probably be "short" that day, meaning that the animal is not prepared to exert the total effort often required for a win. It's simply another part of the sport's immense unpredictability; if you overhear someone at a racetrack moaning about "boat races" and "stiffed" horses, you can be reasonably certain that the complainant has wagered on an animal which just wasn't good enough—that day.

At a racetrack even the laws of time may be overridden by this inherent unpredictability. When we finally reached Monmouth that day, a parking attendant assured us that the fifth race had already gone off, since it was by then a minute or two past the scheduled post time. But sometimes horses require a change of equipment, or a jockey is thrown from his mount during the post parade. So while the tote board may indicate that there are zero minutes left before the start of the race, there might actually be a sufficient grace period to dash across the parking lot and into the grandstand, locate what appears to be a betting window, unfurl a wad of bills, ask the lady in front of you for the number on Power of Choice's saddle-cloth (no betting by name), watch as she then digs into her alligator bag for bills to back the hot tip you've just given her, get to the teller, and cry out the long numbers while fumbling for the cash—only to hear the sound of a buzzer, followed by the words "Sorry, you're shut out. . . ." (I had never been to the races before, but it did not require much horse sense to discern my only recourse: pray like a madman for Power of Choice to lose. While still drooped over the betting window counter, I could see a television monitor hanging from the rafters overhead; moving images on its screen indicated that somewhere nearby actual horses were circling a racetrack. One of them was running much more smartly than the others, scornfully propelling dirt back at his rivals until they all but abandoned the chase.) It seemed not an eternity, but exactly one minute, eleven and two-fifths seconds, before the teller casually added, ". . . and it's too bad."

I had never made a bet in my life (and still had not, of course, despite the intentions of my boss). I had never even *thought* about making a bet in my life. My father had not become the first person in the history of his family to proceed past the eighth grade so that a member of the next generation might one day embrace only the family's horseplaying tradition (so how's about another beer?). "Most Irish laborers died penniless," wrote Daniel Patrick Moynihan in *Beyond the Melting Pot*, "but they had been rich one night a week much of their lives, whereas their white-collar children never know a moment of financial peace, much less affluence. A good deal of color goes out of life when a group begins to rise. A good deal of resentment enters."[45] I've always believed that Moynihan knew what he was talking about, but I was amazed one day years later to hear my mother ask what a "scratch sheet" was doing in the backseat of her car. I still don't know exactly what a scratch sheet is, other than a racing term from bygone days for something similar to today's "program." The atavisms bred by social mobility make for a fascinating ingredient in our cultural stew. We've all known people who, after a few too many drinks or in the midst of crisis, would revert to a little brogue or its equivalent, remember words they're not supposed to know, or even ask a teller at a racetrack betting window to sign a voucher with his ID number on it as proof that a caddyshack syndicate had not been robbed.

Power of Choice paid $18.80 for every two-dollar wager on him that day. The Pepsi Man was probably the only person at the track holding more tickets than I was supposed to be cashing in right then for the fellows back at the club. Instead, my friend and I dragged ourselves across the street to a chicken shack where I called Peewee, who expressed a strong desire never to behold my Irish mug again. Nevertheless, when I returned to Monmouth a year later, it was as a passenger in Peewee's Eldorado. One of the club members had a horse entered in a stakes race. It lost, naturally, and the Cadillac broke down in Red Bank (hometown of Count Basie *and* Edmund Wilson) on the way home, but I learned two things that day: (1) if you pull into a repair shop in an expensive automobile, caddymaster or otherwise, you're going to get instant respect; and (2) genuine horseplayers will trade a quick and easy score for a good story so long as it colorfully fills the downtime between dispensations of racing luck.

In April 1989, a three-year-old colt named Easy Goer ran at Aqueduct in the Gotham Stakes, a one-mile prep race for thoroughbreds headed toward the Kentucky Derby. The 1980s were a terrible decade for American racing, as rampant inflation in the stallion market—fueled in part by Middle Eastern oil billionaires who raced most of their horses in Europe—diverted attention from the track to the breeding sheds. By the time of Easy Goer's Gotham a decade had passed since Spectacular Bid, the last great colt, had failed in his attempt to become the fourth horse of the 1970s to win the Triple Crown (the Kentucky Derby, Preakness, and Belmont Stakes). Seattle Slew (in 1977) and Affirmed (in 1978) had accomplished that feat, but neither approached the level of Secretariat's 1973 performance. The first Triple Crown winner in twenty-five years, "Big Red" not only won the Belmont by thirty-one lengths, but sheared two seconds—roughly ten horse lengths—off the previous stakes' record time, leaving even the most wizened horsepeople struggling to find a standard with which to compare him. Finally, Charles Hatton, whom many considered the Secretariat of racing writers, simply proclaimed: "His only point of reference is himself."[46]

Since Easy Goer was, like Secretariat, a regal chestnut, the inevitable, if unfair, comparisons began to be made as soon as he "broke his maiden" (won for the first time) with a blazing performance at Belmont as a two-year-old in the summer of 1988. His luster had been tarnished somewhat by a defeat on Breeder's Cup Day that autumn. (Launched in 1984, the Breeder's Cup is a kind of Super Bowl for thoroughbreds, a series of seven championship races under a wide variety of conditions.) But even Secretariat had lost occasionally, including a defeat at Aqueduct in his final Derby prep—a performance so tepid that Pete Axthelm had predicted Secretariat would finish no better than third in the Derby. For the Gotham, Easy Goer was the overwhelming favorite in an unbettable race, although that did not prevent the multitudes from trying to at least come up with a second-place horse to round out the exacta. By the time the horses rounded the far turn that April day, two different races were unfolding. Far behind the spring shadows cast diagonally across the track by Easy Goer, a number of animals were doggedly churning in an awkward formation, their jockeys shifting and thrashing, urging more from them than they had to give. From my position at the end of the grandstand, the procession of also-rans looked to be groggily weaving toward us rather than skimming along the rail in the effortless manner of the horse in the lead, whose grace in motion presented a disconcerting counterpoint to the cacophony in his wake.

There had been a brief shower earlier that day, but now the dingy track near
Jamaica Bay—ordinarily the site of a long, grim winter's cheap racing—
was awash in brilliant color, especially once Easy Goer had powered into
the stretch alone, his supporting cast no longer even in the field of vision.

Horses used to make me hear songs all the time. The tune from that
race was The Byrds' "Eight Miles High," but I can't say with certainty if
that chimey *whooosh* in the song was already building as Easy Goer—his
jockey, Pat Day, crouched in a tightly coiled arc—roared with enormous
strides toward the finish line beneath an aura of seagulls. I know I'll never
forget the feeling when the sound in my head became the sound of the
world at Aqueduct, for as Easy Goer crossed the line thousands of seasoned
horseplayers managed to avert their eyes just long enough to see the tiny
numbers instantly appear on the tote board: 1:32:2.

The "whoosh" that rose up from the track and washed over the grandstand then was the sound of the betting public's instant recognition that
Easy Goer had, as Steven Crist reported in the *New York Times*, "missed
Dr. Fager's 1968 world record of 1:32$\frac{1}{5}$ at Arlington Park near Chicago, the
most hallowed standard of time in American racing, by only one fifth of
a second." Racing writers are on the whole intensely loyal to the integrity
of the sport and its history, so when Crist conscientiously noted that other
races at Aqueduct that day had also been run "much faster than usual,"
he was resisting the temptation to rhapsodize—before yielding enough to
add: "Even so, what the chestnut-colored son of Alydar did was something
special."[47]

A few weeks later, on the first Saturday in May, the heavily favored Easy
Goer ran second in a muddy Kentucky Derby to an equally brilliant but
nimbler colt named Sunday Silence. They dueled again two weeks later
in the Preakness at Pimlico; this time Pat Day managed to let Easy Goer
get pinned to the rail by Sunday Silence and his jockey, Pat Valenzuela.
The contrast between Easy Goer's Gotham majesty and the trapped animal
being flayed by his jockey in the Preakness (though still coming within
a nose of victory) will always define the legacy of this supremely powerful thoroughbred that—perhaps as a result of mishandling or even a tiny
flaw in temperament—had left his many fans unfulfilled in their quest for
another Secretariat. (While Easy Goer's smashing victory in the Belmont
prevented Sunday Silence from garnering the Triple Crown, the blackish
colt would settle the issue for all time in the Breeder's Cup Classic at Gulf-

stream Park, leading some to conclude that *this* lionhearted champion was the true superhorse of his era.)

The beauty of thoroughbreds and the feelings they arouse in humans is what kept Pete Axthelm and many others coming back to the races. An appreciation for the sport seems to be inherited (even if it sometimes skips a generation), just as musical or academic interests are often passed down. During my stint as a New York taxi driver, I was always amazed to witness the endless lines of theater, movie, and museum buffs awaiting entry on Sunday afternoons to the culture palaces of Manhattan. The patrons reminded me, in their reverent anticipation, of church goers; but while it is easy to understand why religious folk object to horse racing (such born-again Christians as Pat Day and other prominent jockeys and trainers notwithstanding), the vague disdain of many intellectuals for the sport of kings reveals nothing more than a simple difference of aesthetic traditions. Still, it came as no surprise (to me) when Paul Mellon, one of the world's leading art collectors, responded to a *Time* interviewer's query as to whether "anything in life" gave him more pleasure than seeing one of his horses win a race: "I don't think so. I can't think of anything."[48]

By the time I met Pete Axthelm on the boat returning from Monmouth Park to New York Harbor's Pier 11 in the summer of 1990, the *Herald–Tribune* had been dead for nearly twenty-five years. I liked to treat my occasional excursions to Monmouth as mini–field trips: arriving on the first Saturday morning train into Grand Central, I'd take a leisurely four- or five-mile hike southward along the East River, where airplanes with their little pontoons skimmed across the briny surface. I'd pass a dozen or more ballgames already under way in the parks wedged under the FDR Drive, then detour through Chinatown—where, with a little effort, you can find a grocery that stocks the *Daily Racing Form* in between the crates of produce—before finally making my way to the South Street Seaport in plenty of time to read the *Form*, under the Brooklyn Bridge, while pondering the adventures that lay ahead. When Axthelm strolled aboard the boat that day, it was already well past the scheduled departure time, but he was smiling and in no hurry. He looked heavy yet frail. I thought of Pete at that time primarily as the author of the first classic work on American basketball, *The City Game*, who had later chosen to sell himself to television as a more urbane version of Jimmy "the Greek" Snyder, the house tout on the CBS Sunday morning NFL pregame show. I had only the vaguest memory of Axthelm's career at NBC, although I loved his later work on ESPN's racing telecasts. It turned out that I was dead wrong about his career after *The City Game*: he had written brilliantly for over two decades in *Newsweek* on topics ranging from country music to the Kennedys, while pursuing his desire to "improve the breed" both at the betting windows and in his frequent columns devoted to racing. Only later would I discover that Axthelm's career at the *Herald–Tribune* had prefigured all that was to come, for better or worse.

His guide in preparing *The City Game*—which movingly linked the basketball ascendance of African American New Yorkers to "the dreams of the Irish athletes on famous playgrounds such as the one on 108th Street in Rockaway, Queens," as well as to "Kingsbridge Road in the Bronx, where tough, aggressive Jewish youths grew into defense-minded, set-shooting stars"—had been Al McGuire, a Queens native then building a legend as the coach at Marquette University.[49] They had met when Axthelm was profiling Al's brother John, the "real McGuire," in 1967 for *Sports Illustrated*, Pete's first employer following the demise of the *Trib*. Al and his other brother, Dick—a basketball Hall of Famer who was then coaching the New York Knicks—were blessed, John McGuire told Axthelm, with "tremendous ability. And they have no weakness to hold them back, like I do."[50] "John McGuire's weakness is gambling," wrote Axthelm of the former New York policeman–turned–nightclub owner and semipro horseplayer. His brother Al lamented that "he's got the talent to make a fortune at anything he tries. . . . It's a shame he has to waste it." Axthelm, however, found it hard "to feel sorry for John McGuire for very long."

> No one will ever run any benefits for him. At those times when he can't get even-money favorites home, John still lives at twin-double prices. His five children—he has been a widower for four years—are as good-looking as he is, and considerably sounder fiscally, and he enjoys the finest places, the most impeccable clothes and the most laughs available in New York. "If I ever let winning or losing affect my standard of living," he says, "I'll figure I'm in serious trouble."[51]

John McGuire was one of those people who lived "on his own terms," a phrase that would reverberate over and again in Axthelm's writing, just as it would be invoked redundantly in obituaries of him. His talents and his sympathies were always focused on those who answered a call from deep within and never complained about the consequences. In a 1965 piece for the *Herald–Tribune* on jockey Con Errico, for example, Axthelm described the career of punishment endured by this battered rider:

> Errico is thirty-eight years old and he's been riding in races for 20 years, a lot of them interrupted by injuries. When a horse kicked him in the right leg last month, it was just one more in a series of ailments that included broken bones all over his body. Yesterday he came back again to ride Joyful Sails, a $3,500 claimer, in the second race. People hardly noticed that he'd been gone.[52]

After describing the ritual in which Errico taped his bruised legs after losing his last race of the day, Axthelm commented, "In the competition among Aqueduct riders, there aren't many openings for a 38-year-old who is better known for injuries than for winners. 'I haven't got the big name,' Errico said. 'But I feel very good and I hope to keep riding for a while.'"[53] It was this willingness to tempt fate with an understated recklessness that Axthelm admired in a Con Errico or a John McGuire. Among the "Runyonesque tales" recounted at a "cocktail tribute" held at the New York Yale Club just days after Axthelm's death, someone recalled "the one about the Yale undergraduate who played cards through the night and then remembered he had to take the law school admissions test that morning; who achieved a perfect score on the test, anyway, but went to Aqueduct instead of law school."[54]

While the tradition Axthelm invoked was obviously a gendered, "White ethnic" one, his own brand of practical liberalism was highly inclusive, in the true spirit of New York popular journalism, and he ardently supported gender equity in both collegiate and professional sports. As a winter resident of Florida, he became friendly with tennis champion Chris Evert and paid tribute to her in a 1975 *Newsweek* column: "Perhaps it is time, at last, for people to see women in sports in a fresh perspective. And once we put aside all the cliché titles like Cinderella and Ice Maiden and America's Sweetheart, we just might find that Chris Evert is our best-known example of the woman athlete's effort to grow, to excel and to adapt."[55] Julie Krone, a jockey who has competed against male professional athletes more successfully than any woman in history, paid tribute to Axthelm in turn, saying that she "really got interested in race-riding" after reading *The Kid.*

Axthelm's chronicle of teenage phenomenon Steve Cauthen, who piloted Affirmed to the Triple Crown in 1978, "so turned Krone on that two years later she rode her first winner."[56]

Axthelm's advocacy journalism on African American athletes, however, had more mixed results. His first serious encounter with racism in sports occurred when he covered track meets sponsored by the New York Athletic Club, an organization dominated by Irish Americans, who had until recently been shunned by older sporting clubs in New York. In distancing himself from one of the symbols of New York sporting life, Axthelm had acted "on his own terms," but he may not have recognized the comfort zone his own privilege could afford him in a fall from grace with "the Goddess." He covered the Mexico City Olympics in 1968, when "he was 24, adventurous and guarding the ramparts of the downtrodden," recalled sports columnist Melvin Durslag in 1991. Durslag also claimed that "Pete played a role in one of the most celebrated affairs of the modern Olympics," the black-gloved fists raised by Tommie Smith and John Carlos on the victory stand after being awarded their gold and bronze medals, respectively, for the 200-meter sprint. "Pete knew it was coming off," wrote Durslag. "He knew because it was suspected he was one of the architects of this unique protest shaking up the planet."[57] In 1974 Axthelm wrote a brutally candid *Newsweek* column in which he recalled the incident, describing the experience of walking into the Olympic stadium with the wives of Smith and Carlos as they struggled to ignore jeering fans and officials: "The scene projected a strength that seemed great enough to overcome all the threats and reprisals." Yet, six years later, he conceded that the athletes and their families had suffered not just at the hands of racists, quoting Carlos's bitter words to him:

> You were willing to listen to our point of view once, and we needed you to help get our feelings across. You needed us, too, so you could write the best stories. I guess we used each other. But when your career went along just fine and old 'Los slipped out of sight, did you ever pick up the phone to find out how he was doing? . . . Maybe we were never real friends—just runners and writers.[58]

"No journalism review could have drawn the issue more clearly than the street-wise Carlos," Axthelm confessed. Yet ultimately he could only respond in conventional terms to this athlete's ongoing ordeal: "Carlos hasn't found his own career yet, and he insists he won't accept anything less than his own terms."[59] Axthelm seemed to believe that Black athletes should enjoy not just the same educational and professional opportunities as middle-class Whites, but should be entitled—even expected—to confront the existential challenges that were a condition of freedom. In the end, he related best to moderate individualists like Chris Evert: "Many young people raised in conservative Catholic families like the Everts might tend to rebel when they discover ideas like liberation, but it is a tribute to Jimmy and Colette Evert that they have given their oldest daughter room to expand within the framework they drew for her."[60] The heroes of *The Modern Confessional Novel* manifested Axthelm's modest ideal of personal liberation, beginning with Augustine and Thomas Merton—the great confessional figures, ancient and contemporary, of his own tradition. Quickly passing into the imaginative world he had come to claim as his own, Axthelm then cited Gide, Sartre, and Camus, concluding with the "full perception" of Saul Bellow.

Pete Axthelm lived "on his own terms" right up to the end. In 1982, Bryant Gumbel recounted a not atypical episode with Axthelm while both men were covering professional football for NBC. After working on a postgame show, "we went to dinner, and we never did get to bed, and we had rehearsal the next day at 9 A.M. for the Cleveland–Oakland game. Then we covered that, after 18 hours with the same clothes on. Axthelm kept telling me, 'It's no fun if you can only do it sober. Anybody could do it sober.'"[61] A bartender at a New Haven establishment on the former site of Jocko Sullivan's, one of Axthelm's favorite college hangouts, recalled that Pete was the type of drinker whose demeanor never seemed to change once a certain point in the evening had been reached. In a tragic sense, then, he was perhaps temperamentally suited to precisely the life that would kill him. As Andy Beyer noted, "The natural habitat of the people he liked to associate with was the barroom."[62] Axthelm worked hard to convey the impression that his drinking was a natural part of living "on his own terms," as though any alternative would have constituted some kind of betrayal.

Axthelm's gambling (i.e., his wagering on thoroughbreds) represents a somewhat thornier issue. He was a very good handicapper, and it was exciting to learn, on my boatride home from Monmouth with him, that he focused primarily on the physical appearance of horses because that was one of the first secrets my friend Barry Lipinski had taught me about the game, along with the significance of bloodlines, especially in the turf racing which he, like Axthelm, greatly preferred. (On our first trip to Saratoga in 1987, it was not until the last race that Barry spotted a horse which was "on the muscle," or clearly superior in fitness to her competitors. When this filly, Crystal Blaize, romped home at fifteen-to-one in a maiden race—defeating at least three future stakes winners—I suggested that my friend add "the body language of horses" to his areas of competence on his resume.) The moral objection to gambling on horses must be based on more exacting grounds of purity than those applied to other financial dealings since, in ethical terms, any investment that entails risk would properly belong to the same category. Any act of wagering—whether on preferred stock or racing stock—is capable of producing the adrenaline rush that some crave above all other stimulants. If this sounds like casuistry, just ask anyone who was there what the air felt like in the vicinity of Wall Street on weekday afternoons during the mid-1980s. The fact is that stockbrokers are not the only ones who support themselves by gambling; individuals can be found in every racing jurisdiction in North America who make their living by betting on thoroughbreds. For some reason, many people doubt that this is possible, as though sin could not profit a man over the long haul. But professional horseplayers are generally among the most sober, methodical individuals imaginable, which is why Pete Axthelm never showed much interest in them. Their livelihood depends upon identifying "overlays"—plausible winners made more attractive by the public's habit of betting heavily on undeserving favorites—and they not only pay their income taxes, just as their amateur counterparts do, but they support the breeding and racing industries upon which the livelihoods of many hundreds of thousands depend.

Professionals rely upon a bewildering array of mathematical calculations, many of which have been popularized in recent years by such well-known handicappers as Crist and Beyer, both Ivy Leaguers like Axthelm, but with greater powers of analysis and more sober habits. The real issue in gambling, according to William Murray, is *losing*: no one should bet on horses or anything else with money they cannot afford to spare.[63] Even without compiling the elaborate "speed figures" that Beyer and Crist use, however, Axthelm was more than capable of holding his own at the track, so perhaps the real issue is one of balance, or proportionality. Axthelm made a significant contribution to his favorite sport by fostering an appreciation of its folklore, its traditions, its literature: a modest contribution perhaps, but one that was marked by equal proportions of talent and integrity, or generosity of spirit.

Axthelm's gambling on football was another matter altogether. It was never clear whether his understanding of that game even extended beyond the numbers, since his commentary was often devoted to dissecting point spreads. In any case, the NFL owed its existence in large part to such legendary gamblers as Art Rooney, who founded the Pittsburgh Steelers while flush from one of his frequent racetrack betting coups. And it was Rooney's fellow Irish American sportsman Tim Mara, one of New York's most prominent bookmakers, who gambled $500 in 1925 on the future of professional football by purchasing a franchise that became the New York Giants.[64] As the NFL's popularity soared in the 1960s, Commissioner Pete Rozelle sought to distance the game from such roots as these, even as the league was attracting illegal wagering of an unprecedented magnitude. Rozelle's strategy was a brilliant one: since the league could not stop the gambling, it would raise the image of the game to such a transcendent level that the frenzied economic activity transpiring on each autumn Sunday would be virtually sanitized of its patent illegality. The league thus managed to avoid a gambling scandal after several franchise owners had become a bigger problem than organized crime in the 1970s; one club owner, by his own admission, lost several million dollars in Atlantic City casinos. At the same time, the league did what it could to support the "industry" by providing newspapers with weekly (sometimes even daily) lists of injured players whose status might affect the outcome of the next contest. (Who else besides gamblers really needed to know about the pulled groin muscle of an inside linebacker?)[65]

While Jimmy the Greek projected an image that was somewhat farcical, Axthelm offered his betting advice in dead earnest, as though to undermine the NFL's sanctimonious, if not hypocritical, stance toward gambling. Pressure from the league may in fact have contributed to his being fired by NBC in 1986. In any case, Axthelm was as ill-suited to that medium as he was, in Thompson's words, "a prince in the realm among sportswriters."[66] Yet he took no particular pride in his writing abilities and regarded his move to television simply as a greater opportunity to cover football and racing with the literal immediacy for which his journalism had always strived. By the end, however, he was plainly demeaning himself. When ESPN capitulated to the NFL in 1990 and prohibited Axthelm from referring to point spreads in his predictions, he responded: "Those absolute filth-bag rap groups that get censored—if they were playing in my living room, I'd move out—they have a right to talk dirty. I have a right to talk point spreads."[67]

But neither point spreads nor anything remotely connected to gambling ever came up during our boat trip from Monmouth. I asked Pete all sorts of questions in the roiling manner that often drives my auditors to the nearest exit, but with Axthelm it was different; I felt as if we were sharing a collective memory. I was amazed that a man who was only in his forties could have witnessed so many legendary moments in the culture of postwar America. We talked mostly about sportswriting in the 1960s, about *Sports Illustrated* in its most gloriously literate period, about the body language of horses. He was magnanimous and funny in a fashion that was rarely conveyed by television. I remember feeling somewhat guilty that I had not followed his career more closely, but I was determined to make up for lost time.

Yet when I next saw him, broadcasting from the Bristol, Connecticut, studios of ESPN only a few weeks later, he was doing the Ax routine again on behalf of a professional football league that had become about as colorful as IBM. (In fairness, I should say that I rarely watched him on Sundays, and I later heard that his interview with the coach of his beloved Dolphins, Don Shula—whose wife was losing her battle with cancer—was a remarkable display of empathy and compassion.) One of my own last glimpses of Axthelm was on ESPN, doing an interview with thoroughbred trainers Bobby Frankel and Nick Zito at a racetrack somewhere: "Here are a couple of real New York guys," he bellowed, almost defiantly. Frankel and Zito were still viewed as racing upstarts after decades of successful work—outsiders who continued to operate "on their own terms." But Frankel had been training horses in California for twenty-five years by then, while the sport itself had come to be profoundly imperiled by a proliferation of "simulcast" facilities, which threatened to turn racetracks into casinos and, in pandering to a desire for constant action, to render the unique visual and hermeneutical aspects of the horseplaying tradition extinct.

When the NFL playoffs rolled around in January, I caught another glimpse of Axthelm on ESPN, by then, as his friend Ashbel Green wrote, "grievously thin in the neck, his voice eroded."[68] He died awaiting a liver transplant in Pittsburgh on 2 February 1991. Some of his friends seized upon the occasion to issue defiant statements of solidarity for a way of life they shared with Axthelm: "Doctors who hectored him and warned solemnly of death were idly dismissed as quacks who didn't get the point. They had no sense of fun. 'Who do they think I am?' he would shout. 'Methuselah? No! In my heart I am Peter Pan, and in my dreams I am a sixteen-year-old jockey riding winners at Churchill Downs."[69] In the course of a well-lubricated "wake" that spilled over from the Yale Club to Runyon's, a Manhattan bar frequented by media and sporting types, some of those friends also condemned Jimmy Breslin, who had appeared on an ESPN talk show to express his bitterness over Axthelm's role in hastening his own demise. The evidence of his writings suggests that Breslin's lifestyle had begun to change nearly two decades earlier, and he proceeded to castigate Axthelm for squandering his talent at the racetrack: "How can you tie your being to a jockey?" he cried. "You're angry," interrupted the show's host, Dick Schaap, a former *Herald–Tribune* colleague of both men. " 'Yes,' replied Breslin. 'It's a terrible thing. This is a great waste of ability. And then I'm standing here in a place, and this is where he spends his Sundays. Worrying about some sport that they play for twelve minutes. . . . I was very close to him, and I don't like it, that's all. And I'm not going to get teary-eyed over something I detest.' "[70]

The thirteen years that separated Breslin and Axthelm deeply colored their relationships to a journalistic tradition they purportedly shared. For all the mystique with which he was suffused, Breslin was the quintessential pro; a child of the Depression with a large family to support, he could be as skeptical as Axthelm was romantic. He did not write starry-eyed profiles of journalists from an earlier generation. When he became a pitchman for Piel's Real Draft beer in the early 1970s, he was probably not troubled by the fact that more people saw one of his commercials than had read all of his books combined; the brewer helped pay his bills. Breslin championed the cause of African Americans and Latinos, as he once had the Irish, partly because he cared about the neighborhoods in which he had grown up. From that foundation he expanded his focus outward, to the American South, to Vietnam; but he always came back—spiritually at least—to Queens.

Axthelm's roots were both spatially and temporally at the fringes of Breslin's world. His need to immerse himself totally in the milieu of horse racing (which Breslin always viewed with metaphoric detachment, if not with literal disdain) was anachronistic yet representative of the way that his generation was drawn to the "action." Like many products of the 1960s, he would live "on his own terms" until such time as the world came around to a new dispensation. In many ways Axthelm was a transitional figure: while committed to upholding and extending a tradition "his way," he lacked the resources acquired by his predecessors through years of devotion to the calling of urban journalism; at the same time, his intellectual grounding in existentialist modernism offered none of the flexibility his successors would enjoy as they reconstituted "tradition" only in such ways as they found suitable (as evidenced by the contrast between Axthelm's overly earnest handicapping and the "postmodern" antics of his broadcast partner, Chris Berman, the host of ESPN's *Game Day*). When Axthelm's ambitions propelled him into a career in television, he became even more protective of his print idols. This conflict was the subtext of his famous loud, boozy brawl with Howard Cosell in a Baltimore hotel bar during the 1979 World Series, a hot exchange that combusted when Cosell derided Red Smith's legacy.[71]

If Axthelm was a prisoner of tradition, it also made him something of a mystic. He would have loved the astounding colt Holy Bull, partly for his name but more so for the way this "freak" (as too many racing people insist on labeling horses with talent that exceeds the expectations of their modest breeding) sparked the same ineffable desire inscribed by the poet James Wright after encountering a somewhat slower pony in a Minnesota pasture:

> Suddenly I realize
> That if I stepped out of my body I would break
> Into blossom.[72]

Holy Bull's jockey, Mike Smith, was no less eloquent when asked to describe the almost unfathomable burst of acceleration by his mount, unleashed and headed for home, in the Woodward Stakes at Belmont in September 1994. Suddenly departing from a pack of champions as though to enter a realm known by precious few, Holy Bull "just grew wings," Smith explained. No one could have known that five months later Holy Bull would sustain a career-ending injury in a Florida race—this time Smith had no words to go with his tears. But anyone who loved horses the way Pete Axthelm did would have learned to savor the richness of those special moments that hinted at mysteries of a complex variety.

Alan Baker, a former television executive and Axthelm's close friend, offered a highly meaningful variation on the standard tributes and obituaries: "I never knew a guy who lived on his own terms as much as Pete did," he told a *Boston Globe* reporter. "Yet he wasn't selfish. He did things no one knew about, like assigning speaking honorariums to the Covenant House for homeless kids."[73] While Axthelm's spirituality is properly a matter for "the edge of the page," the paradoxical personal code that Baker ascribed to him was at the heart of a spiritual economy whose sources and claims may have constituted a subtradition unrecognized by Pete himself. He once described Mario Cuomo as "a concerned Roman Catholic theologian,"[74] but would have scoffed at any such designation for himself. In fact, Hunter Thompson emphatically denied that Axthelm was "a religious man. He was a black priest in a family tradition that openly worshiped gambling and had no regard for money." Yet Thompson nevertheless claimed that the last time he saw Pete, he "was sipping a Bombay gin magnum and reading aloud from the Book of Revelation as he often did while he studied the *Racing Form*." Moreover, Pete "sometimes asked morbid questions, which eventually led him into a place that some of his friends called 'the gray area.' It was an essentially Buddhist concept based in karma, laughter, and occasional human sacrifice."[75]

The apparent contradictions in these glimpses of Axthelm's spirituality are actually constitutive of a subcultural theology—resolutely ecumenical, though more common among the urban Catholic laity formed in the postwar era—which might be crudely described as a "preferential option" for the hip, the downtrodden, and the outcast. Most people at the racetrack lose, when they are not simply lost. "He loved the whole subculture of gamblers, bookies, hustlers, loansharks, touts, crooks and assorted wiseguys," eulogized Andy Beyer. "He might moralize in print about the Soviet invasion of Afghanistan . . . but he'd never condemn a con man or hustler."[76] Axthelm once introduced the writer Ashbel Green to his friend, trainer Buddy Jacobson, who, Pete insisted, had "a great book in him." Jacobson would later be convicted of murdering the lover of his recently estranged girlfriend, a New York model.[77] Axthelm also wrote a book and several articles about O. J. Simpson, whom he greatly admired for "the hints of music in every gesture . . . the grace and balance of a great dancer." Simpson told him: "I've often said that all great runners have to be insane. . . . I mean, they can't be acting out of logic or thought. They get into a certain rhythm and make instinctive moves without any reason for them."[78] Ultimately, Beyer told me, Axthelm's life made for a "very sad" story. While the reasons why may be obvious, we should also keep in mind the power of certain traditions to debilitate as well as to ennoble, especially when their deeper sources remain obscure.

In August 1992, still on Ax's track, I stepped into the King's Tavern in Saratoga Springs, just across Union Avenue from the main entrance to the race course. As at Monmouth, I was anxious to hear what patrons of another Axthelm landmark felt about the loss of "one of us," as Thompson had called him. The Saratoga meet lasted only a month in those days, so Pete had actually been gone for just a brief spell in racing-calendar time when I stepped up to the bar and inquired about him. The busy bartender, distractedly pointing to Ax's favorite stool, said, "He'll probably be in later."

Notes

My thanks to Ellen Raben, Inter-Library Loan Department, Pius XII Memorial Library, Saint Louis University. This essay is dedicated to that most real of sports, Barry V. Lipinski.

1   Jack Beatty, *The Rascal King: The Life and Times of James Michael Curley, 1874–1958* (Reading, MA, 1993), 428.
2   Hunter S. Thompson, "Death of a Sportsman," *Esquire* (April 1991): 152; David Heckerman, "Gambling with a Life on the Edge," *Thoroughbred Times*, 8 February 1991, 17.
3   William Murray, *The Wrong Horse: An Odyssey Through the American Racing Scene* (New York, 1992), 161–62.
4   *New York Times*, 11 August 1987.
5   Ibid.
6   *Washington Post*, 4 February 1991.
7   Ibid.
8   See the *Chicago Tribune*, 24 June 1990; and *Newsday*, 8 February 1991.
9   *New Haven Register*, 15 March 1959; 16 March 1959.
10 Thompson, "Death of a Sportsman," 152.
11 Ibid.
12 *Washington Post*, 10 February 1991.
13 James E. B. Breslin, "Terminating Mark Rothko: Biography Is Mourning in Reverse," *The New York Times Book Review*, 24 July 1994, 3.
14 Ibid., 20.
15 Ibid. Ironically, perhaps, Breslin's death (on 6 January 1996) was, like his father's, due

to a heart attack. "For Breslin, reinventing himself proved something of a habit," noted his *New York Times* obituary. "At the time of his death, he was working on a biography of John Coltrane"; see "James E. B. Breslin, 60, Poetry Specialist," *New York Times*, 16 January 1996.

16 *Yale Daily News*, 17 October 1963.

17 Ibid.

18 Jimmy Breslin, *Damon Runyon: A Life* (New York, 1991), 6.

19 *Yale Daily News*, 6 January 1964.

20 Ibid.

21 See the *New York Times*, 26 October 1993.

22 Peter M. Axthelm, *The Modern Confessional Novel* (New Haven, 1967).

23 Germaine Bree, "Axthelm, Peter. *The Modern Confessional Novel*," *Studies in the Novel* 1 (1969): 90–91.

24 *The World According to Jimmy Breslin*, ed. Michael J. O'Neill and William Brink (New York, 1984), xv. On the last days of the *Trib*, see the remarkable account by Richard Kluger, *The Paper: The Life and Death of the New York Herald–Tribune* (New York, 1986), 671–741.

25 Quoted in Ira Berkow, *Red: A Biography of Red Smith* (New York, 1986), 128.

26 Ibid., 229.

27 *New York Herald–Tribune*, 14 June 1965.

28 Ibid., 1 June 1965.

29 Ibid., 2 June 1965.

30 Quoted in the *Washington Post*, 18 January 1995.

31 See Carlo Rotella, *October Cities: The Redevelopment of Urban Literature* (Berkeley: University of California Press, forthcoming).

32 *Washington Post*, 10 February 1991.

33 Pete Axthelm, "Everybody Wants a Piece of the Action," *Newsweek*, 10 April 1972, 48.

34 Ibid.

35 *New York Herald–Tribune*, 20 June 1965.

36 Ibid.

37 Berkow, *Red*, 216.

38 *New York Herald–Tribune*, 16 July 1965.

39 Ibid., 17 July 1965.

40 *Spirit of the Times*, 12 August 1882, 48; see also Frederic Hudson, *Journalism in the United States, From 1690 to 1872* (New York, 1873), 341–42.

41 *St. Louis Post–Dispatch*, 5 February 1972.

42 Thompson, "Death of a Sportsman," 152.

43 Murray, *The Wrong Horse*, 17–18.

44 Ibid., 67–70.

45 Nathan Glazer and Daniel Patrick Moynihan, *Beyond the Melting Pot: The Negroes, Puerto Ricans, Jews, Italians and Irish of New York City* (Cambridge, 1964 [1963]), 262.

46 Quoted in William Nack, *Secretariat: The Making of a Champion* (New York, 1975), 325.

47 *New York Times*, 9 April 1989.

48 Sam Allis, "The Fine Art of Giving," *Time*, 18 September 1989, 86.

49 Pete Axthelm, *The City Game: Basketball in New York* (New York, 1970), xi.

50   Pete Axthelm, "When the Real McGuire Stood Up," *Sports Illustrated*, 20 March 1967, 76.

51   Ibid.

52   *New York Herald–Tribune*, 20 June 1965.

53   Ibid.

54   *Washington Post*, 10 February 1991.

55   Pete Axthelm, "How Chris Has Grown!" *Newsweek*, 18 February 1975, 43.

56   *Chicago Tribune*, 1 November 1992.

57   Melvin Durslag, "Axthelm's Career Left the Gate at a Gallop" (syndicated column, c. 5 February 1991).

58   Pete Axthelm, "John Carlos's Unlowered Fist," *Newsweek*, 10 June 1974, 55.

59   Ibid.

60   Axthelm, "How Chris Has Grown!" 43.

61   *Washington Post*, 4 January 1982.

62   Ibid., 4 February 1991.

63   See Murray, *The Wrong Horse*, 168–75.

64   See Myron Cope, *The Game That Was: The Early Days of Pro Football* (New York, 1970), 121–22; and David Harris, *The League: The Rise and Decline of the NFL* (New York, 1986), 82.

65   See Harris, *The League*, 556–57.

66   Thompson, "Death of a Sportsman," 152.

67   *St. Louis Post–Dispatch*, 25 August 1990.

68   Ibid.

69   *Thoroughbred Times*, 8 February 1991.

70   Quoted in the *Atlanta Journal and Constitution*, 4 February 1991.

71   See Berkow, *Red*, 218.

72   James Wright, "A Blessing," in *The Norton Anthology of Modern Poetry*, ed. Richard Ellmann and Robert O'Clair (New York, 1988), 1284.

73   *Boston Globe*, 5 February 1991.

74   Pete Axthelm, "The Great Conciliator," *Newsweek*, 17 March 1989, 36.

75   Thompson, "Death of a Sportsman," 152.

76   *Washington Post*, 4 February 1991.

77   *New York Times*, 13 April 1980.

78   Pete Axthelm, "O. J.—The Juice Really Flows," *Newsweek*, 26 November 1973, 67–70.

Notes on Contributors

PATRICK ALLITT teaches American history at Emory University and coaches the Tornados, a girls' soccer team in Decatur, Georgia. He is also the author of *Catholic Intellectuals and Conservative Politics in America, 1950–1985* (1993), which he updated in his *SAQ* (summer 1994) article, "The Bitter Victory: Catholic Conservative Intellectuals in America, 1988–1993."

PHILIP DELORIA, Assistant Professor of History, University of Colorado, plays basketball on his department team, which rules the intramural C League. He is also the author of *Playing Indian: Native People and the Creation of American Identities*, forthcoming from Yale University Press.

ANN FABIAN originally planned to become the next Vince Scully. Instead, she is currently a Fellow at the Shelby Cullom Davis Center, Princeton University, and the author of a book on gambling, *Card Sharps, Dream Books and Bucket Shops* (1990).

JAMES T. FISHER, Danforth Chair in Humanities at Saint Louis University, is the author of *The Catholic Counterculture in America, 1933–1962* (1989), and *Dr. America: The Lives of Thomas A. Dooley, 1927–1961* (forthcoming, University of Massachusetts Press). From 1968 to 1970, he was a slick point guard (and head case) on the St. Bridget's Junior High School basketball team.

GASPAR GONZÁLEZ is a Ph.D. candidate in American Studies at Yale University.

ROBERTO GONZÁLEZ ECHEVARRÍA, Sterling Professor of Hispanic and Comparative Literatures, Yale University, plays first base and catches for the Madison Ravens of the Connecticut Senior Baseball League. Author of the award-winning *Myth and Archive: A Theory of Latin American Narrative* (1990) and, most recently, of *Celestina's Brood: Continuities of the Baroque in Spanish and Latin American Literatures* (1993), he has also edited the forthcoming *Oxford Book of the Latin American Short Story* and coedited the three-volume *Cambridge History of Latin American Literature* (also forthcoming). He is currently writing a cultural history of Cuban baseball.

PAMELA HAAG is an Orioles devotee who believes that a grave injustice was rectified when the NFL returned to Baltimore this year. She is an independent scholar with a Ph.D. from Yale and was recently awarded an NEH grant to write about how the sexual revolution has shaped American life and politics in the 1990s.

MICHAEL ORIARD, Professor of English, Oregon State University, played football for Notre Dame and the Kansas City Chiefs. He is also the author of *Dreaming of Heroes: American Sports Fiction, 1868–1980* (1982), *The End of Autumn: Reflections on My Life in Football* (1982), *Sporting with the Gods: The Rhetoric of Play and Game in American Culture* (1991), and *Reading Football: How the Popular Press Created an American Spectacle* (1993).

KENNETH L. PARKER is Assistant Professor of Church History at Saint Louis University, where he also plays squash, lifts weights, and swims. He is the author of *The English Sabbath: A Study of Doctrine and Discipline from the Reformation to the Civil War* (1988).

STEPHEN RACHMAN teaches in the Department of English at Michigan State University and is the coeditor of *The American Face of Edgar Allan Poe* (1995). He is also a road runner, tennis bum, weekend warrior, and couch potato—a real all-American sport.

CARLO ROTELLA, Assistant Professor of English and American Studies at Lafayette College, is the author of *October Cities: The Redevelopment of Urban Literature*, forthcoming from University of California Press.

SAQ

Sports Community

Album

Golden
Phil Deloria
in 1972.

Junior equestrienne
Priscilla Lane in
1944.

Being "like Mike"
Oriard at
Notre Dame
in 1969
(Bradley
Photographers,
Dallas).

Cross-country runner James J. Fisher (Jim's father) in 1946.

Quarterback Steve Rachman at about the same age as his number.

Margaret McAllister
(Candice Ward's
grandmother)
riding in
New York City
(c. 1908).

566

Young urban
wave catcher
Carlo Rotella in
1971.

Pari-mutuelle
Pam Haag
at the races.

Fin-de-siècle
catcher Roberto
González
Echevarría.

Coach Patrick Allitt
(and daughter,
Frances, seated in
front of him) with
The Tornados.

Squash courtier
Kenneth Parker.

Pétanque player
Isabelle Smeall
(Ann Fabian's
daughter).

Movie
marathoner
Fred Jameson.

Duke

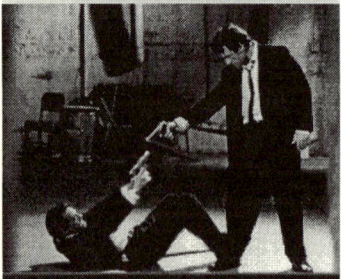

Home
and
Away

The Jamesonian Unconscious: The Aesthetics of Marxist Theory

Clint Burnham

Burnham negotiates Jameson's major works by way of his own working-class, queer-ish, Gen-X background and sensibility.
272 pages, paper $17.95, library cloth edition $42.95
Post-Contemporary Interventions

At Home in the World

Michael Jackson

This book chronicles Jackson's experience among the Warlpiri of the Tanami desert and takes a new look at what it means to be "at home."
200 pages, 3 maps, cloth $21.95

Now in Paperback
Macropolitics of Nineteenth-Century Literature: Nationalism, Exoticism, Imperialism

Jonathan Arac and Harriet Ritvo, editors

The essays in this collection explore the relationship between politics and culture by examining developments in a wide range of nineteenth-century writing.
328 pages, paper $16.95

Duke University Press

Box 90660
Durham, North Carolina 27708-0660

Teoría Literara: Texto y Teoría

Volume 19:
BEATRIZ PASTOR BODMER

El jardin y el peregrino
Ensayos sobre el pensamiento utópico latinoamericano 1492-1695

Amsterdam/Atlanta, GA 1996. V,366 pp.
ISBN: 90-5183-934-0   Hfl. 120,-/US-$ 80.-

INDICE: I: EL JARDIN Y EL PEREGRINO. Cap. I: América: Figuración del locus utópico. Cap. II: Pensamiento utópico y alteridad. Cap. III: Sobre el discurso utópico. II: LOS BUSCADORES DEL REINO. Cap. IV: Las claves simbólicas de la historia. Cap. V: Ojos interiores y visión utópica. Cap. VI: Utopía y revolución. III: LA MUJER: CLAUSURAS HISTORICAS Y ESPACIOS SIMBOLICOS ALTERNATIVOS. Cap. VII: Figuraciones del miedo. Cap. VIII: Los espacios simbólicos alternativos. Cap. IX: El círculo y la espiral. IV: COLAPSO SIMBOLICO Y FIGURACION UTOPICA.
Cap. X: La escritura del trauma. Cap. XI: El sueño de la razón. Cap. XII: El mundo al revés.

USA/Canada: Editions Rodopi B.V., 2015 South Park Place, Atlanta, GA 30339, Tel. (770) 933-0027, *Call toll-free* (U.S. only) 1-800-225- 3998, Fax (770) 933-9644, *E-mail:* F.van.der.Zee@rodopi.nl
All Other Countries: Editions Rodopi B.V., Keizersgracht 302-304, 1016 EX Amsterdam, The Netherlands. Tel. + + 31 (0)20-622-75-07, Fax + + 31 (0)20-638-09-48, *E-mail:* F.van.der.Zee@rodopi.nl

NEW FROM DUKE

THE USES OF LITERARY HISTORY
Marshall Brown, editor

Twenty leading literary critics appraise the current state of literary history in provocative, sometimes combative essays on the writing of literary history, the nature of our interest in tradition, and the ways that literary works act in history.
316 pages, 4 illustrations, paper $16.95, library cloth edition $49.95. Expanded/revised from inaugural issue of *MLQ: A Journal of Literary History*

VISION AND TEXTUALITY
Stephen Melville and Bill Readings, editors

The essays in this anthology address the emergent terms and practices of contemporary art history, examining the discipline's distinctness from and community with literary theory.
409 pages, 90 illustrations, paper $17.95, library cloth edition $49.95

UNIVERSAL GRAMMAR AND NARRATIVE FORM
David Herman

In a major rethinking of the functions, methods, and aims of narrative poetics, Herman exposes important links between modernist and postmodernist literary experimentation and contemporary language theory.
296 pages, paper $19.95, library cloth edition $49.95
Sound and Meaning: The Roman Jakobson Series in Linguistics and Poetics

Duke University Press Box 90660 Durham, North Carolina 27708-0660

Three from Duke

Bad Objects: Essays Popular and Unpopular
Naomi Schor

"As one has come to expect from Naomi Schor, the arguments she advances are forceful, challenging, and above all, elegant. Highly individual and distinct, these essays consistently achieve their aim of reposing the essential questions of feminist theory."—Peggy Kamuf, University of Southern California

232 pages, paper $15.95, library cloth edition $45.95

Troubadours, Trumpeters, Troubled Makers: Lyricism, Nationalism, and Hybridity in China and its Others
Gregory B. Lee

"This is an innovative book clearly destined to become the object of debate and discussion, both within the particular field of Chinese studies, in the wider and expanding field of cultural and postcolonial studies, and in interdisciplinary critical analyses of present-day metropolitan and global cultures."—Iain Chambers, Istituto Universitario Orientale, Naples

200 pages, paper $17.95, library cloth edition $45.00
Asia-Pacific

Phantasmic Radio
Allen S. Weiss

"Putting a stethoscope to the chest of mass-culture's first darling medium, Allen Weiss draws radio art out of electromagnetic obscurity and onto the stage of current debates on subjectivity and technology, primitivism and vanguardism, psychology and textuality."
—John Corbett, author of *Extended Play*

136 pages, paper $13.95, library cloth edition $34.95

Duke University Press • Box 90660 Durham, NC 27708-0660

Colonialism *and* Desire

Race and the Education of Desire: Foucault's History of Sexuality *and the Colonial Order of Things*
Ann Laura Stoler

"This is an important book, probably the only reading of Foucault that seriously tracks and takes up his probing, restless and recursive leads. Instead of reducing him to an icon of one or more ideas to be either uncritically embraced or irresponsibly discarded, as others have done, Stoler engages Foucault's dynamic, nervous, and passionate moves towards focusing the interdependence of ideas and forces."—Doris Sommer, Harvard University
248 pages, paper $15.95, library cloth edition $45.95

The Ruling Passion: British Colonial Allegory and the Paradox of Homosexual Desire
Christopher Lane

"Lane's work displays a quite astonishing intellect. *The Ruling Passion* is expertly researched, demonstrates an authoritative command of theoretical knowledge, and advances our understanding of the complexities involved in representing cross-cultural and cross-class homosocial and homosexual desire. It is a highly original work of considerable academic stature in the rapidly developing field of gay male cultural criticism."—Joseph Bristow, University of York
344 pages, paper $16.95, library cloth edition $49.95

Duke University Press Box 90660 Durham, NC 27708-0660

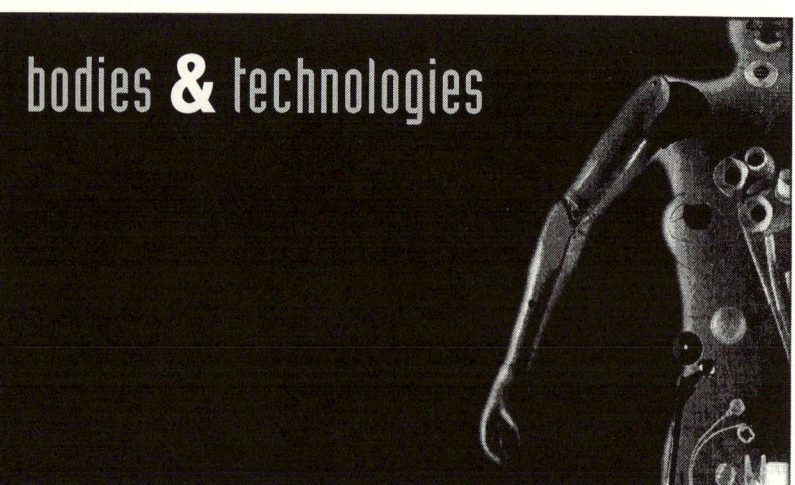

CALL FOR PAPERS

First International and Eleventh National MELUS Conference

Multi-Ethnic Literatures Across the Americas and the Pacific: Exchanges, Contestations, and Alliances

The University of Hawai'i at Mānoa • April 18-20, 1997

Hosted by the College of Languages, Linguistics, and Literature;
the Center for Pacific Island Studies; the East-West Center;
and the Department of Ethnic Studies

The Society for the Study of the Multi-Ethnic Literature of the United States (MELUS) will hold its first international conference at the University of Hawai'i in 1997, in acknowledgement of both Hawaii's central location between East and West and the increasingly complex relationship between the Pacific and the Americas. We invite proposals for papers, panels, etc. (less than 500 words). In addition to papers on the multi-ethnic literatures of North America, we welcome comparative perspectives that address the growing cultural or textual connections between America and the Pacific.

possible topics

new frontiers? *ethnic literatures of the u.s. • immigrant literatures • border identities • critical regionalism • new directions in feminism • multiculturalism*

emerging literatures & languages *pacific island literatures • literatures of hawai'i • creole languages & cultures • protest & resistance literatures • why standard english? • theorizing asian/pacific literature • cultural nationalism • The languages of dance • non-u.s. ethnic literatures • & europe?*

narrating north america & the pacific *oral literatures & popular traditions • film & theater • representations of indigenous culture • colonialism, neo-colonialism, post-colonialism • transnationalism & cultural production • representations of hong kong 1997 • tourism & homo ludens • sovereignty & first nation movements • the black atlantic and the asian pacific*

reconfiguring american literary & cultural studies *african american literature • asian american literature • chicano/a literature • euro-american literature • native american literature • the critique of nation & nationalism • cnn, www, & capitalist world culture*

The conference will advertise internationally. Special sessions for K-12 teachers. Reduced registration rates for high school teachers, students, and international scholars. Presenters should be members of MELUS. For conference information, contact 1997 MELUS Conference Chair, University of Hawai'i, Mānoa Dept. of English, Honolulu HI 96822; fax (808) 956-3083; e-mail: rhsu@hawaii.edu

deadline for proposals: October 15, 1996